THE WARS OF THE BUSHES

THE WARS OF THE BUSHES

A Father and Son as Military Leaders

By
STEPHEN TANNER

CASEMATE
Philadelphia

Published by
CASEMATE

ISBN 1-932033-32-7

Cataloging-in-Publication Data is available from the
Library of Congress.

First edition, first printing.

PRINTED AND BOUND IN THE UNITED STATES OF AMERICA.

CONTENTS

For
Emily and Annie

PREFACE

There are times when current events can be more fascinating than history, but I've yet to see an occasion when familiarity with history has not been invaluable to one's perception of current events. This may be more true than ever now that the United States has adopted new doctrines in foreign policy following the disaster of 9/11. Dually spurred by a frightening new sense of vulnerability, and by the fact that we are are now, in absolute terms, the strongest nation in history, able to wield military power anywhere on the globe, America has recently entered new territory.

Military concepts like pre-emption and pre-eminence have now entered our political discourse as if they are new ideas. Actually they are, when professed by the United States. But to the rest of the world they are old, and they are concepts that many had hoped that the New World democracy would never adopt. The very word "America" once stood for something more promising, and it is not just a large part of our public, but millions of people around the world who have begun to look with dismay at an America that has become a reactionary power, instead of a leader and an example which other nations could follow.

The terrorist attacks of September 11, 2001 transformed the United States, but it now looks as if they transformed it too much. Beneath the smoke and ashes of World Trade, much chaos has ensued. While the perpetrators have gone free, new wars have been created, new doctrines have been declared, and a great deal of paranoia has clouded America's traditional goal of being an agent for peace and international justice. In the past year we have launched our first pre-emptive war, re-evaluated our traditional alliances—in fact, questioned the need for allies at all—and announced a determination never to let another nation match our currently overwhelming power.

This is quite a departure, as the Wizard of Oz would say, for the land of E Pluribus Unum. There seems to me to be an accelerating trend among the public to view current events with a very narrow focus, as if each is unprecedented, calling for its own rule book. As the airwaves become flooded with breaking events, and reporters hang on to every word of our current president, there is an increasing danger that our public will forget about the past, even if it is recent.

This book is an attempt to step back for a slightly larger view. To acquire a perspective on events during George W. Bush's administration we don't need to dive back deeply in history. Our current president did not spring from nowhere, like some unknown political populist from the hinterland who suddenly seized the enthusiasm of the populace; he instead sprang from the seed of George H.W. Bush, who served as president just eight years earlier, and who was the first modern president to wield American military power outside the constraints of the Cold War. Since the end of that long, scary stand-off, the father and son have been the only two presidents to date who have launched U.S. forces in aggressive, decisive actions against foreign powers or threats. To acquire an historical perspective on the son, we need only look back at the father, who very much embodied traditional American ideals during his day, and at this juncture, in my view, is very much missed.

It's an odd twist in American history that our presidents at very critical times—the collapse of the Berlin Wall and the collapse of the World Trade Center—have been a father and son, George H.W. Bush, and George W. Bush. Americans had elected one previous father and son duo, John and John Quincy Adams, back at the beginning of the republic. John Adams held office for four years when the quasi-war with France was about to rage, and then his son was elected 25 years later, when our biggest foreign policy problem was the Cree Indians. The Bushes have assumed office more closely together, and as such have dominated the military history of the post–Cold War era. Alone among the presidents of the past 30 years, the Bushes have waged full-blooded war, at this writing two apiece, while other presidents—Ford, Carter, Reagan and Clinton—were never able or inclined to do so.

The American public is currently, and justifiably, obsessed with how the second President Bush is faring with his occupation of Iraq, as well as with the broader War on Terror. But too many among us have taken to viewing George W. Bush as if he alone is inventing military history, propelling it by his unshakeable moral convictions, while we have forgotten the battles, the lessons, and the achievements that have come before.

To gain a better perspective it is important to consider the wars waged by the father as well as those of the son. Prior to the 2003 invasion of Iraq, and the quasi-war in Afghanistan, there was an American president who led an unprecedented global coalition, and who waged war in swift, decisive fashion. He held no claim to divine moral clarity but only to a surehanded grasp of American strength, and to its essential principles.

"The Wars of the Bushes" is the story of how two presidents have diverged in the way they have wielded American military power. That they are a father and son adds poignancy to the tale, and perhaps a degree of personal complexity which can best be left for psychiatrists to examine. Our purpose here is to lay out the operations, at a time when America has gotten into trouble, with thousands of its soldiers being killed and wounded in a foreign land for a cause that is still unclear.

We primarily wish to change the focus from the current pre-eminence of Bush the son, to look once again at the father, whose example has recently been neglected. If this is finally a Freudian issue, so be it. But it is more importantly an American issue, which as it unfolds will have enormous consequences for millions of people around the globe. The multicultural force of history cannot be determined by an American president's willpower; it can only be influenced or guided through his skill and understanding, regardless of the relative merits of our military power. And in the wars waged by the father and son, we can clearly see the difference between these two approaches

THE WARS
OF THE BUSHES

INTRODUCTION

Pillars of smoke blotted the April sky when the armored columns broke into the capital. The invaders had expected, and feared, a block-to-block fight like a latter-day Stalingrad, a final effusion of blood to mark the culminating battle of the war. But so far defending soldiers had run away, surrendered, or, in most cases, simply stripped off their uniforms and blended back into the population. Across the city, foreign fighters and operatives scrambled to escape. The invading tanks tore up the streets, crushing cars, fruit stands and market stalls in their path. Inside the 40-ton monsters, highly trained crews stared through their optical sights, ready to spit fire with machine guns or deliver devastating blasts from their main cannon. The turret of the lead tank swiveled ominously from side to side as if greedily looking for a chance to fire. Finally the column, composed of the most lethal mechanical behemoths of a superpower, arrived at its destination: the opulent presidential palace that had once served as a nerve center for the enemy's power. The battle-hardened men inside the machines didn't bother to dismount to open the gates. They simply crushed their way through and one after another the tanks spread out on the grounds, their guns trained on the palace. Minutes later, the nation of South Vietnam ceased to exist. Saigon had fallen! The Communist victors renamed it Ho Chi Minh City.

And so ended a long, unnecessary war.

Several decades later, in the new millennium, a similar scene took place in Baghdad, Iraq. But on this April day it was American tank

1

columns overrunning an enemy's capital against surprisingly feeble opposition. The American tankers called it a "thunder run," and we should leave open the possibility that the Vietnamese, too, had a nickname for their daring drive into the enemy's final stronghold. The major difference was that while the Communist tanks in 1975 had ended a war, the Americans in 2003 had only started one. While the fall of Saigon marked the end of America's effort to occupy a country through military means, bending a foreign culture to its will, the fall of Baghdad marked the start of a new attempt, with an entirely different culture.

Already phrases like "hearts and minds," "credibility gap," and the dreaded word "quagmire," are being respoken, none perhaps very sinister to the half of the population born since 1975, but foreboding to their elders, who once witnessed a tragically slow slide into failure. America's military history over the last 60 years can be divided into two parts. For three decades after 1945, the American military sought to duplicate the unconditional triumph it had earned in World War II. It spent the next three decades, after 1975, trying not to duplicate the excruciatingly prolonged strategic defeat suffered in Indochina. Both the 1945 victory and the 1975 defeat were unprecedented in America's experience, and the object has since become how to judge the difference between the two—the capability of U.S. power versus its inherent limits.

For the United States, the long road from Saigon to Baghdad has consisted of a series of dips and rises, with no shortage of rest stops. And though America has made rapid progress, it has been pursued throughout the journey by the spectre of failure with which it once came face to face. There have been dynamic twists and turns on the road where it seemed as if the phantom had finally been lost for good. But the majority of our military and political leaders have realized that all it would take is one tragic misjudgment—just one terrible stall—to allow it to overtake us.

Among American presidents who have held office since 1975, only two—the Bushes, father and son—have waged full-scale wars against foreign nations. Yet the wars waged by the Bushes have been entirely dissimilar in the way they were fought, what they meant for America's global position, and in their degree of success.

The first President Bush—as evidenced by the invasion of Panama and the Gulf War—specialized in quick, decisive victories. He had a surehanded grasp of U.S. military capability and didn't fear to use overwhelming power. The troops would promptly return home, leaving a new democracy or a liberated country behind, as the case might be. He also had a firm belief in the value of broad-based alliances, sensing that American ideals were never so well projected as when the United States was considered the moral as well as the military leader of the world.

The second President Bush—as evidenced by Afghanistan and the invasion of Iraq—has not shown such a firm grasp of American military capability. When not overly relying on foreign "proxies," he has shortshrifted U.S. combat troops after misjudging the task he assigned them. Rather than identifying an achievable goal and bringing the troops home, he has left them to sit on their objectives, suffering more casualties in occupation than during their supposed victories. Though professing to fight a War on Terror, he has allowed the world's leading terrorist to live free for years, while invading a country that did not practice terror. (Now it does.) In the process, the latest Bush has alienated traditional allies, villainized the United Nations, and through arrogant ultimatums such as "You're either with us or against us," all but placed demolition charges beneath the Pax Americana.

Since Bushes famously don't like to be "put on the couch," we can leave psychological issues out of it. Suffice to say that sons are not always the best imitators of their fathers and in many cases endeavor to be the opposite. This need not indicate a lack of affection but only a process designed to learn from the father's mistakes, and to the degree that the relationship is competitive, perhaps an acute need for the son to gain, on his own, his father's admiration. The main risk in such an apparently complex relationship between father and son is that the latter may behave in a contrary fashion even if his father's example was worth following.

All of this leaves the phantom in the rear-view mirror—Vietnam—which the father left behind, and which the son has allowed to catch up. It is a truism that the word "Vietnam" has been invoked as a warning at the start of every military venture, large or small, that the United States has undertaken since 1975. The cry usually comes from the remains of the contemporary anti-war movement, which by 1970 claimed a majority of young people. This generation, now middle-aged, continues to dominate the culture, and has yelled "Vietnam" everywhere from Grenada to the Kuwaiti desert, generally without reason.

But as these words are written in Spring 2004, the American public is noting the first anniversary of its ongoing war in Iraq. We have been there for over a year, and politicians on both sides of the aisle are claiming that we can not possibly withdraw. They may be correct, and there may indeed be a justifiable end in sight. But what was that word again? For those with poor memories, or those younger people who wonder about the meaning of this terrible word, "Vietnam," that so spooks a large segment of the population, we should take a brief trip back to the beginning.

Like most wars, Vietnam began on a fiery wave of patriotic idealism. It was set alight in 1961 by the most charismatic of U.S. presidents, John F. Kennedy, who declared in his inaugural address, "We shall pay any price, bear any burden, meet any hardship, support any friends, oppose any foe, in order to assure the survival and the success of liberty." The premise of his statement was that liberty depended primarily on a country not going Communist or otherwise aligning itself with Moscow. And so the less remembered, next paragraph of his speech may be more pertinent today:

> To those old allies whose cultural and spiritual origins we share, we pledge the loyalty of faithful friends. United there is little we cannot do in a host of cooperative ventures. Divided, there is little we can do—for we dare not meet a powerful challenge at odds and split asunder.

Americans took Kennedy's entire speech to heart at the time, and before Kennedy had time to reflect on the old saw, "easier said than done," he was killed by a sniper in Dallas, Texas. Two months later, the Beatles invaded America, staging their own inaurgural on the Ed Sullivan show with the words "Yeah, yeah, yeah." Kennedy's death combined with the Beatles' arrival ushered in the "Sixties." The following year, U.S. Marines came ashore at Da Nang, South Vietnam, following up Kennedy's original vision. But as it turned out, the 1960s and the Vietnam War didn't mix.

Part of the problem with Vietnam was that the American culture that went in was entirely different from the one that came out. In the interim the United States had been wracked by a sexual revolution, a drug revolution, a Civil Rights revolution—that truly looked like a revolt, with violent riots in the cities—and a huge divide that opened between young people, especially those of draft age, and their elders. To the post–World War II baby boomers who had seized control of the culture, Kennedy's successor, Lyndon B. Johnson had no inspirational influence. They looked instead to rock icons, because music, along with fashion and drug use, became the unifying elements of the new counterculture. Aside, that is, from opposition to Vietnam.

The war began well enough, because the North Vietnamese had not braced themselves for the American onslaught, and the indigenous Viet Cong were purely guerrilla fighters who hid more than they fought. Meantime there were millions of South Vietnamese citizens who genuinely welcomed American help, including civic programs, jobs and medicine as well as arms. Once the Communists regained their balance the war escalated, however, and soon the population was forced to migrate en masse to the cities while the countryside became a brutal free-fire zone. For over two years U.S. troops supported by aircraft scoured the country, achieving any number of tactical successes while unsure if the total was adding up to victory.

The turning point in Vietnam was the Communists' Tet Offensive in January 1968, when 70,000 Viet Cong guerrillas backed by North Vietnamese regulars suddenly rose from hidden base camps in a devastating attack. Over 100 cities were assaulted, including 36 of 44 provincial capitals, and Viet Cong sappers penetrated the walls of the U.S. Embassy in Saigon.

If one has difficulty remembering the psychological impact of Tet on the American public, picture a similar situation occurring in today's Iraq. During a couple of months of lull, officials would paint rosy pictures of imminent victory, or in the terminology of the time, "a light at the end of the tunnel." Then picture, say on the first night of Ramadan, every major city in Iraq suddenly overrun by thousands of resistance fighters inflicting 3,500 American casualties in a gigantic burst of bloodshed. The point would not be the eventual defensive victory won by U.S. forces, but the fact that political leaders had either lied or had misjudged the situation, or more likely, had no idea themselves what they had gotten into.

The Tet Offensive was defeated by the Americans and South Vietnamese, and the Communists later admitted they had lost 40,000 men, over half their forces. The Viet Cong had been nearly gutted and thence the North Vietnamese Army had to take over the war. But no matter how one turned the military side, the fact remained that Kennedy's original concept of projecting the happiness of liberty around the world had come to a dead end.

Two months later, on March 31, 1968, President Johnson effectively waved a white flag when he somberly addressed the nation in prime-time, declaring a bombing halt of North Vietnam above the 21st parallel, and stating that he would not seek re-election. Eugene McCarthy, the Howard Dean of his day, had already been rallying young people against the senselessness of the war. Once Johnson dropped out a truly formidable anti-war candidate, Robert F. Kennedy, entered the Democratic race, but he was assassinated shortly afterward, killed while celebrating victory in the California primary. His assassin was a Palestinian, Sirhan Sirhan, and the result left the race to two Minnesotans, Johnson's vice president, Hubert Humphrey, who leaned liberal, and McCarthy, who had remained in the race, albeit somewhat on the fringe.

On the Republican side, Richard Nixon pragmatically maneuvered between the Goldwater right, then personified by California governor Ronald Reagan, and the eastern liberal wing under billionaire New Yorker, Nelson Rockefeller. Nixon won the nomination and then narrowly defeated Humphrey in the 1968 election.

Nixon was a far better war leader than Johnson, with an instinctive distaste for quagmires. In order to solve the problem he proceeded on several tracks. First, he began drawing down the troop levels as soon as possible. These had reached a high of 543,000 in March 1969, due to reinforcements LBJ had put in the pipeline, but Nixon immediately threw it into reverse. The codename for the general withdrawal was "Vietnamization," and there was indeed some hope that the

South Vietnamese army could be trained, armed and supplied in order to take over the war.

Next, Nixon departed from the sprawling occupation policy to deliver heavy blows at the enemy's strategic vulnerabilities. LBJ had declined to target the NVA's supply and base network in the jungles of neighboring Cambodia and Laos, respecting international law while allowing the Communists to defy it. Nixon dispatched B-52s to obliterate the network and in 1970 launched a ground offensive to overrun base camps in Cambodia. The incursion was successful, but was misinterpreted domestically as an escalation of the war when it had really been designed to provide breathing room for the retreat. The antiwar movement exploded, causing such a domestic uproar that Nixon was forbidden by Congress from waging any more cross-border attacks. In 1971 South Vietnamese troops invaded Laos to block the Ho Chi Minh Trail, but without U.S. combat strength on the ground they were defeated by a confluence of NVA divisions.

Nixon's third track, and the most important, was to project American strength beyond the jungles into the capitals of the opposing powers that supported the North Vietnamese war effort. Nixon went to Communist China—the first U.S. president to do so—where he and his his National Security Adviser, Henry Kissinger, held discussions with Mao Tse Tung and Chou En Lai in Beijing's Forbidden City. Nixon and Kissinger then traveled to Moscow where they sat down in the Kremlin with Leonid Brezhnev and the Soviet Politburo.

These détente initiatives were primarily designed to relax tensions between the superpowers in order to reduce the chance of global nuclear holocaust. A side benefit was that when Nixon turned again to Vietnam he was able to remove restrictions from the U.S. bombing list. Haiphong harbor was finally hit from the air and sewn with mines. Hanoi was plastered with bombs and supply routes near the Chinese border were attacked. The North Vietnamese, fearing they had been sold out by their patrons, launched a massive attempt to conquer the South quickly with conventional weapons. During this "Easter Offensive," U.S. aircraft caught NVA tanks, trucks and artillery in the open en masse for the first time in the war. The multiple prongs of the offensive were defeated and the Communists slunk once more back to their jungles.

At the end of the year Nixon launched waves of B-52s against Hanoi in the "Christmas bombings" and the following month, January 1973, the North Vietnamese finally signed a peace treaty that allowed the remaining American military to vacate the country with a semblance of achievement. In reality, the agreement provided what Kissinger termed "a decent interval" for the United States to get out prior to the inevitable collapse. Two years later the South Vietnamese army crumbled before another Communist offensive and North Vietnamese tanks finally rolled into Saigon.

Though the United States military had not been technically defeated in the war, its failure to achieve its strategic goal—unrealistic as that goal might have been—and the fact that it had pulled out of the war without having defeated the North Vietnamese amounted to the same thing. Ironically, Nixon's years of withdrawing forces and trying to hold down casualties had a more devastating effect on the army than Johnson's years of build-up. Until Tet, at least U.S. troops thought they were there to win, and they had in fact wreaked massive destruction on the Communists. By the time Nixon arrived it was obvious that America was conducting a retreat under the ephemeral concept "peace with honor," while morale among the draftees still fighting the war went into a tailspin.

Vietnam had presented an array of military, social, economic and cultural dilemmas that even in retrospect defy clear answers. In military terms, however, the lesson was clear that the incremental use of force without a clear objective, together with an absence of political will, could only lead to failure. The larger question, disguised at the time by the apparently stark battle lines of the Cold War, was whether a foreign culture could ever be subjugated by pure force.

In Vietnam, by applying military power gradually—even stopping and starting the cautious bombing campaign—the enemy had been allowed to incrementally increase its own measures, leading to a drawn-out war of attrition. At that point Napoleon's maxim, "The moral is to the material as three to one," took precedence, and even though the Communists, by their own admission, lost a million dead compared to 58,000 U.S. soldiers, it was the Americans who gave up.

This lesson was codified some two decades later in the "Powell Doctrine," which held that if the U.S. military was sent to war it must be enabled to use decisive, overwhelming force from the outset. Enunciated by General Colin Powell, who became foremost among a generation of officers schooled on the battlefields of Vietnam, the doctrine's tacit corollary was that if America couldn't summon the political will to supply its military with such force, then war should not happen at all. An additional corollary was that clear strategic objectives had to be in sight. The U.S. military was trained to defeat opposing armies on the battlefield. Plopping it into the fog of a foreign culture for months on end, where troops could not tell friend from foe, could only have tragic results on both sides.

The Vietnam War lasted so long—eight years between the Tonkin Gulf Resolution and the signing of the Paris Peace Accords—that the anti-war movement had grown to an unprecedented magnitude. An entire generation had come to despise all things military, and once the draft ended the services were short of recruits. The Army lowered its standards so it could at least attract ne'er-do-wells. These were sometimes supplied by judges who spared young men from jail (usually for cannabis possession) if they would join the Army instead. Many officers resigned from the service, and the professionals that remained struggled with the dregs that they were supposed to whip into combat shape. Of course no one, including the recruits, expected that the United States would try to fight another war anytime soon.

Nixon, who by 1973 had probably become the most publicly vilified man in history, was chased out of office by scandals in 1974. His vice president, Spiro Agnew, had been forced to resign the previous year, and his second vice president, Gerald Ford, was unable to hold onto the presidency in the 1976 elections. America had fairly yearned for a fresh face from the countryside to clean up the spiteful mess in Washington, and the public found its man in the Democratic ex-governor of Georgia, Jimmy Carter.

A brilliant intellectual with deep Christian convictions, Carter had graduated from Annapolis and served in the nuclear submarine force. Recognizing that the United States was no longer the idealistically unsullied nation that Kennedy had exhorted to bestride the globe, Carter tried instead to exert American power through its good intentions. High on his agenda was cleaning up the CIA, which had gotten its hands dirty with all kinds of mayhem in Indochina and Latin

America. The Spanish-speaking Carter attempted to put U.S. financial and diplomatic strength behind democratic movements in South America, and in the Mideast he negotiated a peace treaty between Israel and Egypt. This treaty still stands as the only permanent diplomatic success in the region.

Unfortunately for Carter, the American economy went down the tubes during his administration, the American military (except for the start of some weapons programs) was neglected, and his idea of projecting moral influence unsupported by true strength turned out to be a mistake. In November 1979 Iranian revolutionaries overran the U.S. Embassy in Tehran and took its personnel hostage. The following month the Soviet Union invaded Afghanistan, an action that took Carter by surprise. The nadir of his presidency came in April 1980 when Carter tried to rescue the hostages in Iran with what remained of the U.S. military.

The operation was daring enough. But while the Navy had helicopters it didn't have the pilots. The Marines had pilots but they were unfamiliar with the helicopters. The Air Force had transports, but then the Army Delta and Ranger troops inserted into Iran were not on the same page. Rangers on the perimeter blew up a passing fuel truck, jeopardizing the secret base, called Desert One, near Tehran. Three helicopters malfunctioned while en route from aircraft carriers, forcing the whole mission to be aborted. But during the withdrawal a remaining helicopter accidentally crashed into a transport plane at Desert One, causing both to explode in a huge fireball.

The next morning Iranian soldiers and reporters milled around the Desert One site, lining up eight charred U.S. bodies, gazing at abandoned helicopters and wreckage, while wondering to themselves if this was the best that America could do.

In the 1980 election Carter was defeated by Ronald Reagan of California. Reagan was heir to the conservative, Goldwater wing of the Republican Party, which had once scared everyone to death in 1964. Goldwater had seemed too militant at a time when America and the Soviets had their nuclear daggers drawn, but now a bit of militancy seemed like a good idea.

The gray complexity of Carter thus fell to the shining simplicity of Reagan. Thereafter presidential aides in Volkswagens were banished from the capital and the new administration unabashedly rode in limousines. In contrast to young aides forged through the sixties, Reagan was accompanied by a phalanx of self-made men, all of them wealthy and accustomed to power and influence. No one expected Reagan, like Carter, to carry his own bags in airports, but only to give a cheery thumbs-up before boarding Air Force One.

Reagan benefited from the fact that Ayatollah Khomeini released the U.S. hostages in Tehran the second Carter left office, so that he did not have a foreign policy albatross around his neck. Instead he focused on the economy, which was in a shambles due to double-digit inflation and usurious interest rates around 20 percent. Reagan's prescription was a huge tax-cut which in its effect primarily benefited wealthy individuals and corporations.

During this period the United States suffered its bleakest economic days since the 1930s. Amidst the idle or decrepit factories of New Jersey a troubadour arose, Bruce Springsteen, who defined the era in popular culture, singing, "Badlands, you gotta live 'em every day." In the midwest, John Cougar Mellencamp similarly lamented the plight of the farm belt.

But then inflation started falling, as did interest rates. The remaining problem was unemployment, the most painful economic problem of all, which was still through the roof. But then that indice, in an event that prompted jubilation in the White House, similarly began to fall. Two years into the Reagan administration, America had broken its fever. "Voodoo economics" had actually worked. And boom years were on the way.

Across the pond, Reagan had a counterpart in Margaret Thatcher of Great Britain. No less conservative than Reagan, she had become prime minister in 1979 and had similarly endured a dire economic crisis. But Britain, which had prudently steered clear of Vietnam, still had a fine-honed military establishment. In 1982 a crisis arose when Argentina arbitrarily seized a British possession, the Falkland Islands, just off the coast near the tip of South America.

The Falklands, which had originally been Spanish, then French, and seized for the Crown 150 years earlier, were now populated by 1,800 British subjects. According to Royal Marine officer Ewen

Southby-Tailyour, who had recently gone down for a survey, the islands were mainly populated by "a drunken, decadent, immoral and indolent collection of drop-outs." So the question arose: would Mrs. Thatcher consider the interests of Argentina, and by extension 300 million citizens of South America? Or would she attempt to reclaim the Falklands? The question didn't really need to be asked, and in April 1982 Americans were astonished to see the British Royal Navy at full steam, charging hellbent down the Atlantic toward the Falklands.

The commanders of the British Task Foce had no plans for what to do when they got there, but sailed into the fray with Mrs. Thatcher's declaration ringing in their ears "I do not know the meaning of the word defeat." As it turned out, the British had underestimated their foe. Many had thought Argentina would be a third-world pushover that would cave in at the first taste of first-world might. But Argentina had long been the home of tens of thousands of Italian and German immigrants, and as one commander reflected later, had for years been producing some of the best race car drivers in the world. When the British fleet set up shop near the islands it was beset by waves of French-built Mirage III and Super Entendard fighters, as well as American-made A-4 Skyhawks. Royal Air Force and Navy pilots rose to the challenge in Harrier jet fighters from the aircraft carriers *Hermes* and *Invincible*, but were unable to prevent 16 British ships from being sunk or heavily damaged during the campaign.

The skill of the Argentinian conscript army did not match that of its fighter pilots, and the Falklands soon returned to British hands thanks to SAS, SBS, and Royal Marine Commandos, along with other units that landed on the barren rocks to seize them back. The war had cost the British 255 dead and 777 wounded. The Argentinians suffered some 650 dead, over half of them from the cruiser *Belgrano* that was sneak-attacked by the nuclear submarine *Conqueror*, a controversial event that continues to be debated, not least in Britain, for its apparent lack of fair play.

Politically, the war provided a tremendous boost to Mrs. Thatcher. The Union Jack, which had been meekly folding up around the globe, had unfurled once again to symbolize courage, daring and a still-potent ability to straddle the hemispheres. The way these things work, Mrs. Thatcher found herself transformed from the most despised person in Britain, due to her ham-handed approach to economic problems, to the most admired one. Britain's own national malaise had been cured, and on a wave of new popularity based on martial pride, soon all the domestic cards began to fall her way.

The amazing thing about the Falklands War at the time was that it was waged as if the Cold War didn't exist. While the Americans were still shell-shocked by Vietnam, and the Soviets were just beginning to realize what a snakepit they had stepped into in Afghanistan, the British had merrily embarked on a martial adventure with limited goals and clear-cut lines. The conflict looked like an anachronism even as it was taking place, like some modern reenactment of the Napoleonic Age. Who could have guessed that the Falklands would not turn out to be a blast from the past, but instead a clarion call for the Anglo-Americans to once more assert themselves in the most forceful terms? A few years later, in fact, the Cold War did cease to exist, leaving the English-speaking peoples completely unfettered.

After conquering his economic problems Ronald Reagan had a good deal of political capital. While Goldwater had held claim to a minority of public support, the Gipper's success in restoring not only prosperity, but the tangible perception of a "new morning" in America, raised the conservative ranks into a near-majority. Many people who had feared Reagan, voting for Carter in 1980 despite that presidency having every woe imaginable, began to warm to the genial Californian.

The U.S. military was also beginning to shape up again. Each year hundreds of dedicated young people were graduating from the service academies, all untainted by the mess in Indochina and looking toward the future. After suddenly switching to a volunteer system after Vietnam, the de facto recruiting slogans, "Go to the army or go to jail," or "Enlist for three meals a day," had given way to a brighter motto that flooded the national airwaves: "Be all that you can be." Not only had the high school graduation rate in the army risen from less than half to more than 90 percent by the end of Reagan's terms, recruits were attracted specifically for their technical ambition and interest in higher education. The new influx of bright young people into the services also allowed officers to hammer down the drug problem.

Given the few opportunities available to him, Reagan did not distinguish himself as a military leader. In the last week of October 1983 two contrasting events took place: one a defensive disaster suffered by conventional forces and the other an offensive operation with Special Operations Forces.

The previous year Reagan had committed U.S. Marines, alongside troops from Britain, France and Italy, to quell factional chaos that had erupted in Beirut, Lebanon, after the Israelis had invaded that country. The Marines, under fire from all sides, had no clear mission of their own and simply took up positions at Beirut's airport. In October 1983, Arab Shiites, employing a new tactic, rammed a truck packed with over 10,000 pounds of explosives into the Marine barracks, collapsing it completely and killing 241 men. Across the city, another suicide truck bomber hit the French barracks, killing 60 paratroopers.

The carnage was sickening, and even worse, it was not clear how to retaliate, or against whom. The battleship *New Jersey* pounded Arab militia areas with 16-inch shells, but the indiscriminate fire created as many enemies as it killed. By the following March the Marines had pulled out of Lebanon, following the European contingents which had already left. Though it is difficult to find a silver lining in the Beirut disaster, the fact is that since then U.S. forces have not been caught similarly unawares in combat zones, despite far larger commitments in the Middle East. In 2003 Iraq, the only serious hit of that kind was suffered by the Italians, who lost 19 men. The lesson learned in 1983 may have saved the lives of many American soldiers later.

Just two days after the Beirut bombing, the United States launched an invasion of the tiny Caribbean island of Grenada. A Communist named Maurice Bishop had taken control of the island and Cubans had begun building a large airstrip suitable for strategic bombers. When an even more radical Communist, Bernard Coard, took power, by murdering Bishop and his cabinet, Reagan ordered an invasion. It was the first significant offensive undertaken by the U.S. military in over a decade, and the rust showed.

Navy SEALs were paradropped offshore for a scouting mission, but they were overladen with equipment and four of them drowned.

Army Rangers were assigned Air Force transports on which their equipment wouldn't fit. When they arrived over Grenada they couldn't decide whether to land their planes or parachute, and finally scrambled out in a chaotic jump. Three Army Black Hawks piled up and crashed at an enemy installation that turned out to be undefended. A brief flurry arose when the Navy refused permission for Army helicopters with wounded to land on its carriers. Altogether, the only positive note was that resistance had been so feeble, and there had been no regular Cuban troops as feared. In the days before the SNAFUs emerged, the public also took some pride that the United States was finally willing to reassert itself.

While Beirut had been a tragedy, Grenada revealed a larger, more systemic problem, and both the armed services and Congress set about to fix it. That this process took place over a period of years may seem odd—in World War II, Eisenhower had only two months to solve all the fiascos that had plagued the invasion of Sicily before the invasion of Italy got underway—but then again, during the 1980s America was at peace, unthreatened in its own homeland, and with no major urgencies. Barry Goldwater, together with Senators Sam Nunn and William Cohen, took the lead in refashioning U.S. military doctrine, and one of the results was Special Operations Command, a new branch of the armed services that placed units like the SEALs, Green Berets, Rangers, and Air Force SpecOps under one roof. There would be no more inter-service confusion during quick-reaction contingencies. At the same time Reagan continued to fund U.S. conventional forces, providing nearly everything they could ask for.

Reagan spent much of his presidency obsessed with Communist movements in Central America, and the U.S. became covertly involved in a series of messy, murderous wars until a combination of scandals and Congress finally called a stop. During his second term he openly projected U.S. power again to the Mideast.

In 1986 the U.S. Navy began bullying the rogue state of Libya whose leader, Colonel Muammar Qaddafi, was a sponsor of terrorism. When Qaddafi responded by blowing up a Berlin nightclub, killing an American soldier and wounding many more, U.S. F-111s based in England swooped down on several Libyan targets, including Qaddafi's personal tent. The surprise bombing, which may have killed one of Qaddafi's daughters, seemed to force the dictator to mend his ways. It wasn't till much later that the U.S. learned that the destruction of Pan Am Flight 103, which exploded the next year over Lockerbie, Scotland with 270 dead, had been the work of Libyan intelligence agents.

Beginning in 1987 U.S. naval forces began protecting Kuwaiti oil tankers in the Persian Gulf against Iranian attacks. Navy SEALs created two floating bases from which they could sally out with helicopters or small boats against enemy raiders. This otherwise successful effort ended in tragedy when the Navy accidentally shot down an Iranian airbus, killing 290 civilians. The U.S. would have blamed Qaddafi sooner for Pan Am 103 except Intelligence assumed it had been the Iranians avenging their airbus.

In military terms, Reagan is most remembered for escalating the decades-long stand-off with the Soviet Union to the point where they could no longer compete. He began in 1982 by declaring the Soviet Union an "evil empire." He then pressed for the deployment of intermediate-range, tactical nuclear weapons in Europe, as if he just couldn't wait for the long, cold confrontration to become hot. Europeans and American liberals protested loudly, but Reagan got his deployment, forcing the Russians to shift their resources likewise, though they had no intention of enduring, much less initiating, a nuclear conflict. Then Reagan unveiled his Strategic Defense Initiative, SDI, or as it was commonly called, "Star Wars." By that time, U.S. scientists had written enough theoretical papers so that Reagan believed the United States could build a space-based missile shield. Thus America would be invulnerable—which Reagan interpreted as a peacemaking prospect—while the Soviets would be made to cower under its sword.

In 1972 Nixon had negotiated an Anti-Ballistic Missile (ABM) treaty with the Soviets, on the theory that defensive systems had the same effect as offensive ones. Any missile that could be knocked down by a defense would only prompt two more to be created on the offense, where the more established technology was available. So if the world could already be destroyed 12 times over by the superpowers' combined 50,000 warheads, there was no point in erecting defensive systems that could be easily evaded by each side creating 100,000 warheads. Nuclear holocaust had to be avoided diplomatically, in his view, rather than by accelerating the technological race.

But Reagan chose to raise the stakes, and though his Star Wars was a chimera it spooked the Soviets enough to call off the arms' race. The American economy was booming and was far bigger than the Soviet one, so that while the U.S. had to devote, at most, five precent of its GDP to arms, the Soviets had to devote 30 percent just to keep up. And the American system called for a profit motive within defense, which fed back in taxes or political contributions, while the Soviet bureacracy was wasting billions on weapons they had no intention of using, at the expense of their infrastructure and consumer economy. In some quarters, Reagan, or Ronaldus Maximus, as radio talk-show host Rush Limbaugh calls him, is given credit for forcing the Soviet Union to collapse.

But as we now know, the USSR had severe internal problems of its own. In short, and literally, the Communist system was not working. Reagan's truculence and continual escalations of the nuclear poker game might have had an influence in the Kremlin. Devoting even more resources to a military arm that could not possibly be used except as a contribution to apocalypse might have been dismaying. On the other hand, since the CIA had consistently overestimated Soviet strategic potential for years, it could have been a simple matter for the Soviets to have faked a Star Wars of their own without expending serious resources. On the American side it was widely suspected that "Star Wars" was a figment of Reagan's imagination in the first place. By then America's oldest president wasn't inclined to pore through engineering reports, and the Soviets wouldn't have been hard-pressed to create their own anti-missile defense. (In the 1991 Gulf War, it turned out that the U.S. with its latest technology wasn't even able to knock down Iraqi Scuds, based on the old German V-2.) But the problems in the Soviet Union had by then extended far beyond matching American one-upsmanship in strategic weapons.

Reagan had come into office when the American military and economy were in shambles, and he left with both at unprecedented heights. Though his military operations had been modest, and not always successful, his strategic achievement of increasing American power relative to its potential enemies was impressive. And it had begun to look as if America's primary antagonist, the Soviet Union, was about to say uncle, ending a stand-off that had endured for over 40 years.

By 1989 it was clear that the world was about to enter a new phase. In some ways the Cold War had been the scariest conflict in history, since the survival of hundreds of millions of people—perhaps the human race itself—had been at stake. And though from a fortunate reservoir of common sense neither side had triggered a thermo-nuclear holocaust, enough lives had been shed during the hot flashes. In Korea, Vietnam, Greece, the Horn of Africa, Cambodia, Angola, Latin America, Malaysia, Hungary, Afghanistan and elsewhere, millions of lives had been lost as Moscow and Washington had wielded proxies against each other or at selected points had committed their own forces. And in the meantime much of the world had been filled to the brim with modern weapons. Villagers in the Congo now possessed SA-7 anti-aircraft missiles while Arabs drove T-72s and Afghan tribesmen had become schooled in heat-seeking Stingers. The "Kalashnikov-ization" of dozens of ex-colonies had become complete, when those militias weren't armed with U.S. M-16s.

The Cold War would end without climactic conflagration, but in the meantime it had militarized the globe, placing great quantities of modern arms in societies where indigenous industry was far from inventing them. Conversely, the arms makers in industrialized countries enjoyed excellent business and became leading exporters

The big question as the Cold War drew to an end was what kind of world would replace it. Without the Soviet Union trying to instigate proletarian revolutions everywhere from El Salvador to Somalia, the United States, too, could relax its support of every dictator, monarch, or oligarch who professed determination to resist Communist rule. The U.S. armed forces could be drawn down, in what politicians termed a "peace dividend," but which, at the same time, was not such a boon to defense contractors.

Idealists pointed to the example of the former Axis Powers in World War II. Germany and Japan, the "evil empires" of their day, had transformed into democratic states under American tutelage. With their armies disbanded they had reasserted themselves instead as economic powers, where they ranked second and third in the world behind the United States. Russia, too, seemed inclined to head in that direction, as did China, albeit with very careful incremental steps.

With the demise of the Soviet Union, there would be only one superpower, and that was in the New World, where Americans had invented a system of government from scratch, after drawing on the best philosophies of prior democracies from ancient Athens to the Swiss Confederation to Britain's Glorious Revolution. America had emerged into the 20th century after difficult travails on its own raw continent, and thence had grown strong enough to project its principles outward, against any imperial, aggressive or totalitarian designs.

But America had never occupied such a high strata of pure power by itself before. Would it continue to act in concert with allies, like a sheriff in a western town who led posses to take action on behalf of the public good; or had it now become so strong that it could act according to its own interests, without a need for allies, fully aware that no one had the power to stand in its way?

It is one of the odd twists of history that in the world's leading democracy this question would be answered by a father and son. Ronald Reagan was ill-equipped to wield military power in the early 1980s. His several ventures backfired, he never had the opportunity to wage a hot war, and in the last days of his administration he was probably not capable of decisive action at all. During the 1990s Bill Clinton triangulated mightily, trying to sublimate American strength into the multilateral crowd, while eliminating combat deaths in honorable consistency with his own past of having dodged military service during Vietnam. Clinton took office on the cusp of an economic boom, won two terms, and then left just as the economy went south again. He was either the most brilliant U.S. president or the luckiest; in any case his reign resulted in so much media attention on minutiae that he barely escaped with his dignity intact.

So we are left with the Bushes, father and son. To date they are the only two men who have wielded American military power confidently and decisively in battle since the haunting experience of Vietnam. But like strangers, one Smith and the other Jones, they have operated under separate guiding philosophies, not just about how and when to project American might, but over the very nature of American leadership in the world.

One thing that ties the presidencies of the father and son together is that soon after taking office, each was greeted by the sudden collapse of a massive physical structure. For the father, the event was the fall of the Berlin Wall, a once impregnable barrier, the ruin of which unleashed a wave of liberty around the globe. For the son, the autumn event was the fall of the World Trade Center in New York, a heinous surprise attack that laid bare America's vulnerability.

While the father took advantage of the Berlin Wall's collapse to enact his vision of a new international order, based on moral as well as military leadership, tying the world together under traditional American principles, the disaster of 9/11 caused the son to take a different view. The collapse of the World Trade Center, in conjunction with America's great military-technological leap beyond other nations, indicated to him that new rules were in order. Pre-emption and preeminence would become his guiding concepts. The arsenal of democracy would now become its avenger. While the father believed that the American example alone could encourage freedom, the son perceived that that example could be enforced.

America's military history since Vietnam consists of many stops and starts, some half-hearted efforts, and an even greater deal of hesitation. But four major projections of U.S. power have taken place since 1975, two each by the Bushes, father and son. They are the only two presidents since Vietnam who have triggered offensive warfare, on the ground as well as in the air. The fascinating thing is how different their concepts of leadership have been, as if the two men were not related at all.

1

BUSH 41

George H.W. Bush took an unusual path to the presidency. He was not very successful as a politician, serving only two terms as a Congressman from Texas in the late sixties and failing in both of his runs for the Senate. He did not win another election on his own until he reached the White House. In the meantime, however, he had gained a vast wealth of experience through appointed positions, the most prominent of which was his designation as Ronald Reagan's vice-president in the 1980s.

Bush was born an eastern blue-blood in 1924, the son of investment banker Prescott Bush, who in middle-age would go on to become a senator from Connecticut. He was named George Herbert Walker after his maternal grandfather, who by that time was called Pop, so young Bush was saddled from birth with the family nickname "Poppy." He split his childhood seasons between family houses in Connecticut, South Carolina and Maine, and attended exclusive private schools. He was 17 years old, in his senior year at Andover, when Pearl Harbor was attacked, and he then counted down the days to both high school graduation and his 18th birthday. On that day he enlisted in the naval air force and so became the youngest pilot in the U.S. Navy.

After training, he was assigned to the aircraft carrier USS *San Jacinto*, flying the Grumman Avenger. This was not the luckiest of results for Bush, since the Avenger was probably the homeliest, least agile plane fielded by the Navy in World War II. While hundreds of other U.S. pilots were flying elegant Corsairs or tough Hellcats, Bush piloted a craft that resembled a pregnant pheasant, with a three-man crew (pilot, radio operator, and rear gunner) and a big belly to store bombs or from which to hang torpedoes. In the Pacific War, this craft's primary fame resulted from the Battle of Midway, where the Japanese annihilated an entire attacking squadron.

Bush nevertheless piloted the plane on dozens of missions, earning an excellent reputation for skill. Part of this came during the Battle of the Philippine Sea when his plane was hit and he executed a very difficult landing on the ocean. This meant keeping a tiny fraction of elevation while the tail hit the water first to create drag. The most miniscule slip on the nose would have smashed him and his crew into a veritable brick wall, but he was able to guide the plane down. Bush's luck ran out over the island of Chichi Jima in 1944, when Japanese anti-aircraft fire hit his craft while he was dive-bombing a blockhouse containing an enemy radio transmission station.

His cockpit filling with smoke, Bush remained steady long enough to deliver his bombs, and then veered out to the sea. His wing was on fire with the flames approaching the gas tanks, and the controls were slipping, so he yelled "bail out" through the intercom to his crewmates. The Japanese recorded two parachutes emerging from the plane before it crashed into the sea; however, only Bush, who had just made his first parachute jump on a few seconds notice, survived the fall. It's remarkable that he also gashed his forehead against the tail section of the plane when jumping, since this had been the demise of many another World War II pilot, including the legendary ace, Joachim Marseilles. One quarter inch, as Bush was swept back against the vertical stabilizer, made all the difference.

In the water Bush found the plane's liferaft but looked in vain for his comrades. He tried to paddle as fast as possible from the island while Japanese boats came out from the shore. His squadron mates had seen the crash and swooped in to keep the enemy at bay. After the war it was revealed that the Japanese commander on Chichi Jima had practiced cannibalism on the eight other U.S. flyers he had captured.

Bush did not have a happy time alone on his raft, and was startled again when a submarine began to broach the surface just yards away. "God, I hope it's one of ours," he thought, as the huge steel craft rose from the depths. Indeed it was. The Navy had realized the perils of

Chichi Jima and had positioned a submarine to retrieve shot-down fly-ers in what today is called Combat Search and Rescue. The skinny, shaky Lieutenant Bush was pulled aboard the sub and guided to the conning tower. Little did any of the sailors realize they had just retrieved a future president of the United States.

Bush had the option to sit out the rest of the war, but instead returned to the fleet to fly eight more missions, making 58 in all. After the war he returned to his sweetheart, Barbara, and attended Yale University, where he became captain of the baseball team and was inducted into the secretive college fraternity, Skull and Bones.

After graduating from college, Bush could have strolled into any number of lucrative professions in the East, but instead decided to invent his own part of the family legacy by moving to west Texas. This was not such a daring venture as is sometimes portrayed, because fol-lowing the war it was widely perceived that oil would be the new fount of fortune for ambitious young executives, and the brushweed territory around towns like Midland and Lubbock became the Silicon Valley of its day. A number of Ivy Leaguers moved west to get on top of the new wellspring of the economy.

After his successful launch of an oil business in Texas, Bush felt drawn to follow his father into public service and became a Con-gressman. His 1970 bid for the Senate, in those years when Nixon had just formulated his "Southern Strategy," was turned back by the native Texan Lloyd Bentsen. These two would clash again when Bush ran for president and Bentsen was the vice-presidential choice of Massachusetts' Michael Dukakis. In the meantime both their eldest sons served in the same unit of the Texas Air National Guard.

Bush proceeded to take on a series of jobs on behalf of his party. First, Nixon appointed him the American ambassador to the United Nations, at a time when two-thirds of that body consisted of newborn Third World nations who dominated its general assembly. This was his first direct foreign policy experience and the foundation for what would become first-name familiarity with a remarkable array of world leaders. Bush then became the Republican national chairman during the Watergate crisis. In that role, untouched by the scandal, he man-aged to keep a respectable veneer on the party. He was afterward appointed U.S. envoy to Red China, a remote post where his eldest son reportedly tried and failed to meet girls. Then, in a true dead-end appointment, President Ford named him head of the CIA. The Democrats were wary of approving a Republican party operative in the post, which had just been wracked by scandals, so Bush had to renounce any political ambitions of his own in 1976 in order to be approved by Congress.

The upside to his various appointments was that Bush continued to be prominent in one way or another, all the while building his network of contacts, both domestically and abroad. He was not bombastic in public, but had a real talent for forging personal relationships, based on trust, intelligence, and a sure-handed grasp of American imperatives. These could be based on either pragmatism or principle, but Bush was capable of negotiating the difference. He had a habit of keeping his cards close to his chest, while respecting the confidence of others. He was what Victorian British officers, with their highest compliment, would have called "a steady man."

In 1980, freed from the strictures of Ford, Bush ran for president, giving Ronald Reagan a good run for his money in the primaries. At the Republican convention, Reagan was still at a loss whom to pick as his vice-presidential nominee. Negotiations were held with Ford's people who suggested a kind of co-presidency in which Ford would handle foreign policy while Reagan focused on domestic issues. This held no attraction for the Gipper, and at the last minute he turned to George Bush, genially overlooking the fact that during the primaries Bush had called Reagan's tax proposals "voodoo economics." At that point Reagan's most important imperatives were achieving a demographic/political balance on the ticket—and Bush not only represented Texas but the moderate Eastern establishment wing of the party— and second, which was Reagan's big gamble, enlisting a VP who would sublimate his own ambitions to support Reagan's agenda.

As it turned out, Bush considered loyalty a high virtue, and for the next eight years devoted himself to making the Reagan administration a success. Any differences he had with the president were discussed in private, never made public, and even when Reagan was badly wounded in an assassination attempt in 1981, Bush stayed discreetly behind the scenes. The vice president's staff was naturally drawn from his loyalists, but like Eisenhower in World War II, who forbade his officers to express Anglophobic sentiments, Bush prohibited his staff from openly criticizing the president.

When Reagan interviewed Bush at the 1980 convention, the only promise he exacted was that Bush would back his pro-life view on abortion. Bush was happy to comply, since like many middle-aged male politicians he had always fluttered around the issue, mainly hoping it would go away. Bush maintained a pro-life stance throughout his own presidency, though he was not the kind of person that partisans could count on for passion, and word eventually seeped out that Barbara Bush was pro-choice.

An oddity attached to Bush's political career is the word "wimp" that his political opponents often used to describe him. For a volunteer fighter pilot who gained more combat experience than any other 20th-century president, who also captained his school sports teams, and founded a successful business in west Texas, the term is hard to fathom. Bush's supposed wimpdom is commonly attributed to his Eastern upper class expressions as well as a modest lack of macho carriage. But these reasons hardly suffice to override his actual physical and philosphical toughness.

The real source of "wimp" is probably that Bush—both physically and through his self-effacing manner—just viscerally reminded everyone of Darrin on "Bewitched," Major Nelson on "I Dream of Jeannie" or other sitcom figures who were constantly befuddled by more clever wives or servants. Barbara Bush, whose great youthful beauty was supplanted by pugnacious character in middle-age, may have contributed to this perception. It's ironic that "wimp" was eventually thrown around most often by those who opposed Bush's military initiatives and his refusal to bend his course to prevailing winds while drawing down the Cold War.

A related sneer at Bush came from a female journalist who said, "He reminds every woman of her first husband." This slur was widely repeated, though hardly anyone knew what it meant.

As Reagan's vice president, the joke was that Bush was "mourner in chief," due to all the funerals of foreign leaders he attended on the president's behalf. In fact, these foreign trips, which also included inaugurations, anniversaries, treaty signings and the like, allowed him to increase his already considerable familiarity with foreign leaders, and in turn to familiarize them with American policies. Bush also headed the administration's crisis management team, which was tested during 1983's short-notice invasion of Grenada. This was Bush's first experience with wielding U.S. military forces and the results were mixed. After the almost simultaneous Marine disaster in Beirut, Bush was instrumental in persuading Reagan to withdraw U.S. troops. The intervention in Lebanon had been a classic case of over-reaching, leaving American forces without clear strategic goals, merely with the status of sitting ducks.

After Reagan finished his second term, Bush ran for president, successfully fending off a serious primary challenge from Senate Minority Leader Bob Dole. At the 1988 Republican convention he chose youthful Indiana Senator Dan Quayle as his running mate. This often-criticized choice was vindicated not by Quayle's qualities as much as by the leap in stature Bush gained by standing next to him. Bush had just emerged from Reagan's shadow (where columnist George Will had labeled him a "lap dog") and if he had chosen the ascerbic ex-infantryman Dole or an ex-football quarterback like Jack Kemp as his running mate, the so-called "wimp factor" might have lingered on.

Bush's acceptance speech at the convention was notable for his call for "a kinder, gentler America." In fact, the late Reagan years had been characterized by Gordon Gekko's motto, "Greed is good," a concept that resulted in widespread corporate scandals and a growing income disparity between wealthy people and the middle class. Bush's "kinder, gentler" prescription was viewed as suspicious at first by the Reaganites, who had never fully accepted Bush and now wondered if he was subtly criticizing the Gipper. But they need not have worried.

The 1988 presidential race turned into a romp as the Republican right-wing that had been steadily invigorated for eight years by Reagan suddenly burst out on Bush's behalf against the hapless Democratic candidate, Michael Dukakis. Bush's campaign manager, the impish Lee Atwater, played up every symbolic issue for all it was worth, from Dukakis' ingenuous claim to being a card-carrying member of the ACLU to his veto of a bill requiring students to say the Pledge of Allegiance, to his parole of Willie Horton, a murderer who went on to commit further mayhem. The latter issue was echoed in one of the presidential debates, when Dukakis gave an incorrect answer to the question how he would react if if his wife Kitty was raped and murdered. The most famous image of the campaign was of the card-carrying guy from Massachusetts, attempting to establish defense credentials, riding around in circles in a tank while wearing a helmet double the size of his head.

For his part, Bush stressed his utter conviction that what the United States really needed was a Constitutional amendment to ban flag burning. The Republican right had had their doubts about Bush, but the 1988 campaign evolved into their coming out party. While the term "conservative" had become a byword during the 1960s and 1970s, now the term "liberal" was demonized to the point where it could hardly be spoken, referred to instead as the "L-word." Bush, though actually a moderate, provided as much red meat to the right as he could. With the Soviets on the decline, conservatives had found an equally heinous villain in domestic taxation (not entirely illogical since both represented "big government"). Playing to this fervor, Bush fiercely declared, "Read my lips: no new taxes!" If he had left out the "read my lips" part, the vow would probably have not have been so well remembered.

After taking the oath of office in January 1989, Bush put his foreign policy team in place. The State Department went to his old friend from Texas, James A. Baker, III. Baker had managed Bush's 1980 run for the presidency and then, to the surprise of many, had been appointed Reagan's first White House chief of staff. In 1986 he switched jobs with Donald Regan and became Secretary of the Treasury (while Regan went on to take much of the brunt of Iran-Contra and then was forced to resign). Baker was a hard-nosed pragmatist, an excellent negotiator, and had an easy familiarity with Bush based on 15 years of friendship.

The position of National Security Adviser had been pumped up by Henry Kissinger and its prominence continued by Carter's Zbigniew Brzezinski, until, under Reagan, the office collapsed into scandal. Bush chose former Air Force General Brent Scowcroft as his NSA. A brilliant analyst and theorist, Scowcroft had served under Nixon and Ford and had no desire for personal limelight. He saw his job as simply to advise the president, and the two men eventually achieved a seamless intellectual partnership. When Bush wrote his post-presidential foreign policy memoir it was co-authored by Scowcroft.

For Secretary of Defense, Bush wanted Senator John Tower of Texas, but after a painful series of Congressional hearings alleging drunkenness and womanizing, Tower removed himself from consideration. Bush settled on Dick Cheney, a congressman from Wyoming who had risen to become the Republican Whip, and who had formerly been Ford's chief-of-staff at the age of 34.

Baker, Scowcroft and Cheney were fine players, but the catalytic piece of the puzzle arrived on September 30 when Colin Powell was vaulted above fourteen other four-star generals to become Chairman of the Joint Chiefs of Staff. Powell's entry into the inner circle of the Bush administration was noteworthy for several reasons. Replacing Admiral William Crowe, who had provided more a brake to military dynamism than encouragement, Powell was the first Chairman to take office after the Goldwater-Nichols Act, which had elevated the Chairman to be the sole spokesman for the service chiefs. Powell would take council from the heads of the Army, Air Force, Navy, and Marines, but he alone was now empowered to represent the broader military's view to the government.

Second, Powell had been promoted after serving as commander of U.S. Armed Forces, or the domestically-based military, but just a year earlier he had been Reagan's National Security Adviser, and before that Caspar Weinberger's aide at Defense. A more political general, intimately familiar with how the White House worked, could not be found. In addition, while the administration was stocked with veterans, Powell was the only senior participant whose combat experience had come from Vietnam.

Finally, as an African-American, Powell was a media magnet, and had even been suggested as a running mate for Bush in 1988. Though as Chairman of the Joint Chiefs Powell was officially subordinate to Cheney at the Department of Defense, he was in an excellent position to have an influence in Bush's councils.

The Bush administration's first task—and arguably its greatest achievement—was to draw the Cold War to a close through pragmatic cooperation with the Soviet Union. Historically, the end of the Cold

War was no less important than the defeat of the Axis in World War II or the Central Powers in the Great War. In fact, considering the dangers involved, the strength of the opposing powers, and the fact that the end of the conflict involved almost no bloodshed, it was a more impressive achievement.

The process had been set in motion by Mikhail Gorbachev, who in 1985 had become head of the Communist Party, thus the most powerful man in the USSR. In his own society Gorbachev had initiated the twin concepts of glasnost (openness) and perestroika (restructuring). Both policies seemed eminently worthwhile, and even surprisingly in line with Western principles. The first question for Bush was whether Gorbachev was sincere or if he was actually pursuing new tactics to increase Soviet strength. During the 1970s American power had declined and the Soviets had taken advantage of its weakness by spreading its own influence and even launching a military invasion, in Afghanistan. By the time Reagan was through, America was once more in the ascendant and Soviet economic problems had become acute. Personally, Gorbachev was a dynamic, charismatic figure, and younger than previous Soviet leaders, but it was difficult to tell if his true goal was only to regain the Soviets' advantage.

Assuming Gorbachev was sincere in his desire for peace and for an open society, another question for Bush was how to provide cooperation without overly encouraging Soviet-occupied states to jump the gun. Impromptu liberation movements had arisen in Hungary in 1956 and Czechoslovakia in 1968, both of which had been brutally suppressed by Red Army reflexes. And if Gorbachev was suddenly assailed by chaos it was unclear if he could retain power.

Bush ultimately trusted the Soviet leader, but it turned out that Gorbachev had misjudged several essential factors. First, once he opened Soviet society it became clear that the economy was much worse off relative to the West than anyone had imagined. And by stripping off the layers of entrenched bureaucracy it only sank into a deeper mess.

Gorbachev was also blind-sided by ethnic and cultural forces that burst to the fore the minute he relaxed the Kremlin's grip. He may have assumed that Communism had rendered ethnicity as a political force obsolete, except for perhaps the occupied nations of Europe. But now, led by the Baltic states, which had always held onto a theoretical lifeline of independence through the West's refusal to recognize Russian sovereignty, even the Soviet republics themselves were champing at the bit for freedom. Long-suppressed nationalism in Ukraine, Moldova, Georgia and the Muslim republics in the south had risen to a cacaphony of political clamor. Finally, Gorbachev's persistent belief that a modified form of Communism could still provide a solution to the USSR's problems was a view shared by almost no one else, inside his country and without.

One of the chairman's dilemmas was that just as he unleashed the ethnic genie in his own domain he had also made great strides in rapprochement with America and the West. The West thus became a restraining factor as Gorbachev contemplated how to deal with his restive republics. It was not exactly feasible for him to invade Latvia with one hand while grasping the Nobel Peace Prize in the other. And for his own goal of perestroika, close ties with the West were vital for improving his people's standard of living.

During this period there was no shortage of reactionary elements in the USSR's military and society who were appalled at the proceedings. Germany, which had once ravaged the Soviet Union to the tune of 20 million dead, was now contemplating reunification. In the East, China was calmly gathering its strength while Japan had emerged as the number-two economic power in the world. Across the ocean America, which still had 15,000 nuclear warheads aimed at the USSR, was obviously on the rise. If, at this juncture, the U.S. administration had begun proclaiming a doctrine of world hegemony or pre-emptive war—or even repeating Reagan's "evil empire" view—the Soviet Union might have collapsed into a military dictatorship rather than an explosion of ethnic self-determination.

In the White House, Bush, Baker, and Scowcroft were intent on easing the transition. Defense Secretary Cheney went off the rails one day by expressing his own view, that "Gorbachev will ultimately fail," but he was quickly corrected, and as a good team player went on to contribute to the administration's program.

Domestically, Bush was able to fend off criticism from the right that he wasn't "hard enough" on Gorbachev, while deflecting criticism from the left, that he should press the Soviet leader faster and harder for the liberation of Eastern Europe and the Baltics. Instead, Bush kept a steady hand on the situation. As a centrist, Bush recognized the pressures Gorbachev was under from both sides of his own political spectrum. The prime imperative was to stay the course.

Indeed, 1989 was a heady year for the United States and the world. In May Bush went to Europe where he put American weight behind the concept of German reunification. This meant breaking the tight bonds that Reagan had forged with Britain's Mrs. Thatcher, who was still suspicious of Germany. But Bush thought that Western Europe had evolved beyond its bloody competitions of the past, and that Germany could now be a rock for democratic principles and peaceful commerce. Beyond that, he hoped that a reunified Germany's safe integration into a peaceful network of global commerce would serve as a model for Russia, its dependencies and clients, who could similarly join the world community.

The following month, the world was astonished at images emerging from China, where hundreds of thousands of people had taken to the streets, some of them carrying homemade replicas of America's Statue of Liberty. But the scenes of triumph turned to tragedy when the Chinese government finally quelled the demonstrations with firepower, killing hundreds of demonstrators in Beijing's Tianamen Square. The world was mesmerized by the act of one young man who, armed with nothing but courage, stood before a government tank, not permitting it to go around him. It became an iconic image of the end of the Cold War, and also a harbinger for the future of freedom in China.

In Washington, Tianamen Square was one of those occasions when both the left and right hammered the administration, demanding stern punitive measures against the Chinese government. But in Bush they were dealing with a man who knew more about the country than they, having served as U.S. Envoy after Nixon had opened relations. Though expressing disapproval and slapping on certain sanctions, Bush refused to revoke China's Most Favored Nation trade status, knowing full well that interaction with the West was the best guarantor of China's progress in human rights, rather than shutting off the Middle Kingdom into isolation once again.

In November 1989 the Berlin Wall was torn down by joyous

crowds, and across Europe the Iron Curtain both physically and sym-
bolically bit the dust. In Prague, Warsaw and Budapest, the scenes of
liberation resembled those in Paris and Amsterdam when U.S. tanks
had finally come rolling in after years of brutal fighting. But this time
it had been bloodless, the Russians and Americans acting carefully in
concert without using troops. It was not only a triumph for diplomacy
but for civilization.

For 40 years the U.S. military's primary task had been to prepare for
a war with the Soviet Union. But in the meantime it had adjusted to
the times and prepared for other contingencies. A new generation of
weapons, including Black Hawk helicopters and the M-1 Abrams
tank, had been launched under Carter. When Reagan took office the
soldiers themselves were given priority so that the services had become
not just a refuge for what Wellington, referring to his British conscripts, called "the scum of the earth," but a career for many of the
best and brightest in American society. In 1987 Special Operations
Command, or SOCOM, was created as a new branch of the armed
forces, giving the United States a new dimension in hard-hitting,
quick-reaction forces.

And they would soon be needed. In strategically vital Panama, a
thug dictator had taken control and had become increasingly dangerous to his own people and to vital American interests. A product of his
times, Manuel Noriega had built his career upon the chaos of the Cold
War, and had enriched himself further through the drug offensive
mounted by South American cartels. Regardless of the earthshaking
events happening in Europe and Asia, President Bush knew that sooner or later he would have to deal with this problem closer to home.

2

THE INVASION OF PANAMA

President Bush knew Manuel Noriega personally. He had called him on the carpet first when he was CIA director under President Ford, and had encountered him afterward during his travels as Reagan's vice president. Noriega had been a CIA "asset" ever since the late 1950s, and had reached his height during the Reagan administration's Cold War obsession with Latin America during the 1980s. But he had suddenly become a villain in the United States after the influx of cocaine from the south began to loom as a more dangerous threat to American society than the threat of Communism from the east.

During the 1988 presidential campaign, the Democrats had tried to tar Bush with his connection to Noriega, and it was indeed one of their best issues. Bush was able to fend off the sometimes sinister accusations, while at the same time he had difficulty defending so many years of U.S. policy. In the wake of the Reagan administration's secretive, bloody, and ill-advised fixation on Cold War issues in Latin America, the Bush administration was left with one of America's most vital strategic possessions threatened by the control of a violently criminal dictator.

PANAMA

Panama was founded for Spain during the great wave of exploration that followed Columbus's initial voyage to the New World. The first settlement, established by Columbus himself in 1501, fell to disease, but some ten years later Vasco Balboa founded an enduring colony among a native population estimated at over half a million.

In the wake of the revolutions led by the great South American patriot Simon Bolivar, Panama broke free from Spain in 1821 and became part of Colombia. At the time there was a vision that the ex-Spanish colonies could unite to form a great state, and Venezuala and Ecuador were also part of a short-lived federation. But skill at government did not follow Bolivar's ambitions and the region was wracked by violence, repeated coups, despotism, and widespread poverty. Only Brazil, which had been a Portuguese colonial project, emerged from the chaos as a formidably large state, albeit one largely buried under impenetrable rain forest.

Part of the problem was that the demographics the Spanish left behind did not argue for coherence. Whereas the English in North America had arrived in sufficient numbers to evict the native population, the Spanish were only able to implant a ruling class, along with a number of African slaves. And while the English had encountered true primitives in the north, the Spanish had encountered remnants of powerful empires such as the Aztecs, Mayans and Incas, who had once built great cities. The demographics eventually hardened into a strata of a European-descended ruling class, an even smaller percentage of indigeous natives who steered clear of civilization in forests or mountains, and the great majority, mestizos, who were sedentary people, often of mixed race, who comprised the poor and mostly uneducated masses. Politics in Latin America naturally flowed from the educated, land-owning class, resulting in a series of oligarchies, while the bulk of the population, not so privileged, engaged in constant revolutions and civil wars.

Panama was blessed by geography as the last and thinnest leg of the Central American isthmus, and beginning with the 1849 Gold Rush to California, found itself a desirable short-cut for hordes of United States citizens rushing to the Pacific. The idea soon took hold of cutting a canal through the country that would drastically shorten the treacherous route that ships had to travel around the tip of South America. In 1869, Fernando de Lessups completed the Suez Canal, and ten years later started the Panama Canal, the perfect twin that would have effectively chopped the world in half for seafaring commerce. But conditions in Panama were far more difficult than in the arid sands of Egypt and his laborers died of disease faster than he could hire new ones. The project was dropped.

In 1898 the United States fought the Spanish-American War, an easy victory that put to death once and for all the remnants of Spain's global empire. The Monroe Doctrine, which declared the Americas off limits to Europe, gained a corollary that allowed the United States to assert its own interests. In 1903 Teddy Roosevelt dispatched gunboats to help sever Panama from Colombia. Later that year the United States began building the canal. An enormous project, it was well worth the cost in both money and lives, because now the two halves of the continental U.S. could be quickly connected by sea, and in addition America could now project power more quickly to both of its surrounding oceans. The canal was completed on August 15, 1914, two weeks after the start of World War I. At the time, British and French armies were desperately trying to stave off a German juggernaut aimed at Paris, while the Germans and Austrians were concerned with a Russian drive descending on them from the east. The United States would refrain from that conflict for three more years, but in the meantime the Panama Canal had empowered it considerably.

Its commercial benefits aside, the Panama Canal really paid off in World War II, when the United States fought simultaneously against Germany in Europe and Japan in the Pacific. While Suez was partially blocked off during the war, the Axis Powers could not get close to Panama, where the canal was protected by over 60,000 American troops. In return for its independence, Panama had granted U.S. sovereignty over a 10-mile strip on either side of the waterway called the Canal Zone.

Like other Latin American states, Panama underwent a revolving door of governments in a process that accelerated after World War II. Europe's degradation in that conflict put an end to the colonial age, but now there was Communism to rouse the ambitions of the masses. In 1968 the last aristocratic leader of Panama was overthrown in an army coup and General Omar Torrijos took control. Torrijos subsequently became the model of a "good" dictator. To the degree that democracy equaled chaos in the mainly poor, illiterate Third World, and Communisn represented a fearsome sort of institutional control, as well as Soviet strategic advantages, the West's hopes frequently rest-ed on benevolent dictators, who could achieve stability while not imposing such a strict totalitarianism that would preclude an evolution to democracy and its necessary partner, individual prosperity. Torrijos, who was decent as well as ambitious and who aspired to be a hero to the Panamian people, was just such a good dictator. For his dirty work he relied on his chief of intelligence, Manuel Noriega.

Noriega hardly knew his parents, a maid and the employer who had impregnated her, but was warmly raised by a friend of his mother. He was unimpressive physically, being squat and stricken with severe acne, but was bright and industrious. He was able to enroll as a military cadet in a Peruvian school where in the late 1950s he first began providing information on other cadets to the CIA. Eisenhower's was thus the first of seven successive U.S. administrations to keep him on their payroll. (Jimmy Carter, in his effort to clean up the CIA, took him off for awhile but he was reinstated under Reagan.) Like many other Latin officers from regimes friendly to the U.S., he received training at a special school at Fort Bragg, North Carolina, and worked closely with American troops and advisers in Panama, where the U.S. Southern Command (SOUTHCOM) was based.

Noriega had a true talent for intelligence work. In fact, he spied on everyone, from his countrymen to the Americans to the Communists to the South American drug cartels, keeping massive amounts of files while covertly making himself valuable to all sides.

In 1976 he was called on the carpet by George Bush, who was then director of the CIA under President Ford. During negotiations over the Panama Canal, the U.S. had bugged and wiretapped Torrijos but Noriega had bribed Spanish-speaking U.S. sergeants to obtain copies of the tapes. What the U.S. knew about Panama was possibly less than what Noriega, if not Torrijos, knew about the United States. More seriously, after a stall in the Canal negotiations, Noriega, at Torrijos' behest, had set off three bombs in the Canal Zone. When Noriega appeared for his meeting with the CIA director, the two intelligence chiefs struck a stark contrast—on one side the tall, confident patrician Bush representing the world's greatest espionage resources, and on the other the short, homely Mestizo who had a natural genius for the spy game. Both men knew not to reveal all their cards, and Noriega denied having anything to do with the bombings. He only questioned why (how) Bush knew he was involved. Bush didn't fall for the bait and concluded simply by stating that he didn't expect such incidents to occur in the future.

Noriega felt he had dodged a bullet. With his patron, Torrijos, determined to acquire the Canal it would have been a simple matter for the U.S. to have demanded his head as part of the price. Noriega subsequently tried to be as valuable to the Americans as he could, a task made easier when the Communist Sandinistas took over Nicaragua in 1979 and the Americans suddenly needed local allies. That year he also took the deposed Shah of Iran off America's hands for a while, providing a beach house and nonjudgmental political refuge, though the Shah considered his Panamanian experience distasteful.

Jimmy Carter signed the Panama Canal Treaty in September 1977 and it was ratified by the Senate the following year, despite virulent right-wing opposition led by Jesse Helms. The Canal would be handed over to Panama at the start of the year 2000. As part of the deal, Torrijos agreed to hold democratic elections in 1984, largely because he was fully confident he would win them, since he was the national hero who had gained the Canal.

The troubles began when Torrijos died in a plane crash against a foggy mountainside in 1981. Everyone from the Sandinistas to the CIA to Castro to Noriega has been accused of engineering his death, but it may well have been an accident. After two years of jockeying with fellow officers, Noriega rose to the head of the army, called the Guardia Nacionale, which made him the most powerful man in Panama. Unlike Torrijos, however, he was uncomfortable with being a front man, and for the next six years he would rule behind a succession of presidents beholden to him for their position.

As Latin America gradually became a Cold War hotspot, Noriega entered his heyday. A great admirer of Israel, he renamed the Guardia Nacionale the Panamanian Defense Force (PDF) after Israel's IDF. He hired an ex-Mossad operator to train an elite special forces group, the USEAT, while he hired Cubans to train other contingents. Through bribes and intimidation with paramilitary forces he was able to steal the 1984 election for his own presidential candidate, Nicholas Barletta. The U.S. suspected fraud but was pleased there had been an election at all, and Barletta had once been a student of Secretary of State George Shultz, who flew down to attend his inauguration.

The Reagan administration had increasingly become obsessed with Latin America, where in El Salvador it was supporting the government in beating back a Communist revolution, and in Nicaragua was supporting a counter-revolutionary group, called the Contras, against the Communist government. Noriega, who provided bases, logistics and intelligence for the U.S. efforts, was invited to meetings with Vice President Bush, Secretary of Defense Caspar Weinberger, and on several occasions with Colonel Oliver North, who directed covert—or as some would say, "cowboy"—operations from within the White House.

For his part, Noriega was playing a multi-cornered game to enrich himself. With the grand old man, and chief anti-gringo, of the Caribbean, Fidel Castro, he traded gossip and intelligence. With the rising drug cartels of Colombia he provided the same kind of base and transport services he provided North, as well as the same money-laundering services. Noriega worked mainly for the Medellin Cartel, but in typical careful fashion he kept in good graces with the U.S. Drug Enforcement Agency by providing tips on other drug operations, invariably Medellin competitors.

In 1984 Noriega seemingly betrayed the Medellin Cartel by swooping in to destroy a secret camp and airfield it had bought permission from him to build in the Panamian jungle. Fearing for his life, Noriega suddenly left on a trip to Europe. According to investigative reporter Frederick Kempe, Fidel Castro mediated the dispute by setting up a meeting between representatives of the cartel and Noriega in Havana. It turned out that American DEA agents had accidentally caught wind of the Medellin installation and Noriega had decided to quash it before it became operational. This not only put another feather in his cap with the DEA but allowed him to eventually release the prisoners and captured equipment, since no actual drugs had been found. With peace restored, Noriega resumed his position as a kind of early warning system for the cartel about DEA designs.

Domestically, Panama sank into ruin under Noriega's criminal dictatorship, and democratic elements began to seek reform. A popular opposition figure, Dr. Hugo Spadafora, openly accused Noriega of misdeeds and in 1985 his horribly beaten and tortured body was found tossed across the Costa Rican border. Investigators, including American journalist Seymour Hirsch, tied Noriega to the crime, causing both a foreign and domestic outcry.

By 1988 the Cold War was on the wane and the Reagan administration, lucky enough to have survived the Iran-Contra scandal, had been forced to shift its focus away from the vicious wars still being waged in Nicaragua and El Salvador. Simultaneously, Colombia's drug dealers, the foreign terrorists of their day, were wreaking havoc in America, mainly through a cheap derivative of cocaine called crack. Murder rates in U.S. cities were topping 2,000 a year while the proliferation of drug-dealing gangs threatened to overwhelm law enforcement. Jesse Helms, the crusty conservative from North Carolina, soon found an unlikely bedfellow in freshman Senator John Kerry from Massachusetts, who chaired a subcomittee on narcotics and terrorism. Looking at Noriega, Kerry began to realize Helms had a point in that the U.S. was dealing with a criminal regime. He was soon joined by Ted Kennedy and other liberals, creating a two-pronged opposition to Noriega in the Congress.

In February 1988 crusading U.S. attorneys in Tampa and Miami won indictments of Manuel Noriega on various drug-running and money-laundering charges. Though making the respective DA's famous, the indictments only complicated the government's problem. The State and Defense departments might have wielded enough weight to talk Noriega out of power. But now Noriega was faced with a prison sentence the second he relinquished his grip on Panama. Naturally he held on more fiercely than ever.

After the indictments, U.S. Deputy Secretary of State Elliot Abrams convinced Panama's puppet president, Enrico Delvalle, to go public to dismiss Noriega as head of the PDF. Delvalle, a rich businessman who was widely despised in Panama, weakly complied, but Noriega ignored him. The U.S. slapped economic sanctions on the country, but these primarily hurt average Panamians. In March, Noriega missed a payroll and the next day PDF officers tried to overthrow him in a coup. Noriega crushed it so easily that it appeared he had caught wind of the attempt.

The United States had hit a dead end. The question now became whether the U.S. should drop its criminal indictments in order to persuade Noriega to voluntarily step down. A heated debate subsequently took place in the White House, in which for the first time in eight years Vice President Bush argued openly with President Reagan. Originally supportive of the idea, Bush had had an epiphany while visiting Los Angeles, where police chief Daryl Gates had described how his men were risking their lives every day to battle the drug plague. Bush heatedly told Reagan's National Security Adviser Colin Powell, "I have never been so sure of anything in my life, and I will do whatever I have to do to kill this deal." Later Powell wrote of the incident, "I learned two things about George Bush. First, here was a far tougher man than I had seen before; and second, do not assume you are home free with Bush after the first reading." Nevertheless, Reagan decided to drop the Florida indictments if Noriega would step down.

At first Noriega appeared amenable to the offer, but the more he thought about it the less he trusted it. Giving up power would leave him helpless against any deals the U.S. made with his successor, and by now he also knew too much about his Panamian rivals, the CIA, the Communists, and especially the Medellin Cartel to be left unmolested. If the CIA or DEA didn't get him, Pablo Escobar would.

When George Bush assumed the presidency in January 1989, Noriega still controlled Panama, like a festering sore that no one knew how to cure. The administration focused on the next Panamian presidential election scheduled for May, flooding the country with outside observers to make sure it was fair. Jimmy Carter, who since leaving office had formed the Carter Center to pursue international peace and human rights, was solicited as an observer, as well as a bi-partisan Congressional delegation headed by Senators John McCain and Christopher Dodd. For his part, Noriega prepared the PDF to nudge the vote in his candidate's favor, subtly if possible, just as in 1984.

The election turned into a fiasco. It soon became apparent that the opposition candidate, Guillermo Endara, was beating Noriega's man, Manuel Palma, by a three to one margin. PDF troops in and out of uniform simply started seizing the ballots at gunpoint, prompting equally chaotic countermeasures by Endara's people. Carter estimated that Noriega had been prepared to cheat about 10 percent but had been unprepared for the opposition's strength.

Three days later Endara and his two vice presidential candidates, Guillermo Ford and Arias Calderón, led a protest march in Panama City. Bands of Noriega's henchmen carrying clubs and whips met them and a violent riot ensued. At one point Ford's bodyguard was shot dead, covering Ford with blood. Ford tried to stagger away under the blows of Noriega's thugs. A graphic photo of the scene made the cover of Newsweek magazine.

As Noriega annulled the election, Bush withdrew the U.S. ambassador and dispatched 1,900 additional troops to the Canal Zone, increasing the strength there to about 12,000. Responding to reports from Senator McCain and others, he also replaced SOUTHCOM's commander, General Frederick Woerner, with General Mark Thurman, who was highly respected within the army as a dynamic general. Woerner was a Latin American expert, fluent in Spanish, who had been superb in his role as a mentor and liaison with America's allies in the region. Since the Canal Treaty, Panama had been meant to be one of those allies, and U.S. and PDF troops shared bases, many of the Panamanian officers had been trained at U.S. schools, and Noriega himself had frequently gone to Woerner for consultations. But as James Baker put it, Woerner had acquired a case of "clientitis," meaning that the cop had gotten too close to the criminal. It was a tricky situation in Panama because not only were the primary U.S. and PDF forces entwined, many of them based a stone's throw away (Noriega's Comandancia was only 600 yards from SOUTHCOM's command center at Quarry Hill), but some 34,000 U.S. civilians and dependents were living in the vicinity. Woerner's staff had come up with a military contingency plan, dubbed Blue Spoon, which called for Marines and an aircraft carrier to buttress the troops in the Zone. This was sensible enough, except that it called for five-days of highly visible preparation. Surprise would be difficult and in Panama the potential for hostage-taking was enormous.

On September 30, 1989 General Thurman took command of SOUTHCOM, and the next day, a Sunday, General Colin Powell took office as Chairman of the Joint Chiefs of Staff in Washington. That evening, CIA agents in Panama were approached with news that another coup would be staged on Monday. All the plotters required was that U.S. forces block a road against PDF troops based at Fort

Amador, and at the Bridge of the Americas to prevent reinforcements coming from Rio Hato, an air base 65 miles on the other side of the Canal. Rio Hato was the the home of one of Noriega's most loyal infantry units, the Macho de Monte (mountain men). Trained by Cubans, they were heavily bearded soldiers who dressed in black t-shirts.

All of this was unwelcome news to Thurman, who thought it was a Noriega trick to make him look like a dupe on his first day on the job. Powell also disapproved of the U.S. military supporting a "Brand X" plotter from the PDF, sight unseen. The leader of the coup, in fact, was Major Moisés Giroldi, who had been the head of Noriega's security detail when he had quashed the previous year's coup. Confidence was hurt further when the plotters announced a day's postponement.

On October 3 the coup began, and according to Bush's directive, U.S. units moved to seal off the two routes. When Noriega arrived at the Comandancia, Giroldi's men took him prisoner. Giroldi had an infantry company and a contingent of riot police called the Dobermans in support. At Rio Hato the Macho de Monte, learning that the bridge was blocked off, piled into an airliner and flew the short distance to Tocumen airfield on the other side of the Canal. From there they went to Fort Cimarron to team up with Battalion 2000 (whose commander, hedging his bets, had sent part of his unit away on maneuvers) and then headed for Panama City. Just a couple of U.S. planes or helicopters could have prevented this maneuver, but Thurman had no orders. As Bush held a meeting in the White House to discuss contingencies, the Machos poured out of their vehicles around the Comandancia. Firing broke out and Giroldi's men began to slip away or defect to the other side.

Inside the Comandancia a drama unfolded straight out of Al Pacino's "Scarface," the 1982 movie that has come to epitomize the era of Latin narco-kings. Giroldi held an automatic weapon on Noriega while trying to persuade him to step down for the good of the people. Noriega not only refused but taunted Giroldi for not having the cajones to kill him. In truth, pulling the trigger was Giroldi's only option as the Macho de Monte swarmed the headquarters, but he couldn't bring himself to do it. Weeping, he finally put his gun down. One of Noriega's men burst in, and, grabbing a pistol, Noriega put it to the temple of one of Giroldi's officers. "I'm tired of these bastards," Noriega said, and shot the man in the head.

Much worse was in store for Giroldi, who was kept alive until he revealed all he knew. His body was later found with a fractured skull, multiple broken bones and a number of bullet holes.

But the unfortunate major accomplished more than he knew. In Washington, once the failed coup became known, Helms and his anti-Canal allies on the right, and Kerry with his anti-drug and human rights supporters on the left, converged with new criticisms against the Bush administration. In the center, everyone was appalled by the administration's ineffectualness. This was also recognized in the White House, where Bush's National Security Adviser, Brent Scowcroft, reinstituted a deputies committee so that the principals would be more fully briefed on contingencies when they needed to make quick decisions.

The other effect of Giroldi's coup attempt was to unhinge Manuel Noriega. In the next few weeks he uncovered two more coup plots—imaginary or otherwise—and killed or imprisoned dozens of PDF officers. The way American forces had stirred, obviously intent on his downfall, spelt new handwriting on the wall. He also appears to have increased his drinking at this time and intensified his religious practices, which were a mixture of voodoo and Santeria, with touches of Catholicism and Eastern mysticism.

The worse news for the dictator was that Thurman had brought in General Carl Stiner to revise Blue Spoon, this time in earnest. Thurman had quickly assessed that SOUTHCOM headquarters in Panama wasn't equipped to coordinate a major operation, and he designated Stiner his "warfighter." Though Noriega's intelligence was excellent within Panama and the Canal Zone, U.S. contingency planning had by now passed to the XVIII Airborne Corps based at Fort Bragg, North Carolina, and the dictator had no idea what was in store. Stiner, who had previously commanded Special Operations Command and the 82nd Airborne Division, now commanded the XVIIIth, which was America's most powerful and sophisticated quick-reaction force.

On December 15, Noriega stood before Panama's national assembly and declared himself "Maximum Leader" to loud acclaim from his self-appointed delegates. After years of holding power behind puppet presidents, he had suddenly thrown off the mask to declare himself Panama's native champion. He also declared that a state of war now existed between Panama and the United States.

His PDF troops and paramilitary forces, called Dignity Battalions, were suitably aroused into an anti-gringo frenzy, and the very next evening, a Saturday night, a car full of U.S. Marines returning to the Canal Zone from dinner in Panama City decided to run a PDF roadblock. The circumstances were murky, and either the Marines, the Panamian troops, or both, might have been feeling their oats. The upshot is that the PDF chased the Marines with AK-47 fire and Lt. Robert Paz was killed, another man wounded in the ankle. A Navy lieutenant, Adam Curtis, and his wife Bonnie, had also been stopped at the roadblock and had witnessed the shooting. The couple was whisked to the Comandancia, where Lt. Curtis was brutally beaten and his wife was molested. When Curtis tried to come to her aid he was knocked down and repeatedly kicked in the groin. After four hours they were released. And the report of their detainment soon made it to the White House.

In this post-feminist age it's interesting to note that the abuse of the lieutenant's wife was probably the deciding factor in President Bush's council. A bunch of marines running a roadblock after a night on the town was not the best cassus belli. The temporary detainment and beating of Lt. Curtis was not quite a cause for national war. But the molestation of 23-year-old Mrs. Curtis produced a wave of pure anger. "I guess the thing that troubles me the most," Bush recorded in his diary, "is the humiliation of the lieutenant's wife."

Blue Spoon had already been prepared and the military said they needed just a couple of days to get it lined up. James Baker appreciated the time to prepare for the post-invasion. Endara was to be sworn in as Panama's president minutes before H-hour, economic sanctions were to be lifted and notifications prepared for other Latin countries and the Soviets. The discussion went around the table, weighing pros and cons, almost rising to a cacaphony of voices. The president listened more than participated, but in the end it was clear that Noriega had finally gone too far. It was time for the U.S. to act.

"Okay," said Bush. "Let's do it."

OPERATION JUST CAUSE

The invasion got underway after dark, with aircraft lifting off from 14 U.S. bases, stretching from North Carolina to California. The soldiers and Marines in the Canal Zone locked and loaded and put on their warpaint. At the last minute Thurman arranged to switch the name of the operation from Blue Spoon to Just Cause, which was probably a good idea.

The fact that the invasion was taking place at night was a watershed for the U.S. military. In previous wars, ever since America began to count on air superiority, darkness had always been the best friend of the enemy. It was the only time they could maneuver large units or supplies without being blasted from the air, and tactically, as in Korea and Vietnam, the best time to attack without being chopped to pieces by superior firepower. The difference between the Germans' fortunes in the Normandy campaign and their Ardennes offensive can be measured largely in the amounts of available daylight. In mid-summer Allied fighter bombers ruled the skies about 15 hours a day, while in the Ardennes in winter, there were only some eight hours of light, and those were largely negated by cloud cover.

During the 1980s, along with the general rennaissance of the U.S. armed forces, a new level of technology had been reached that the military called "own the night." Combining night-vision, radar, GPS and other technologies, it was a complete reversal from conflicts as recent as Grenada. Now not only did America possess vast air and firepower superiority, it preferred to operate when the other side couldn't see. This was a tremendous additional advantage.

Transport planes full of paratroopers were en route that night when U.S. intercepts learned that the Panamanians had been alerted. A PDF officer was heard saying, "The ballgame begins at one." It didn't help that Dan Rather had begun his 6:30 newscast by reporting that transports were taking off from Fort Bragg. He was followed by NBC and then later by CNN showing video of the take-offs. In Panama it was more likely that the massive stirring of troops in the Canal Zone tipped off some of the PDF. After a quick back and forth, Stiner and Thurman advanced H-hour from one in the morning to 12:45. With 27,000 troops intricately choreographed to hit Panama in an overwhelming thrust this was easier said than done.

A number of targets were to be attacked simultaneously, but to Bush none was more important than a lone CIA operative held captive by Noriega in Panama City. Kurt Muse had been caught with a secret radio transmitter, and Noriega had announced that should the U.S. attack, Muse would be the first man to die. He had placed a guard outside his cell to pull the trigger at the first sign of an attack. As ex-head of the CIA, Bush had previously been sickened by the fate of Tim Buckley, the CIA's Beirut station chief who had been tortured and killed in captivity. The invasion of Panama thus began foremost with Kurt Muse.

At precisely 12:45 in his cell at the Modelo Prison, Muse heard explosions and automatic weapons-fire in his building. Minutes later the door to his cell blew up and through the smoke he saw a weird creature looming before him. He wore an odd uniform, and had an exotic gun and head-gear. Muse later said it looked like Darth Vader. It was a soldier from the Army's Delta Force who had come to rescue him. Muse was led to the rooftop, stepping over five Panamanian bodies en route, where other Delta troopers hustled him aboard a waiting AH-6 helicopter. This craft was flown by a pilot from the 160th Special Operations Air Regiment (SOAR), a unit known as the Night Stalkers. Muse was shoved aboard and draped with flak jackets while the Delta operators faced outward on the skids for the extraction. But then the copter was either hit by fire from the Comandancia or tripped some wires when it tried to take off. It fell off the building to the ground, but the pilot still had power and scooted down the street. When it tried to take off again the "Little Bird" was knocked down by PDF fire and crashed to the street.

In the White House, news of the downed helicopter caused some dismay. But it was premature. Four of the Delta operators were hurt, one seriously, but Muse was still safe and the Delta personnel spread out to protect their crash-site. They also radioed word to the 5th Infantry to head to their location, and soon a couple of M-113 armored vehicles arrived to pick them up.

While some elements of the PDF seemed to realize the invasion was coming, Noriega did not. He was half-drunk at the time, finishing up a session with a prostitute at Tocumen airfield, when over 700

U.S. Rangers began parachuting onto the runways. AC-130 gunships were circling overhead, blasting away anti-aircraft sites while the Rangers dropped from a stream of C-141 transports at 500 feet. The dangerously low jump was meant to minimize the Rangers' exposure to defensive fire while floating down.

There was henceforth no question about a coordinated command of PDF units. Some men instinctively fought back and most of the others surrendered or dispersed, while their leader fled like a rat from a trap. Two sedans raced toward a Ranger roadblock, and while the Rangers fired on the first the second made a frantic u-turn and veered down a side street. It later turned out that the second car held Noriega.

There was an unexpected problem at adjoining Torrjios International Airport when a Brazilian passenger jet landed just before H-hour. Some of the PDF tried to take hostages and the Ranger company assigned to the terminal had to fight it out. Most of the defenders surrendered on point of death but a couple of hold-outs took refuge in a women's bathroom. The lead Ranger who stormed it was severely wounded. The Rangers threw grenades inside but the PDF hid in the stalls and the Rangers had to break in. One defending soldier was shot dead while a Ranger grappled hand-to-hand with the other, finally throwing him through a window. The man landed a story down where another Ranger had just set up an M-60 machine-gun. Both the American and Panamanian were surprised, and the latter was then nearly cut in half by a stream of bullets.

At Rio Hato, which housed the Machos de Monte and other units, the U.S. had the option of wiping out the PDF barracks at H-hour, but instead chose to drop a couple of bombs nearby to persuade a surrender. This operation saw the first use of America's F-117 Stealth fighter, a batlike jet that on training runs in Nevada had often been mistaken for a UFO. One of the 2,000-pound bombs hit precisely outside the barracks while the other was off. A battalion of Rangers then came parachuting down, and though nearly all of the transports took anti-aircraft hits (one trooper was killed while waiting to jump), the Rangers soon controlled the airfield. A fluid battle took place on the perimeter as the Americans stalked the defenders. The only verified case of deaths by friendly fire occurred here when an aircraft spotted some troops moving through trees and hosed them down with its chain gun. They had actually been U.S. troops moving to flank a PDF unit. Two Rangers died and four were wounded in this mistake.

The biggest head-to-head battle took place at the Comandancia in Panama City, where elements of the 5th Infantry (Mechanized) and 7th Infantry had sallied out from the Canal Zone to attack the PDF's headquarters, a large complex covering two blocks. As defenders tried to escape, a nearby shantytown caught fire, adding to the chaos. At Fort Amador and other points in the Canal Zone, where American civilian dwellings were only yards, or a golf course, away from PDF installations, U.S. units took the offensive. Indirect fire was forbidden during this operation, but point-blank howitzer fire blasting down walls persuaded many PDF to surrender.

The priority remained to capture Noriega personally, and to this end Navy SEALs were assigned to disable his private ship and jet to prevent his escape. The ship was knocked out by SEAL frogmen who reached the vessel and planted explosives against its propellor shafts. This turned out to be a harrowing operation when PDF troops began throwing grenades into the water. They were surprised 20 minutes later when Noriega's yacht and a patrol boat went up in huge explosions. On the way back to their teammates waiting in rubber boats, the SEAL swimmers had to dive 40 feet beneath a cargo ship that unexpectedly crossed their path.

Another SEAL operation was launched to take down Noriega's private jet, housed at Punta Paitilla airport. There was some prior discussion about this, some SEAL officers maintaining that the jet could be disabled by a small team, or even snipers to shoot out its wheels. Instead a full three-platoon assault was launched, the men arriving at the airfield under cover of darkness in 15 rubber boats. Once they got there the problem was that firing had already broken out in Panama City and defenses were on the alert; further, the SEALs now had to traverse an illuminated 1,500-yard runway to reach the hangar. The result was an OK Corral-style shoot-out once the SEALs had reached the hangar and the PDF inside opened fire. The SEALs finally gunned down the enemy and disabled the jet, but lost four dead and eight wounded in the process.

Marines secured essential points on the Panama Canal, while Army Special Forces were dropped by Black Hawk helicopters to block a bridge across which a PDF vehicle column was on its way to reinforce the Comandancia. The 18 Green Berets landed with only minutes to spare and opened fire. They halted the column, greatly helped by a Spectre gunship that had arrived above their position. Another Green Beret team assaulted and disabled a government broadcasting installation.

An ice storm at Fort Bragg had delayed elements of the 82nd Airborne Division and dawn was breaking by the time some of the final objectives were attacked. Helicopters took a number of hits while ferrying paratroopers after their jumps, but most of the PDF had already melted away. When 82nd troopers attacked the stronghold of the USEAT, Noriega's special forces elite, they found after a brief, hot reception that all the officers and most of the men had deserted. The Americans found a wealth of abandoned equipment, including Uzi submachine guns with night scopes and a heavy, fully loaded Chinese-made anti-aircraft piece.

By nine in the morning the PDF had been toppled, though there were still a few tough fights left on the outskirts, including one in which a chopper went down. In the countryside, the 7th Special Forces Group (Spanish speaking) backed by Rangers undertook what were later called "Ma Bell" operations. These involved calling PDF garrisons on the phone to offer them the choice of surrender or annihilation. Panamanian officers invariably accepted the first choice, and in fact, during the mopping up phase there was a discernible "Ding dong the witch is dead" attitude among the PDF toward Noriega, their once-fearsome leader.

Operation Just Cause had called for 27 targets to be hit simultaneously in the dead of night, many in urban settings, involving thousands of paratroopers, and with over 250 aircraft—from the sleekest fighters to the fattest transports—and scores of helicopters swirling around in the skies above.

And it all came off like clockwork. The American public went to sleep on December 19 and woke up the next morning to find that their armed forces had conquered Panama. It had been an awesome display of U.S. military capability, hardly imaginable to those who remembered 1980's Desert One disaster in Iran, or 1983's twin SNAFUs of Lebanon and Grenada.

As for Noriega, he managed to evade capture for four days while Army Delta troopers and their Navy counterparts, SEAL Team 6, tried to run him down, at one point coming upon burning cigarettes still in ashtrays. Finally on Christmas Eve, 1989, he found refuge in the Vatican Embassy. U.S. troops had blocked off all his potential routes of escape, including the Cuban and Nicaraguan embassies, but it hadn't occurred to them that in his darkest hour Noriega would turn to the Church. Troops surrounded the embassy, called the Nunciatore, and in the next few days began blasting loud rock music to annoy the dictator. They favored songs like "I Fought the Law (And the Law Won)," "Voodoo Child," and "You're No Good," until word came from the White House to knock it off. It looked too much like the troops were having a party, and it was learned that while Noriega remained unruffled the Papal Nuncia couldn't get any sleep.

On January 5, 1990 Noriega surrendered. His only condition was that he be allowed to wear his general's uniform and the request was granted. Once aboard a U.S. transport he was compelled to change into an orange jumpsuit and he is currently serving a 40-year prison sentence in the United States.

An unexpected aftermath in Panama was an explosion of looting, which turned out to be more destructive than the invasion itself. It became apparent that blowing the lid off a poor, tightly controlled society resulted in anarchy. Suddenly with no government, no police, and no authority at all, the Panamians pillaged everything from local stores to government institutions. Entire neighborhoods were ransacked with over 11,000 shops robbed or damaged. The new president, Endara, disbanded the PDF and just as quickly created a national police force. Some citizens nervously pointed out that the personnel in both groups looked the same; but the PDF had been stripped of its heavy arms, its worst rogue elements had been eliminated, and its unbridled power was gone for good. Endara's first problem was to restore order, beyond which everything else would follow. Within a few days the Panamians were able to regain control of their streets.

American casualties in the invasion were 23 dead, eleven of whom were Special Operations Forces and six were airborne. PDF casualties were put at 314 dead in addition to an estimated 300 civilians. From

the American left, accusations came in that the night of firepower had
resulted in thousands of Panamian dead, who were then secretly
buried in mass graves. After investigations by government and humanitarian agencies the accusations were proven groundless, the only germ
of truth being that some of the casualties listed as PDF may have been
civilians, and that during the chaos of the fighting, looting, and the
slum fire next to the Comandancia, it was difficult to get a precise
count. The U.S. assault had been incredibly violent, but free-fall
bombing and indirect artillery fire had been ruled out in advance. The
troops themselves had settled matters in about eight hours, with no
gratuitous deaths of civilians.

Though U.S. military casualties had been less than expected,
President Bush was blindsided by the effect that even a few had on the
public. During a press conference describing the success of the operation he appeared on TV relaxed, relieved, and even jocular with
reporters, while unbeknownst to him CNN was splitting its screen
between the press conference and the arrival of flag-draped coffins at
Dover Air Force Base, the military's East Coast receiving point for
casualties. Thus even a stellar achievement of arms in which every
branch of the U.S. military took pride could be transformed by jour-
nalistic techniques into a grim event. This lesson would be remembered later by Bush's son, who after invading Iraq would ban cameras
from filming the arrival of coffins at Dover, citing "respect for the soldiers' families."

It is worth noting that both the Organization of American States and
the United Nations condemned the invasion of Panama. The United
States had acted unilaterally, secretly, and with overwhelming force to
crush the ruling structure of a foreign nation. This was not ordinarily
allowed, and to some degree, like the Soviet Union's invasion of
Czechoslovakia in 1968, it raised as much fear as respect about superpower capability. But Noriega's Panama was like a Prague Spring in
reverse, in that the United States did not move to quell democracy but
to enable it, and with the same stroke rid the world of a true villain.
International protest was tepid, and in private channels beneath their
governments' pro forma protests, many nations signaled their clear
approval.

All American forces had withdrawn to the United States or back into the Canal Zone by January 31. A fringe benefit arrived two months later when the Communist government of Nicaragua was defeated in an election, the results of which George Bush and Mikhail Gorbachev had agreed to respect no matter which way it went. Former Nicaraguan leader Daniel Ortega said that his government had polled 47 percent prior to the U.S. invasion of Panama but the figure dropped to 37 percent immediately after. After all the bitter blood spilled in Nicaragua during the Reagan years, it was astonishing to see the Sandanistas step down after losing a free election. Meanwhile, a CBS poll had shown that over 90 percent of the Panamanian people approved of the American intervention against Noriega.

Today Panama has still not found prosperity for all its people, and the elusive drug trade still persists. But democratic institutions have taken root with regularly scheduled free elections. On New Year's Day 2000 the Panamian people assumed control of the Panama Canal, one of the world's most valuable strategic possessions, and a good foundation for that nation's prosperity in the future.

Just Cause was America's largest military operation since Vietnam and its largest single-contingency operation since World War II. It set startling new precedents in nightfighting capability and air, ground and Special Operations coordination in one highly complex, expertly timed assault.

The operation had succeeded in all its goals. It had achieved a vital strategic purpose in securing the integrity of the Canal; it had liberated a people from the grip of a brutal dictator; it had been conducted decisively with enough force to ensure a minimum number of casualties; and U.S. forces departed almost as quickly as they had arrived, leaving only a newborn democracy behind.

Most Americans swelled with pride at how America had dusted off its white hat, a piece of gear essential to the American psyche but which had been neglected and somewhat soiled over the previous two decades. The U.S. military held the palm, having reached new levels of proficiency and professionalism that had hardly been envisioned since the war in Indochina. But the military was only as good as its highest leadership, and as the armed forces of a democracy were only as effective as the honorable clarity of the goals that were placed before them.

Operation Just Cause went far toward restoring the reputation of America's armed forces and the country's own self-esteem. It would only be a few months, however, before a far larger, more dangerous challenge arose, this time on the other side of the world.

3

SADDAM HUSSEIN

In mid-July 1990, American satellite reconnaissance revealed that the large Arab nation of Iraq had dispatched an armored division to the border of its small southern neighbor, Kuwait. In the next few days this division was joined by two more, and by the end of the month 100,000 troops were in place, including a special forces division and elite units of Iraqi President Saddam Hussein's Republican Guard. And then they began to spread out, the tank muzzles pointing south.

U.S. analysts were dumbfounded. This was the sort of heavy attack posture they had spent 40 years seeking during the Cold War, but had never found. Of course the North Koreans had sprung a surprise on their southern cousins in 1950, and the Arabs and Israelis had traded surprise attacks in 1967 and 1973. But one had to go back to Poland in 1939 to see such a build-up outside of an existing stand-off. Unprovoked blitzkrieg by tank armies had been considered as obsolete in this day and age as cavalry charges. Yet here was such a build-up in the desert, after all the lessons of the Cold War had indicated such things were no longer possible.

But that was the issue. The Cold War had ended, and nations were no longer shackled to the unpinned hand grenade of global nuclear holocaust, adhering to one side or the other, their ambitions gauged by consequences for the respective superpowers. Like many other countries who once subscribed to the American-Soviet face-off, Iraq was now a free agent. It could pursue its own national goals in its own region, unconcerned that its actions would trigger a berserk chain reaction in the Pentagon or the Kremlin.

Saddam Hussein had emerged from an eight-year war with Iran possessing a million-man army, which in terms of standing troops was the fourth largest in the world. He also had over 5,000 Soviet-made tanks, just as many armored troop carriers, thousands of pieces of heavy artillery, and up to 800 combat aircraft. Notoriously, he also possessed vast stockpiles of poison chemical munitions, which he had used freely against the Iranians and against his own rebellious Kurdish population in the north. Most dangerously, his men were hardened combat veterans, experienced with campaigns and killing.

On August 2, 1990, Saddam Hussein invaded Kuwait, conquering the country in a day. His brazenness took the world by surprise.

In the United States it looked like the mother of all faits accomplis. Though America, as well as the UN, immediately condemned the attack, there did not seem to be anything to be done about it. Democratic Senator Sam Nunn, Chairman of the Senate Armed Services Committee, said, "I don't think we have a military option." Republican James Schlesinger, a former Defense Secretary and CIA director, said, "If military options refer to some way of dislodging Hussein from Kuwait, then there are no military options."

Seven months earlier, Panama had gone a long way toward curing America's Vietnam syndrome, but that operation had been conducted mainly by light troops. Saddam's army was 100 times the size of Manuel Noriega's, with 1,000 times the firepower. It was on the other side of the globe, and would be alert and waiting for any response. And in the U.S. Army, as opposed to in Saddam's forces, there wasn't a soldier remaining who had ever fought a head-to-head conventional armored battle.

Thus nearly all Americans, from the most casual housewife to the deepest administration insider, was startled a few days later when President Bush, after disembarking from a helicopter on the White House lawn, revealed his view to a crowd of reporters. Staring straight into the cameras and raising his hand for emphasis he declared, "This will not stand, this invasion of Kuwait."

What was that supposed to mean? Was the United States supposed to transport its army 6,000 miles away to take on superior local numbers on their own turf, in full-fledged total warfare at the cost of untold billions of dollars and unknown numbers of lives? Were untested U.S. infantry and mechanized troops supposed to defeat hardened Iraqi veterans who had already been inured to the brutal tricks of modern warfare? And all to free the territory of a little Arab sheikdom?

Well, yes. Exactly.

IRAQ

The nation of Iraq holds claim to a heritage of culture and a richness of history that is genuinely unsurpassed. In ancient times its fertile region, nurtured by the Tigris and Euphrates rivers, was known as Mesopotamia, called the "cradle of civilization." Its storied city of Babylon was where King Hammurabai codified the first system of civil law and in the Old Testament where the Jewish people were held captive and where Daniel was thrown into the lion's den. After the sweep of Islam, which began in the seventh century, the city of Baghdad was immortalized as the scene of the "1001 Nights," and became the seat of the Caliph, the spiritual leader of the Muslim world.

Iraq has also been the most invaded land on earth, due to its combination of wealth, central geographic position, and the land's topography, which has been easy to traverse by Assyrian chariots, Greek infantry, Parthian ponies and British armored cars alike. The most destructive invasion occurred in 1258 when Genghis Khan's grandson, Hulegu, arrived with an army from the northern steppe. The Caliph of Baghdad defiantly announced that he would raise all of Islam in resistance. Unfazed, the Mongols sacked the city with their usual excessive slaughter and then, leery of spilling royal blood, dealt with the caliph by rolling him up in a carpet and trampling him.

The medieval rise of Europe was matched by a nearly symmetrical decline in the civilizations of the Mideast, and by the 20th century Iraq consisted of a string of provinces in the Ottoman Empire, which had conquered the region in the early 1600s. During World War I, Iraq was the site of a major British effort to roll back the Turks. The British, as per their long tradition of preceding ultimate triumphs with dismal defeats, marched resolutely up the Tigris and promptly lost an entire army to a Turkish siege at Kut. Falling back on their bulldog determination, they tried again, this time driving the Turks before them. When their troops marched into Baghdad it was the thirtieth time that the city had fallen to invaders.

After the Great War the British and French were tasked with drawing borders for the former Ottoman possessions. France took care of the Levant, creating Syria and Lebanon, while the British carved out Transjordan, Iraq and Kuwait. Britain drew Iraq as a large territory stretching from the Persian Gulf to the Turkish border, containing three major ethno-religious groups, the Sunni Kurds, Sunni Arabs, and Shiite Arabs. This design, though recently much criticized, was logical at the time because just next door was the huge land of Persia, which had evaded European colonial rule and had a history of dominating the region. Iraq's diversity was seen as a hedge against its embarking on aggressive wars, while its size was seen as a deterrent against any future Persian expansion. In 1935, the land known as Persia changed its name to Iran.

The biggest losers in the new design were the Kurds, a non-Arab people who spoke an Indo-European tongue and whose population straddled the borders of modern Iraq, Iran, Turkey and Syria. The Kurds first came to light in the West through the story of Xenophon's "Ten Thousand," a Greek force that in 400 B.C. easily cut its way through Persian hosts in Mesopotamia but then was beleaguered by more fierce mountain tribes up north. One problem with creating a Kurdistan was that so many other groups in the region had fought them for centuries, with the result of lingering loathing and fear; another was that, like other highland peoples, the Kurds were perpetually divided and just as often fought among themselves. This factor was exacerbated during the Cold War when strong Kurdish elements took on a Marxist bent.

The most sophisticated group in Iraq was the Sunni Arabs, who held the geographic center, including Baghdad, and the British installed a Sunni Hashemite king as ruler, as they also did in Jordan. These brothers were said to be descended directly from Muhammed. The largest group in Iraq was the Shiite Arabs, who populated the southern half of the country. More strictly religious than the other groups, there was fear, then as now, that they would turn into natural allies of Shiite Persia, or Iran.

Iraq was released from British mandate control in 1932, but it was quickly reoccupied again in World War II as the political winds in Baghdad—as throughout the Muslim world—blew in a pro-Axis direction. Neighboring Iran was similarly taken over by a joint British-Soviet effort in order to allow Anglo-American supplies to reach the Soviet Union in its battle with Germany.

After the war a number of political parties sprang up, including a Communist one and a tiny group called the Baathists. Founded by a pair of Syrian intellectuals, Baathism combined socialism with pan-Arab nationalism, not neglecting to include a streak of mystical Islamic superiority. Saddam Hussein, who was born in 1937, became an early convert to Baathism, as did most of his extended family from the city of Tikrit.

King Faisal II of Iraq was overthrown (actually murdered, along with his family) by an army general, Abdul Karim Qassim, in 1958. The following year Saddam took part in an assassination attempt on Qassim, but it was beaten off and Saddam was wounded in the leg. He barely managed to evade pursuing security forces, at one point by hiding in a well, and made his way to Egypt where he studied law. In 1963, a joint Baathist-army coup overthrew Qassim and Saddam returned to Iraq; however, the army elements got tired of the quarreling Baathists and tossed them out of the government within a year.

Saddam was imprisoned for almost two years during this period, but escaped and continued to rise in the Baath party, which was led at this juncture by one of his older cousins, General Ahmad Hassan al-Bakr. The Arab world was shaken in June 1967 by Israel's spectacular six-day triumph over Syria, Jordan and Egypt, in which the Jewish state more than doubled its territory. The following year the Baathists sprang a successful coup in Iraq and 31-year-old Saddam became second-in-command to Bakr. His first task was internal security, and he pursued it with brutal efficiency. In fact, Iraq, once wracked by coups, has not endured one since, unless one counts the recent U.S. invasion.

By the late 1960s the Cold War was at its height and Iraq, along with Syria and Egypt, welcomed arms, aid and advisers from the Soviet Union, a process that not only extended Soviet influence but provided them much-needed foreign exchange. During the 1973 Yom Kippur War, in which Syria and Egypt attacked Israel, Iraq dispatched an armored division to help protect Damascus against an Israeli counteroffensive. According to Israeli General Raful Eitan, the Iraqis "wandered into a chaotic situation, straying from place to place with no maps or Syrian guides. They were shot at from all directions and never knew exactly who was shooting at them." Nevertheless, the introduction of fresh Iraqi forces into the war was unwelcome to the bruised Israelis, even as their military contribution became a feather in the cap for Iraq's standing among the Arabs.

Iraq's bigger problem was to the east, where the Shah of Iran, together with the Israelis and the CIA, tried to foment armed uprisings among Iraq's Kurdish population. The Shah also bullied Iraq into sharing possession of the Shatt al-Arab waterway, which formed the border between the two countries in the south. While Iran had hundreds of miles of coastline, the Shatt al-Arab, which flowed into the Persian Gulf after the Tigris and Euphrates joined above the city of Basra, was Iraq's only internal outlet to the sea. For his part the Shah agreed to stop arming the Kurds, marking just one of many occasions when that hardy people was abandoned in favor of outside interests.

The most positive development for Iraq was that after the 1973 war the Arab states united to flex economic muscle, and under the auspices of OPEC nearly quadrupled the world price of oil. Iraq enjoyed a period of great prosperity, and as opposed to many other Arab states, tried to join the modern world. The Baathists, though nodding respectfully toward Islam, were primarily secularists. They stressed education, empowered women (even discouraging the wearing of head scarves) and sought to build modern hospitals and municipal systems. Aware of the fragility of Shiite loyalty, the regime sought to provide jobs and consumer goods in the south. The Kurds were offered a degree of autonomy as early as 1970. Throughout the decade, Saddam Hussein served as first deputy to Bakr, spreading his influence from intelligence and security—where his methods were marked by atrocity—to economic, social, and defense policy.

In 1979, with the international situation becoming urgent and Bakr looking increasingly feeble, Saddam compelled his cousin to resign so that he could take the reins of power himself. It was a rare bloodless transfer of power in Iraq; however, Saddam's acsension was accompanied by murder when he subsequently called an assembly of Baathist officials. On the stage, smoking a cigar, Saddam read the names of 66 people he suspected of opposing his rise to power, each of whom was escorted out of the auditorium. During this weird scene, Saddam alternately wept and made bombast from the podium, while his heavily sweating audience professed as much adulation as they could. Of the 66 men taken away, 22 were executed and the rest tortured to reveal anyone else they knew who might oppose Saddam.

Unlike Noriega, whose vast collection of frog figurines ruefully reflected his own personal repulsiveness, Saddam was a good-looking fellow who projected physical vitality. In fact, he immediately began a personality cult with portraits, murals and statues of himself across the country. These depicted him variously as a modern businessman, a military commander, a traditional Arab in robes, and even as a Kurd. Some depicted him as a hero from Iraq's rich history, like Saladin, the Kurdish hero who had defeated the Crusaders, and the Babylonian king Nebuchadnezzar. The latter was a favorite since he had once enslaved the Israelites. The Iraqi currency, the dinar, gained Saddam's face on all its denominations.

Saddam took office during a tumultuous period in the Islamic world. The previous year, Egypt's Anwar Sadat had signed a peace treaty with Israel, exchanging the return of the Sinai peninsula for full diplomatic recognition of the Jewish state. Thus Egypt, which since the rise of Nasser and its subsequent roles in the Arab–Israeli wars had been considered the foremost nation in Islam, was now cast out of the Arab tent. The strongest confrontrational Arab state that remained was Iraq.

The second big event was the fall of the Shah of Iran in early 1979 to a fundamentalist movement led by the Ayatollah Khomeini. While the West had come to view problems in the Mideast as a perpetual showdown between the Israelis and Arabs, the fall of the Shah unleashed a dizzying series of consequences with deep roots in Islamic history. At first Saddam made friendly overtures to the Ayatollah, who had disposed the hated Shah, a man who had been put in place through CIA connivances and had since made his country a depot for American arms. But it turned out the Ayatollah was even more aggressive than the Shah, determined to cleanse all of Islam with his brand of Shiite fanaticism.

Uprisings began among Shiite populations throughout the Gulf. In

Iraq, Saddam's foreign minister, Tariq Aziz, barely survived an assassination attempt by the Shiite Dawa group that killed several student bystanders. At the students' funeral the Dawa struck again, killing even more. In response, Saddam seized and executed Iraq's leading Shiite cleric, who had openly expressed allegiance to Khomeini. In November, Iranian mobs overran the U.S. Embassy in Iran, taking the diplomatic personnel hostage. This breach of international law marked Khomeini's Iran as a rogue state, not just to its neighbors but to the United States and the rest of the world.

Just two weeks later the Grand Mosque in Mecca was seized by 300 gunmen led by a religious fanatic who called himself the Mahdi (not the first in Islamic history). Against the Mahdi's apocalyptic band the Saudis had no choice but to use force, and in a disturbing development the holiest site in Islam became drenched in blood.

The tumultous year of 1979 ended with an event that shook Saddam's new regime, as well as the Carter administration in Washington. On Christmas Eve, the Soviet Union invaded Muslim Afghanistan. The Soviets had hoped for a quick, relatively bloodless intervention along the lines of their previous invasions of Hungary and Czechoslovakia, to protect an established Communist revolution, Their mistake was that the Red revolution in Afghanistan had been engineered by a small minority of intellectuals in the cities. Once the Soviets got in, which was easy enough, they found that the true strength of Afghanistan existed in the countryside and the mountains, where the people were fiercely resistant to occupation.

As the 1980s began it was clear that the once-firm Cold War lines had begun to blur. America's strongest ally in the Gulf, Iran, was now its main antagonist. While the United States was widely despised among Muslims for its support of Israel, the Soviet Union had gone a step further by invading a Muslim country. And the religious fanatic, Ayatollah Khomeini, was now attempting to engineer the overthrow of the Baathists, the Saudis, and the sheikdoms of the Gulf. His agents spread throughout the Shiite populations to rouse them to revolt. In Iraq, while Saddam countered Iranian-backed insurgents in the south with his characteristic brutality, his artillery dueled with Iranian guns along the border.

On September 22, 1980, Saddam Hussein launched a military

invasion of Iran. His first goal was to knock the Iranians back from the Shatt al-Arab, thus securing the vital waterway for Iraq once and for all. The next object was Khuzestan, an Arab-populated region in southwestern Iraq that he hoped would rise in revolt against their Persian masters. Subsidiary thrusts drove across the borders opposite Baghdad, Basra, and the oil-rich city of Kirkuk in the north.

Now that Saddam Hussein is an American POW, it would be interesting to hear exactly what he hoped to achieve with his invasion. The best guess is that he thought Khomeini had so disrupted Iran that it was no longer capable of concerted military action. While Iran's American supplied and trained army had no doubt been shattered by the fundamentalist takeover (many officers, in fact, had been purged or executed), Saddam's own army was still a tightly held machine. The best guess is that Saddam wanted to punch the Ayatollah in the stomach by way of telling him to back off, and if some valuable territory could be seized in the meantime all the better. The main object was to throw cold water on Khomeini's export of his revolution, which was especially dangerous to Saddam because the majority of his people were Shiite. According to reports from the Iranian exiles and refugees that had reached Saddam's ear, the Shah's former army might even have joined an Iraqi attempt to quell the fanatics.

On two other notable occasions, established powers sought to take advantage of large nations in the midst of revolutionary tumult. The first occured after the French Revolution, when the monarchies of Europe, now called the First Coalition, descended on France to roll back anarchy and punish the practitioners of the guillotine. Unfortunately, the foreign assaults only roused the French revolutionaries to national defense. And in the Wars of the Frontiers that followed the monarchists were soundly defeated.

An unexpected consequence of the conflict was that a great French general emerged, Napoleon Bonaparte. Named First Consul of the revolutionary government in 1799, within five years, in a grand irony that can only be explained by "you had to be there," he was crowned as Emperor of a French nation that was by then far larger in extent than anything the Bourbons had achieved. If not for the monarchical counterattack against the French Revolution, Napoleon would never have risen.

The more recent example of taking advantage of the supposed instability of a revolutionary regime occurred in 1941, when Germany invaded the Soviet Union. In Russia, Stalin had gutted the army's officer corps and imposed a reign of terror to eradicate religion, capitalism, and ethnic identity in the vast spaces of Eurasia. Hitler had said, "Kick in the door and the whole rotten structure will fall down."

Germany's invasion most parallels Iraq's in 1980 because it consisted of a tightly-held dictatorship attacking a larger foe. In fact, unlike the First Coalition and Iraq in 1980, the Germans had a good plan. They intended to wipe out the huge build-up of Soviet armies near the border, which they did with amazing speed, and then topple the government by advancing as far as possible, seizing the capital, other major cities, and the largest industrial areas. The Germans were finally stopped by generals Mud and Winter just short of Moscow, and in the meantime it turned out that instead of forcing the Soviets to collapse they had inadvertently solidified their support. Regardless of what people thought of Stalin, the issue had become a defense of Mother Russia. In the Soviet Union, and now its successor republics, World War II is known as The Great Patriotic War.

The problem with Saddam's invasion of Iran in 1980 was that it fell into the useless gap between being too ambitious and not ambitious enough. In order to intimidate the Khomeini regime into ceasing its provocations, he could have simply concentrated overwhelming force behind some select border clashes, which prior to the war were taking place almost daily. The utter destruction of a few Iranian probes, or the launch of a few quick, unstoppable incursions would have dampened Khomeini's ardor to export his revolution across the Tigris while not inviting full-scale war.

But once Saddam gambled on a major invasion his goals were not big enough. Instead of seeking decisive engagements to cripple the Iranian armed forces, or occupying key territory that would have compromised the enemy's warfighting ability, the Iraqi army basically charged headling into Iran for about 20 miles and then stopped. The Iranians, taken by surprise, had by no means pitted their main strength against the invasion while the Iraqis had committed their best forces. And now the Iraqi army sat in its inconsequential slice of conquered territory while a country three times its size began to mobilize for a counteroffensive, and for vengeance.

The worst news for Saddam Hussein was that all the reports he had heard from Iranian exiles that the Khomeini regime had only a tenuous grip on power turned out to be false. If anything, Saddam's aggression had firmed it up. In response to the invasion the Iranian people rallied to their mullahs and the army dropped any plans it might have had for a countercoup. All elements rose to meet the national crisis.

After a bloody series of counteroffensives, by June 1982 the Iranians had driven the Iraqis out of their country. Now Iraq was on the defensive against a far larger enemy, and naturally Saddam tried to sue for peace. An unusual event occurred in 1982 when an Iraqi intelligence agent killed the Israeli ambassador to Britain, prompting an all-out Israeli invasion of Lebanon. The Israelis had only been waiting for one final spark before going after the PLO, which was in exile there. The Iraqis immediately appealed to Iran on behalf of Islamic solidarity, but to no avail. Moderates in Tehran argued to end the war, but by now Khomeini wanted Saddam's head. The war would continue.

Ayatollah Khomeini had created a new armed force called the Pasradan, known in the West as the Revolutionary Guards. Rather than meld their enthusiasm with the expertise of his regular army, on the French Revolutonary model, he kept them organizationally separate from the traditional army, as Hitler did with his Waffen SS. Eventually he created a third force drawn from the untrained population. This was not unlike Hitler's Volksturm which called on older men, boys and misfits, but the Ayatollah drew primarily on underage boys, some as young as 13. And rather than use them to fill out quiet sectors in defensive positions, he used them as an attacking force. After filling the youngsters with religious fervor, he launched them in human wave attacks against Iraqi emplacements.

By 1983 the Iraqis were under such pressure from superior numbers that they began to use poison gas to ward off the Iranian attacks. They began cautiously at first, with tear gas, but after not hearing a peep from the international community, soon upgraded to mustard gas and then nerve agents. Criticism came in from the UN and humanitarian groups but the world's powers remained mute. In fact they were now busy feeding the conflagration. Israel, entirely pleased to see its two potentially biggest antagonists at each other's throats, was secretly shipping arms and spare parts for Iran's American-supplied arsenal. The Soviets, who had initially cut off arms to Iraq, reactivated their pipeline now that Iraq was on the defensive. The French, British, Germans, Chinese, North Koreans, and even the Swiss, sold arms into the war. The United States was officially neutral, though at the end of 1983 Donald Rumsfeld visited Baghdad for a friendly meeting with Saddam, in part prompting a great body of literature that accuses the U.S. of having secretly supplied Iraq with much of its chemical weapons capacity. This issue would be revisited in 2002 when the United States government claimed with full certitude that it knew Iraq possessed Weapons of Mass Destruction. (In fact, most of Iraq's chemical weapons capability came from the Germans.) The U.S. re-established diplomatic ties with Iraq in 1984, and by the end of the decade trade between the countries had increased from $500 million to $3.5 billion.

The war often took on an aspect of stalemate across the 450-mile front, like a Muslim reenactment of World War I. But then in 1986 the Iranians sprung a surprise offensive that seized the Fao Peninsula along Iraq's tiny stretch of coast. This effectively sealed Iraq off from the Persian Gulf, and despite ferocious counterattacks the Iranians could not be dislodged. Now Iraq was truly in danger, as was Kuwait and the other Gulf emirates. Much of southern Iraq was covered by marshlands which were penetrable by Iranian infantry, often in small boats, but not accessible to Iraqi armor. Saddam began a national program to rip up the reeds of the marshlands, and later began to drain them completely.

Though it may have been in everyone's interest to see the two Islamic beasts fight it out interminably, the prospect of an Iranian victory was worrisome. For one thing, if the southern, Shiite, portion of Iraq had been conquered by the Shiites of Iran, the little sheikdom of Kuwait would have been extinguished far sooner, and perhaps more permanently, than it was by the Iraqis in 1990. Kuwait and Saudi Arabia thus funneled billions of dollars into the Iraqi war effort and shipped oil on Iraq's behalf through their own ports.

For its part the United States initiated Operation Staunch, a diplomatic effort to cut off international arms shipments to Iran. The world was thus surprised in November 1986, when a Lebanese newspaper revealed that the United States itself was secretly shipping arms to the Ayatollah's forces. The news not only marked the Americans as hypocrites to the world at large but caused a huge firestorm domestically, where the U.S. public still despised Ayatollah Khomeini for the hostage crisis. In fact the scandal was worse than that. While Colonel Oliver North, working from the White House National Security Adviser's office, had been selling arms to Iran, he had been using the profits to buy arms for the Nicaraguan Contras, thus evading Congressional prohibitions against doing so. North responded that he wasn't using taxpayer funds for the Contras, he was using the Ayatollah's. Still another aspect of the scheme was that by currying favor with Iran, North hoped to secure the release of several American hostages held by terrorists in Lebanon. This violated longstanding U.S. policy not to bargain with terrorists.

In terms of presidential scandals, one would think Iran-Contra would hold a high place. Nixon's Watergate, where Republican Party operatives tried to spy on Democrats, looked like a campus prank in comparison, while Clinton's Whitewater, not to mention Monica, hardly registers on the scale.

But President Reagan was unruffled by the scandal. Since U.S. troops were not at war he was unburdened by the passionate hatred that had enveloped Nixon, nor by any particularly rabid domestic opposition such as was always on the hunt for Clinton. It is also true, though slightly sad, that when Reagan claimed he couldn't remember the details of some of his most important foreign policy meetings, the public was inclined to believe him. The Gipper, though still genial, had gotten a bit elderly. The big guffaw arose when Vice President Bush said, "I was out of the loop." It was difficult to believe that Bush, the primary foreign expert in the Reagan administration, former ambassador to the UN and ex-head of the CIA, was oblivious to what was going on.

There is actually no reason to doubt that Bush was "out of the loop" regarding Colonel North's schemes. The better question would have been: Was he aware that the loop existed? From what we now know of George H.W. Bush it is difficult to think he was ignorant of what was going on in the NSC beneath Reagan's nose. But it is just as improbable to think he would have taken any part in North's cowboy operation and that it was one loop he purposely stayed out of. As he would say, it wouldn't have been prudent.

As a result of Iran-Contra, the United States abandoned its dealings with Iran and began visibly leaning toward Iraq. Intelligence operatives arrived in Baghdad to share satellite photos showing Iranian military dispositions. The U.S. further encouraged its allies to make sure the Iraqi military was well equipped.

At this point Saddam drew America further into the conflict by igniting what is known as the "tanker war" in the Persian Gulf. Iraqi naval vessels attacked Iranian shipping, compelling Iran, with its larger navy, to attack Kuwaiti tankers, which were known to be shipping oil for Saddam. Kuwait appealed to both the U.S. and the Soviets for assistance. The Soviets leased three tankers to Kuwait while the Americans raised their own flag over Kuwait's existing fleet. U.S. warships and Navy SEALs arrived in the Gulf to protect "their" oil tankers, and for the next year U.S. forces played a cat-and-mouse game with Iranian assault boats, sinking as many as they could.

By this time Iraqi armored, air, and artillery strength had grown to impressive proportions while Iran was forced increasingly to rely on human bodies. Iraqi counteroffensives began to push back the dangerous Iranian incursions around Basra.

While the Iraqis gained strength in the south, the Iranians counterpunched in the north, overrunning Kurdish territory where the populace was even more inclined to rebel against Baghdad than the southern Shiites. In March 1988 Saddam responded with brutal force. At Halabja, a city of 50,000 that had been overrun by Iranian Revolutionary Guards, waves of Iraqi aircraft dropped chemical weapons in an attempt to simply annihilate the town. The Iranians were quick to bring in reporters and video cameras to record the massacre. Dead mothers lay clutching their babies in doorways, and clumps of dead civilians lay in the streets. This event would be recalled by President Bush two years later, and more vociferously by his son 15 years later with the phrase, "Saddam gassed his own people."

In fact, the Iraqi army followed up with a general offensive into

Kurdish territory dubbed Anfal, in which they uprooted hundreds of Kurdish villages and executed thousands of Kurdish men and boys, burying them in mass graves. In this operation there were more uses of poison gas but the Iranian army wasn't there to videotape the results. On the subject of atrocities, it should also be noted that while Saddam's behavior was criminal, Ayatollah Khomeini's practice of recruiting children to send into battle was inexcusable. These boys were used as spearheads for Iranian human wave assaults and sometimes used to charge into, and thence clear, minefields. Barely trained and ill-equipped, they were armed primarily with little keys from the Ayatollah that they hung around their necks which guaranteed them entrance to heaven.

The month after Halabja, the Iraqi army finally took back the Fao peninsula. It had already rooted the Iranians out of the marshlands and relieved the threat against Basra. Due to their horrendous casualties Iranians on the homefront had become disillusioned and support for the government had begun to slip. On a succession of battlefields north to south, the Iraqis were getting stronger while the ill-equipped Iranians were getting weaker. One of the final straws may have come on July 3, when the U.S. cruiser *Vincennes* shot down an Iranian airliner with 290 people on board. On his radar the American commander had mistaken the airbus, which was making a regularly scheduled run across the Gulf, for a fighter plane. Between superior Iraqi armor on the front and trigger-happy Americans in the Gulf, Iran's chances had begun to dim.

The war finally ended in August 1988 with Saddam Hussein's Iraq in the ascendant. Unlike other revolutionary regimes, Ayotallah Khomeini's Iran simply hadn't been able to translate superior passion and numbers into military success. With reluctance and a great deal of sorrow, Ayatollah Khomeini "drank from the poison chalice," and shut down the war in August 1988. The border between Iran and Iraq remained the same as in 1980.

Due to all the close calls and the fact that Iraq had fought a country far larger than itself to a standstill, Saddam Hussein was able to claim victory to his own people and to the Arab world at large. The fundamentalist vision of Khomeini had been held at Iraq's borders, much to the relief of Kuwait, Saudi Arabia, and the Gulf emirates. Iraq had suffered at least 200,000 dead in the war, but had held the Arab line against the Persian fanatics, who had suffered far more casualties in return.

Over the next two years Iraq struggled to reclaim the burgeoning prosperity it had enjoyed before the war. But by now it was out of reach. The country was $90 billion in debt with over double that amount needed for reconstruction. Hospitals overflowed with wounded veterans, many of whom had become permanent government dependants. An attempt to disband portions of the army had to be cancelled when the men fell into a restless pool of unemployed.

In fact, the only useful thing Saddam had gained from the war was a gigantic, well equipped army. Pondering how to solve his new array of problems, he increasingly cast his eye on the tiny, incredibly rich sheikdom on his southern border.

KUWAIT

Like Iraq, Kuwait was a British creation, but unlike its larger neighbor, the tiny sheikdom of Kuwait had managed to evade the firm grip of the Ottomans. This was partly because during the three centuries of the Empire, Kuwait had no value to the Turks. It was an insignificant patch of desert inhabited by Bedouins, governed well enough by the al Sabah family that had emigrated out of Arabia, whose only community of worth was a small, walled town. The Ottomans still considered it part of their domain, nominally under the rule of their provincial capital at Basra, but there was nothing there to bother with.

A bigger factor in Kuwait's favor was Great Britain's nineteenth-century interest in clearing the sea-routes, especially to its prime possession, India. To a maritime empire, Kuwait's position at the top of the Persian Gulf had strategic value. The length of the Gulf was infested by pirates who sallied out to prey on commerce, whether local or European. Britain responded by spotting the sea passages to the East with bases for the Royal Navy.

The Ottomans had no inclination to tangle with the British, who served as a counterweight to the Ottomans' most dangerous traditional enemy, Russia. In mid-century the British and French had joined the Turks to fight a horrific war against the Russians in the Crimea. In

1877, when a Russian juggernaut stormed out of Bulgaria intent on seizing Constantinople, it found the British fleet calmly waiting for it in the Bosporus. This tense stand-off was solved by the Treaty of Berlin, though in the confused aftermath the Second Anglo-Afghan war erupted accidentally.

It was not until the Great War, when the Ottomans threw in their lot with the Central Powers, that the two empires came to odds. By that time, Kuwait had been a British protectorate since 1799. Even when Britain released its mandates on Iraq and other Arab countries it held on to Kuwait, which had meanwhile been found to contain vast quantities of oil. Exploitation of the resource was interrupted by World War II, but afterward it began in earnest.

The British granted independence to Kuwait in 1961 in one of the most painful concessions in their program to retreat from "East of Suez," after the 1956 crisis in which they found that America was not inclined to stand behind a postwar continuation of European colonialism. But the Iraqis under General Qassim immediately massed forces to take over their long-lost province and the British were forced to reinsert troops in Kuwait to prevent them. In 1963 Qassim was overthrown and the new Iraqi government agreed to respect Kuwait's border.

After the Iran-Iraq War, Saddam Hussein gazed covetously at the wealth of Kuwait while he also had bitter complaints about its behavior. The emirate had cowered beneath the Ayatollah's tide, providing money while Iraq had provided blood. Iraq had emerged from the war as a debtor nation and in the meantime world oil prices had plummeted. Kuwait and the United Arab Emirates were exceeding their OPEC quotas to make up the difference for their own coffers. Saddam thought they should not only forgive Iraq's wartime debt but curtail their shipments in order to let Iraq's own industry catch up. In addition, he thought the Kuwaitis had been practicing lateral drilling in the vast Rumaila oil field that straddled the border of the two countries, stealing about $2.5 billion of crude from the Iraqi side.

Again, Saddam's strategic thinking is unknown at this juncture. He might have supposed that America didn't have the stomach to oppose him; the Arab world actually owed him for standing as the front line during the 1980s against Khomeini; and the Soviets were on the decline. A glance at the map also revealed a certain logic in Kuwait being part of Iraq.

From what we now know, Saddam had no intention of going on to invade Saudi Arabia in 1990. His calculation was that any move toward the peninsula would probably trigger a massive Western response. Instead he took care to stop after retrieving Iraq's "lost" province, on the gamble that the geographic logic of his move on the heels of Iraq's vast sacrifice against Iran would eventually be accepted by the Arab League. American fears that he was planning to go on to Riyadh were unfounded; but then, if Bush had not shown such determination to resist his grab of Kuwait, Saddam might well have decided to go to Riyadh later, and in any case would have been able to intimidate the peninsula into compliance with his policies. As Osama bin Laden commented years later, "People instinctively like a strong horse, not a weak one."

In retrospect, Saddam would have been better off launching a limited aggression to seize the Rumaila oilfield and Warba and Bubiyan, the two islands that stand outside the Shatt-al-Arab in the Gulf. This would have enhanced his domestic stature, as well as that of his army, improved Iraq's geographic position considerably, and made it impossible for the American president to assemble a worldwide coalition to "die for Bubiyan," or for a disputed Kuwaiti oilfield. The Arab League would have censured him for awhile, until it was found that the Kuwaiti princes were still richer than Midas, had no other use besides, and that Saddam, the only truly dynamic Arab leader since Nasser, was still their best hope to counter the growing power of Israel.

There was also a possibility that once the furor died down over his partial invasion, Saddam could have grabbed the rest of Kuwait later, just as Hitler had gobbled up the rest of Czechoslovakia after first testing the waters with a takeover of the Sudetenland. Just as he had miscalculated by attacking Iran in 1980, however, Saddam misjudged the situation again in 1990 when he decided to seize all of Kuwait.

It tends to be forgotten that in most circumstances relating to the United States, Saddam would have gotten away with his aggression. It is extremely difficult to imagine a full-blooded military response mounted by the Clinton administration. In fact, during that era hundreds of thousands of people from Rwanda to Bosnia were slaughtered with the administration's sole claim to fame being that it didn't lose a man in response. It is similarly difficult to imagine Reagan rolling back such an aggression, after the Marines' disaster in Lebanon and the rather shaky conquest of Grenada. We need not even talk about Jimmy Carter, whose post-Vietnam military establishment was mainly preocupied with getting its troops off marijuana.

But in one of those odd historical confluences of force and effect, Saddam launched his invasion smack into the center of the first Bush administration. The four years of Bush senior comprised the only period within a quarter century—perhaps longer—when the U.S. military was not only ready for a major fight but had truly expert leadership in place at all levels.

Saddam may not have been able to help his general timing, for example by waiting two years for Clinton; but he also erred with specific timing. He launched his invasion on a day when President Bush was scheduled to meet with British Prime Minister Margaret Thatcher, and Secretary of State James Baker was in the Soviet Union, meeting with Foreign Minister Eduard Scheveradnaze. If he had delayed his invasion a couple weeks, all of Washington and half of the rest of the world would have been on vacation. Instead he presented the crisis precisely when the leaders of the U.S., Britain, and the USSR were in personal consultation.

Bush's meeting with Thatcher has by now become legendary for her supposedly stiffening up the president's resolve. The Iron Lady was gung-ho from the first, still buoyed by her military success in the Falklands and as ever imbued with the former empire's grasp of the importance of the Persian Gulf. If Saddam Hussein considered Kuwait a lost province of Iraq, Mrs. Thatcher considered it a vital outpost of Western strength, even more important for its energy resources in the modern age than it had been when held by the British during the age of Victoria.

At one point she said to Bush, "George, this is no time to go wobbly," as if she privately envisioned Britain and the United States in a Master-Blaster relationship similar to that in "Mad Max: Beyond Thunderdome." Bush's staff was amused by her colorful enthusiasm, though, in fact, Bush needed no further stiffening. His difference of opinion with Mrs. Thatcher concerned only how to proceed. She thought the Anglo-Americans could act unilaterally under Article 51 of the UN charter, which allowed for member states to act in self-defense of their vital interests. Bush wanted to seek broader UN approval by going to the Security Council.

In Panama, and before that in Grenada, the United States had launched surprise attacks from strategic necessity. The British fleet had gone charging down to Argentina with hardly a care for what other countries thought. With the dissolution of the Cold War, however, Bush envisioned an enduring peace that would rely heavily on the sole remaining superpower acting in concert with the world community, leading through its principles and the correctness of its cause rather than by filling vacuums of power with its military strength. In the war to come the British would be foremost by America's side, but according to Bush's vision, the true victory would be earned by leading the world community into a new era of common purpose. Baker reported from Siberia that the Soviets were on board. The next calls went out to the French, the Chinese, and to dozens of leaders on every continent. In the end Bush would assemble the largest, broadest based international coalition in history.

Though many players became involved, the upcoming conflict eventually unfolded as a clash of wills between two men: George H.W. Bush and Saddam Hussein. In the Arab world only Saddam had the strength and ruthlessness to violate international norms with naked military aggression; in the rest of the world only Bush had the power to roll him back. Thus both men sat across the world table and gambled.

Saddam had misjudged his first opponent, Iran, badly, practically ruining his country in the process. He had then used his only remaining asset, his army, to retrieve his fortunes. The conquest of Kuwait had been a negligible military task, and at one stroke it had restored Saddam's prestige, placing him in a position to gain far greater power in the future. His only serious opponents were on the other side of the globe, if they chose to take him on at all, and it was doubtful if the United States would be willing to do it. Indeed, to many Americans, the Iraqi invasion of Kuwait looked like a mission accomplished.

But where Saddam's gamble ultimately failed was in his underestimation of the American president. George Bush, showing more determination than many of his countrymen, performed the classic maneuver of turning a challenge into an opportunity. He knew that for political and historical reasons, the United States would be ill-advised to confront Iraq unilaterally. Even with the British alongside, a purely military response—which by itself was attainable—would have resembled a reassertion of colonialism, a counter-grab for resources, or at worst the rise of a new imperialism.

Bush's true challenge, as the once-fearsome Cold War stand-off dissolved, was what kind of international order he could devise to replace it. Military power by itself was a brittle tool in world leadership, subject to politics at home, resentment abroad, and inevitably, if used without a firm foundation of justice, bloody attrition in endless battle. But combined with diplomacy, American strength could have a lasting influence. Military power supported by a consensus of the world community, with respect for other cultures, international law, and used in the best American tradition of protecting the weak against aggressive predators, might well establish a more peaceful era than the one just past.

Saddam Hussein could not have realized it, but the minute he invaded Kuwait he had lost another gamble.

4

THE GULF WAR

Once George H.W. Bush had decided to roll back Saddam Hussein, the first priority was to secure permission for American troops to take position in Saudi Arabia. This was a sensitive issue because the region still had memories of Ottoman subjugation, followed by British administration, and the idea of foreign armies once again setting up shop on the peninsula of Muhammed was unwelcome. In addition, the Saudis and other ruling families had evolved from Bedouin tribes and still maintained highly conservative societies, intentionally closed off from foreign influence. The Emir of Kuwait himself had resisted Western intervention until the last minute, when Iraqi tank-fire forced him to flee his palace.

The Saudi ambassador to the United States, Prince Bandar bin Sultan, had been a fighter pilot in the Saudi air force and educated in U.S. schools. An open-minded individual, he served as a valuable conduit between the two disparate cultures, and he correctly assessed the threat that Saddam Hussein presented. The challenge was to convince King Fahd that he might be next on Saddam's list.

The preference in Riyadh was that the inter-Arab quarrel be handled by the Arabs themselves. But when a U.S. delegation led by Dick Cheney and CENTCOM commander General Norman Schwarzkopf arrived, armed with satellite photos of Iraqi tanks lined up along the Saudi border, the king agreed to let U.S. troops enter his country. The Western agenda of protecting the world's energy supply did not differ markedly from his own self-defense agenda. And Saddam, with his huge army, was obviously more of a threat than the Gulf states could cope with themselves.

The 2,300 men of the 82nd Airborne Division's ready brigade—always on alert to move anywhere in the world in 18 hours—were the first U.S. troops to arrive in Saudi Arabia. Their job was to plant the American flag, so that if Saddam moved south he would know he was taking on not just the kingdom but the United States. There were some tense days when it was obvious that the small American contingent, along with forward elements of the 70,000-man Saudi army, could be crushed by Iraqi armored divisions. Soon the rest of the 82nd arrived, as did the 101st Air Assault Division with its hundreds of helicopters, and the 1st Marine Expeditionary Force. Squadrons of F-15s flew from the United States, refueled en route by a string of aerial tankers hung high above the Atlantic and Mediterranean. And two naval groups, built around the carriers *Eisenhower* and *Independence,* with a combined 150 strike aircraft, took position in the Gulf.

Some of the pressure was off. Saddam would have to think twice about any move against Saudi Arabia. But if he was indeed intent on further aggression or a pre-emptive strike against U.S. forces, he would have to act quickly. America's conflicts since Vietnam had all involved light, air, or naval forces. Now part of the new generation of U.S. heavies was on the way, led by the 24th Infantry Division. The word "infantry" had by now become an honorific since all U.S. regular divisions were fully motorized. Their cutting edge consisted of armored infantry fighting vehicles and M1 Abrams tanks, and at this point a U.S. infantry division could dwarf the firepower of armored divisions in World War II. The Abrams' 120mm main gun had nearly twice the range of the top Soviet-built tank, the T-72, with far better optics and fire control. In terms of size, and thus crew survivability, it was almost double the weight of the most formidable World War II tank, Germany's Tiger.

President Bush steadily worked the phones while James Baker made marathon trips around the globe, and soon allied contingents began to arrive in the theater. The British needed no prodding and lead elements of their 1st Armoured Division were first to show up, soon followed by France's 6th Light Armored. Naval forces of Britain, France, Australia, Canada, Italy and others sailed into the Gulf. Syria supplied a special forces brigade, followed by an armored division, while Egypt supplied two armored divisions. In a trend that touched some in the Bush administration, newly freed nations in Eastern Europe like Poland, Romania and Bulgaria rallied to the American cause, even though Iraq owed them money and it meant writing off the debt. These countries were just happy to join an American cause after so many years under the Soviet heel. Some 30 nations ultimately provided forces for the operation while others, like Japan and Germany, who still felt constrained from committing troops, provided billions of dollars instead. The Soviet Union acquiesced to the American plan, alternately providing moral support and launching peace initiatives toward Baghdad, while the Chinese did not attempt to interfere.

Bush termed what was taking place a "New World Order." He might have used the word "system" since "New Order" had a Nazi ring. However, his intention was benign and his goal was lofty. What he meant was that in place of the Cold War, which had frozen the world into hostility along the lines of competing economic philosophies, nations from every continent could now unite behind universal principles of self-determination and justice. And America, which had been anti-colonial from birth, which had fought the greatest war in its history to free black slaves, and had entered both World Wars reluctantly, and then with no territorial designs on its enemies, was in a perfect position to lead the international community into the post–Cold War age.

By late October the build-up in Saudi Arabia had reached about 250,000 troops. This was enough to not only deter Saddam Hussein, who was thought to have increased his forces in Kuwait to half a million, but to defeat him if he decided to extend south. But the problem was that Saddam wasn't moving and the U.S. forces alone were costing a billion dollars a month. The debate in the U.S. public and in the Congress was whether to wait for economic sanctions—which included a worldwide trade embargo—to force Iraq out of Kuwait, or to continue to pursue a dangerous military option. Maintaining a huge army baking in the desert in an interminably passive role did not appeal to President Bush. He was more interested in a solution to the aggression, not a stand-off. Yet the military informed him that to switch to an offensive capability would require 200,000 more troops. On October 30 Bush held a council in which the options were aired, and he made a decision about the troop level in the desert: double it. He had already announced that Iraq's invasion of Kuwait would not stand, and he had little faith in economic sanctions. The United States and its allies would prepare for a counteroffensive.

This momentous decision was kept quiet for a week so as not to throw a thunderbolt into the 1990 midterm elections. When it was announced on November 8, the political firestorm broke out. While few had objected to the purely defensive operation, dubbed Desert Shield, many people passionately objected to the prospect of a major war to seize back Kuwait.

"Blood for oil" was the assessment of the anti-war movement that rose across America immediately after Bush revealed his intentions. And the protestors were perfectly correct. Iraq's invasion of Kuwait had been quick and easy, causing not even 100 deaths on either side. The map showed that Kuwait might well have been part of Iraq in the first place, and its existence at the top of the Persian Gulf served to prevent Iraq from having a decent coastline and a deep-water port. Kuwait's exclusionary monarchy only existed because of the "black gold" found beneath its sandy surface, nearly 10 percent of the world's known reserves. And everyone was aware that Bush had been an oil man prior to becoming president. The protestors who said the upcoming war was about oil had a point.

The other side of the coin was that "blood for oil" was also Saddam's motto. It was the reason he had invaded Kuwait, not only to solve his financial difficulties after the war with Iran, but to vault Iraq into a potentially dominant position in the region. By adding Kuwait as a 19th province he would control over 20 percent of the world's known oil supply. Saudi Arabia had closer to 25 percent, but Saddam had a lavishly supplied million-man army compared to the Saudis' miniscule national guard. In military terms, the United Arab Emirates, Oman, Bahrain and Qatar were hardly worth mentioning. Yemen already supported Saddam in all his ventures, as did the PLO and the Pashtun muhajadeen of Afghanistan. Jordan, economically entwined with Iraq, and with a king bound to respect the sentiments of his

Palestinian majority, stayed neutral in the conflict.

The crux was that once Saddam controlled a fifth of the world's oil, he would not only be able to afford an even stronger military but his influence on the global economy would preclude the West from cutting him off from world markets. If they tried, the other Arabian states would not be able to make up the difference with an Iraqi hammer hanging above their heads. The Saudis and other Gulf states would have to purchase their continued independence by compliance with Saddam's policies. It was the ultimate Baathist dream of pan-Arab power, and in Saddam's mind the fulfillment of a concept that harked back to Saladin's uniting the Arabs to victory against the Crusaders.

Much of the anti-war sentiment in the United States had a green tint. Many people felt the country should wean itself from oil anyway for environmental reasons. However, if the entire New World had suddenly switched to electric cars, gone back to coal, and dug up Alaska, that would still have left the Persian Gulf as the source of the rest of the world's energy. Europe and the Far East would continue to draw oil from the Gulf, becoming stronger in the process, while the United States would have abdicated its role as a world leader. The American example, including its democratic ideals and liberal influence, would shrink into insignificance.

Oil aside, there was an element in Bush—the last of our World War II presidents—that simply bridled against bullies and blitzkriegs. As a young man he had fought against aggressive dictatorships and took great pride in America's selfless heritage of allying itself with the weak. He saw the invasion of Kuwait as another clear-cut case where the superpower that wears the white hat should make its strength felt.

Of course one can go only so far with this factor, because if Bolivia had tried to grab some outlying province of Peru, Gabon had made a stab at Cameroon, or even if Libya tried to bully Chad (as did happen), the United States would not have been so exercised. The essential fact was that 20 percent of the world's oil reserves, while not necessarily a subtraction from the West, could not be allowed to become an addition to a rogue regime like Saddam Hussein's. Moral imperatives had merged with geostrategic ones. And there was well-founded apprehension, amounting to probability, that if Saddam got away with his conquest of Kuwait, his ambitions would only grow larger, whether aimed at the Arabian peninsula or Israel. The Munich principle—which held that Hitler could and should have been stopped earlier on his path of aggression—still held sway in Western councils, and the Iraqi invasion of Kuwait greatly resembled one of Hitler's early blitzkriegs.

The other major concern of the anti-war movement was casualties. Reports emerged that the Defense Department had ordered 20,000 body-bags. In Saudi Arabia, Schwarzkopf had ordered 65 hospitals with 18,000 beds. The historical anomaly of Kuwait did not really seem to be worth that much in American blood.

To the new incarnation of the old Vietnam anti-war movement, the Kuwaitis were not sympathetic characters. A tribe of bedouins grown atrociously, arrogantly rich, they relied on imported workers from Palestine to the Philippines to perform the actual labor in the country, and many of these people had cheered the Iraqi tanks that broke across the borders. There was an element to the aggression as if a horde from Brooklyn had marched on Central Park South, forcing Donald Trump and Leona Helmsley to flee in their limousines.

While Kuwaiti princes were not the most endearing underdogs, little was then known about Saddam Hussein except for his war against the Ayatollah, in which most Americans had cheered him on. Though he might be a threat to his small neighbors he was certainly not a threat to the United States, and in any case why not deal with him through economic or diplomatic means? The lives of thousands of young Americans need not be piled up on the altar of power politics.

Still another element of opposition to American involvement came from extremely religious Islamic partisans like Osama bin Laden, a wealthy young man who had become a Saudi national hero for his efforts in combating the Soviets in Afghanistan. Bin Laden thought that Saddam's oil-grab was just as disgusting as the man himself, but that by all means the aggression should be handled by the Arab community without inviting a new influx of Western might. In 1990 bin Laden was fresh from the defeat of the Soviet superpower, in a war that had seen thousands of Muslims from throughout the world rising to resist the invader. Now here were the Saudis and Gulf sheikhs actually inviting the American army to settle into the region in some

satanic deal to maintain their mutual wealth. Bin Laden thought that ✓
once the Americans were invited in they would never leave, and that
less than 50 years since the Arabs had gained their independence, they
would have effectively lost it again. The passion of bin Laden and his
fellow reactionaries was not part of the American domestic argument,
except as contained in Jimmy Carter's warning that war might desta-
bilize the region; but it would be tragically recognized some years
later.

In November and December 1990, U.S. forces continued pouring into
Saudi Arabia. Ironically, the same end of the Cold War that had
allowed Saddam to pursue his regional ambitions allowed the
Americans to strip Europe, the Pacific, and its homeland of forces that
would normally have stood by for emergencies. U.S. armored and
infantry units who had done nothing but wargame and train now
headed for the desert. Carrier groups that had spent decades on station for Soviet contingencies were now dispatched to the Persian Gulf,
where the only action was taking place.

On Thanksgiving, George and Barbara Bush visited U.S. troops in
Saudi Arabia, where the president was impressed by how young they
all looked as well as by their confidence. This was the centerpiece of a
mammoth globetrot in which the president held meetings with the
leaders of Britain, France, the Soviet Union, Turkey, Saudi Arabia,
Egypt, Syria and other allies.

On November 29 Bush went to the UN Security Council to gain
unambiguous international support for the upcoming war. The vote
was 12 to 2 in support, the only naysayers being Cuba and Yemen,
with China abstaining. The Chinese abstention was considered a victory in itself by James Baker, a sort of thank-you for the Bush administration not going haywire after Tiananmen Square. The Soviet Union,
who like China could have vetoed the resolution, voted in favor of the
United States. The UN resolution called for Iraq to voluntarily withdraw from Kuwait by January 15, 1991, or the world community
would enforce the will of the UN by "all necessary means."

As Schwarzkopf fine-tuned his plans for the offensive, domestic
opposition surged. Bush had the backing of the UN but he by no
means had the support of the Democrats. Though they were not sym-

pathetic to Saddam Hussein, their argument was that economic sanctions hadn't had enough time to work, and that force should only be used as a last resort. Why should American soldiers die, when Kuwait's own rulers had fled, and their own army had hardly fought at all? Senator Sam Nunn held hearings of his Armed Services Committee, at which witness after witness provided dire warnings of the bloodbath to come. Most damaging was the testimony of former Chairman of the Joint Chiefs, William Crowe, who stated that he didn't think the U.S. armed forces were ready for such a war.

For his part, Bush began condemning Saddam Hussein personally, relating reports of unspeakable brutality that had emerged from Kuwait, as well as stories about Saddam's ruthlessness toward his own people. Bush spoke of Saddam's chemical and biological weapons, and how in 1988 he had gassed his own people, the Kurds at Halabja. This argument was slightly undercut by the fact that the Reagan and Bush administrations had increased commercial credits to Iraq afterward. Bush's councilors were unhappy with his personal demonization of Saddam, because the UN mandate was to free Kuwait, and it was entirely likely that Saddam would be still be left standing in Baghdad. But Bush did feel a personal animosity toward the dictator. His policies toward Iraq had been designed to modify its behavior through interaction with the United States; and then Saddam had turned around and brutally violated American and international principles.

Legally, Bush could have waged a short military campaign without going to Congress for a prior vote. But he did not want to go to war without the clear backing of the U.S. Congress as well as the world community. In his inner circle he was supported by Baker, Scowcroft and Powell, while Cheney thought going to Congress was too risky. What if the Democratic Senate majority denied the president, leaving half a million U.S. troops in Arabia in limbo? Bush persisted in seeking unambiguous domestic support, and on January 12 the Senate, after passionate speeches on both sides, narrowly went his way, 51–47. Tennessee Senator Albert Gore and Connecticut's Joseph Lieberman were notable among the Democrats who crossed party lines to support the president. In the House the vote went 250 to 183, a more emphatic endorsement.

Saddam Hussein had doubted all this time that post-Vietnam

America had the stomach for a full confrontational war. His own army had waged one throughout the 1980s against Iran, every man "seeing the elephant," and they were now expert with their tanks, artillery and automatic weapons. Saddam anticipated the "mother of all battles" with the new Crusaders, and that just as in Lebanon, an eruption of blood would chase the Americans home. The fact that Bush was trying to arrange meetings for him with James Baker, using the Soviets for back-channel peace proposals, and seeking talks with his foreign minister, Tariq Aziz, caused him to think the Americans were desperately seeking a diplomatic solution, while only bluffing with their military posture.

President Bush's January 15 deadline for the Iraqi army to withdraw from Kuwait passed without incident, adding to Saddam's confidence. In fact, the Soviets had put forth a new peace initiative, and most people thought that diplomacy would still intervene.

What Saddam didn't know was that the deadline had been rendered awkward by the eight-hour time-difference on the American side. "Own the night" technology had provided U.S. forces the tactical advantage of darkness, and Schwarzkopf had slated his intial blows for three in the morning. This would still have been January 15 in Washington, so the offensive was moved to the early hours of January 17, Baghdad time. But it was the early evening of the 16th in Washington, at first opportunity, when Bush made good on his deadline. Operation Desert Shield had ended.

DESERT STORM

The offensive began with two Air Force Special Operations helicopters skimming the dark desert of Iraq at 150 mph, followed by a posse of rocket-firing Apaches. The SpecOps Pave-Lows led the way to a pair of Iraqi radar sites, identifying them on the ground, and then the Apaches blew them to pieces. This opened up an air corridor to Baghdad, into which rushed over 700 fixed-wing coaltion aircraft.

In the United States the scene that broke into TV, about seven in the evening, was spectacular. Against the backdrop of Baghdad's mosques and minarets, streams of tracer fire piled into the sky while white blasts burst from the ground. It was truly an incredible sight as the heirs of Thomas Jefferson appeared on the other side of the world to confront the heirs of Nebuchudnezzar.

After the first day it was seen that Iraq's air defense was not as good as anticipated. Only two aircraft were lost from over 850 sorties flown, a ratio on the first day of the war that would have been considered a milk run in World War II. America's Stealth aircraft had exceeded expectations. Their first combat run, in Panama, had been inconclusive, but it was now seen that the F117A Nighthawks could suddenly appear with their 2,000-pound bombs above sophisticated defense networks undetected.

Over the next several weeks, U.S. and coalition aircraft continued to pound Iraqi installations, paying special attention to knocking out nuclear plants and any chemical or biological warfare facilities. Other targets included the country's electrical and communications network, as well as bridges, waterworks, and Baath party headquarters. In this war the public learned of a new priority target, "command and control centers," a phrase that was never heard during Vietnam but which in Iraq served as a euphemism for "trying to kill Saddam."

After a week of bombing only 17 coalition aircraft had been lost after thousands of sorties, and by now the Iraqis had shot off most of their best munitions and were hunkering down. The only real sore point was Britain's RAF, whose young pilots had practiced daring, low-level attacks on Iraqi airfields, losing five Tornados in the process. Word went out to the British to keep at high altitudes and stop trying to reclaim the glory of their Spitfire and Hurricane predecessors.

The air campaign manifested itself to the U.S. public mainly through Pentagon video of precision-guided "smart" bombs going into the doorways or chimneys of Iraqi installations, a fraction of a second before they blew up. This was amazing to see, and it became apparent that anything U.S. airpower could identify, it could destroy.

Saddam Hussein could only counter with an opposite kind of airpower weapon, the Scud missile. Derived by Soviet scientists from the German V-2, the Scud was an area weapon that could only hit somewhere in a four-mile diameter. The Iraqis had also jerryrigged their missiles, providing them greater range at the expense of their warheads, which were reduced to about 160 pounds. In view of the vast weight of munitions that could be delivered on-target by U.S. airpower, Schwarzkopf scoffed at the Scuds' military effectiveness, which was equivalent to a fleet of light propellor planes flyng around with blind-folded pilots. But it was the very inaccuracy of the Scud that gave it a unique effectiveness. The only targets it could reliably hit were cities, and then with unpredictable mayhem. Saddam fired a number of missiles at Dhahran and other Saudi cities, but he aimed most of them at Israel.

The sad fact is that Israel was considered so toxic in the region, due to its occupation of Palestinian territories, it was the only nation that the United States didn't try to enlist in its coalition. This did not indicate a change of heart toward Israel, and the U.S. was willing to continue its decades-long task of being Israel's sole support at the UN, vetoing Security Council Resolutions against Israeli policies right and left. But the current conflict was about (1) Ensuring world stability through access to energy; (2) Solving a fraternal Arab conflict at the invitation of weaker states who could not by themselves handle a brutally rampaging dictator; and (3) Establishing an international system based on respect for state sovereignty to replace the aggressions and militarization of the Cold War. It had nothing to do with Israel.

So naturally Saddam aimed most of his Scuds at Israel. If he could provoke them to barge into the conflict they would undermine the vast coalition arrayed against him. Saddam's own propaganda line was that the war was not about oil, since the only point of having it was to sell it, or the Kuwaitis, whom no one liked anyway. It was all an American-Zionist plot to destroy the only Arab state capable of matching Israeli power. The Iranians seemed to think something similar; when Kuwait was first invaded, they told the Saudis they would help in any way they could, but when the U.S. took on the job they declared neutrality.

The flaw in Saddam's propaganda was that Saudi Arabia, the Gulf emirates, Syria, Egypt and Morocco, as well as Turkey, Pakistan and other Islamic states, had joined the American-led coalition. The world's instinctive response to his naked aggression hardly looked like a Zionist plot, thus he had to goad the Israelis into the war by any means possible. Once they started attacking him the Arab states would begin bailing out of the coalition and even nations like France, Germany, Japan and the Soviets would start looking at the conflict with a new eye.

In Israel the Scud attacks were galling. The Jewish state had always relied on the principle of responding to Arab violence with double or triple its own, while now it was forced to sit quiescent under a rain of Iraqi missiles. It didn't help to see the Palestinians on their rooftops cheering every one that came over. There was also fear that the Scuds would carry chemical weapons so that half the population was burdened with donning gas masks at every alert.

The United States did everything it could to resolve the Israeli plight. First it shipped batteries of its Patriot anti-missile system into the country to knock down the incoming Scuds. It turned out that the early Patriots didn't work—at best causing the rickety missiles to explode before their target, which they were too inaccurate to hit any-way—but they did much to stiffen morale. The U.S. also diverted a great deal of its air strength to try to hit mobile Scud launchers in the western Iraqi desert. Like the Patriot, this effort was only found to be unsuccessful after the war, when all kinds of destroyed tractors, fuel trucks and fertilizer carts were found across western Iraq. The U.S. also sent in Special Forces teams to spot or destroy the Scud launchers on the ground, resulting in a number of harrowing experiences. In one case a team was inserted at night and built a hide-site near an irriga-tion system. The next morning kids started playing nearby and spot-ted the concealed position. An Iraqi infantry company soon arrived and the Green Berets engaged in a running fight throughout the day, assisted by F-16 strikes on the Iraqis, until two Night Stalker heli-copters extracted them after dark.

Prime Minister Yitzhak Shamir of Israel still agitated for a shot at Iraq, and he had an initial force of 100 jet fighters and elite comman-dos waiting for the word. In Washington, Dick Cheney advised that it was useless to restrain them and that the U.S. would only make the sit-uation worse by trying. According to Brent Scowcroft, "He suggested we let them go, go fast, and get it over with." Bush and the rest of his war council didn't agree. A delegation headed by Deputy Secretary of State Lawrence Eagleburger went to Tel Aviv to invite the Israelis to share targeting intelligence; if they knew where to bomb they could just say so and the U.S. Air Force would take care of it. There was apprehension that the Israelis were actually intent on retaliating against civilians, and a greater fear that if Saddam started loading his Scuds with gas, the Israelis would push their nuclear button.

Though the United States' main priority was holding its coalition together, it was that same coalition that caused Israel to worry. Bush and Baker, who in Tel Aviv were viewed as prototypical Texan "oil men," had already proven far less sympathetic to Israeli military occupations than Reagan had been. And their new alliance, which integrated Saudi, Syrian, Egyptian and other Islamic troops under a U.S. command structure caused some alarm. Perhaps this was a coalition that needed to be broken up.

While Eagleburger was in Tel Aviv the Israelis requested an aid package of $13 billion, which would have been the largest such foreign appropriation in U.S. history. On the verge of a battle in which America was risking thousands of its soldiers against the Arabs' strongest state, Bush thought the request was unseemly. The administration eventually approved $10 billion in loan guarantees and $650 million in reparations for damage caused by the Iraqi Scuds.

In the end the combination of American persuasion and military efforts, together with Israeli restraint, prevented Saddam from drawing Israel into the war. His problem was that none of his Scuds made major hits, and of course he hadn't dared load any with chemical weapons. The Israelis suffered only two casualties from 69 missiles (though some elderly people died of heart attacks) and in the end there was no cassus belli. Just one major hit might have meant otherwise.

On January 29 an Iraqi armored brigade attacked into Saudi Arabia. A battalion feinted to the west while two more converged on Khafji, a Saudi town near the border that had been abandoned by civilians but was still an outpost for U.S. Marine artillery spotters backed by armor. The war's initial ground combat was spotty on both sides. American air power soared in and accidentally destroyed two Marine armored vehicles, killing eleven men. Saudi forces counterattacked to retake the town while Marines held out in abandoned buildings behind Iraqi lines. The Iraqis lacked coordination and fire discipline, and were soon driven out with heavy losses. U.S. airpower hammered their surviving forces, but at the very end of the battle an SA-7 missile scored a hit on a Spectre gunship, which crashed into the Persian Gulf with 14 men.

Khafji had been a tough fight, and one that sent mixed signals about the larger battle to come. And as always with Saddam Hussein it is difficult to assess what he had meant to achieve. The Coalition air campaign had been going on for two weeks and by now Iraq was nearly defenseless against the bombing. Iraqi fighter planes had been wiped from the sky in the few sorties they had attempted, and the Americans had not only knocked out Iraq's radar sites but learned how to avoid its AA fire. In a weird development, over 130 Iraqi aircraft simply fled to neighboring Iran (where the craft still remain). The Khafji incursion may have been an attempt by Saddam to divert Coalition airpower from Iraq to the front itself, even hastening the mother of all battles on the ground, where he thought he had the only chance to win. If so, the attempt failed. After the Iraqis were driven out of Khafji, the Coalition continued with its air campaign.

The air strategy had been designed by USAF Colonel John Warden, who was a firm believer in the concept of strategic bombing that the U.S. had first enacted in World War II. In that war the Germans, Japanese and Russians had constructed tactical air forces, meant to assist their ground or naval operations. The United States (and to a significant degree Britain), had instead prioritized a strategic air force to attack enemy rear areas rather than the front itself. In American history the godfather of this philosophy was William Tecumseh Sherman, who in the Civil War had turned his back on the Confederate Army of Tennessee and decided instead to wreak havoc on the enemy's heartland. His march to the sea, thence through the Carolinas, tore the guts out of the Confederacy, whose frontline armies by that time only comprised a brittle shell.

America's strategic air campaign in World War II essentially followed Sherman's concept that an enemy could be brought to his knees through devastation of his homeland rather than by knocking heads at the front. In Korea and Vietnam, strategic airpower was of limited use because the Communists didn't rely on their own industrial infrastructure, instead procuring arms through hidden supply lines from the Soviet Union and China, which the United States couldn't bomb. But in Iraq, which had become a fairly industrialized nation, cut off from foreign assistance, the strategic concept found a good playing field.

After Iraq's air defense system was suppressed, Coalition airpower destroyed its communications and electrical networks, most bridges and airfields, and its arms-related factories. In retrospect such a strategic campaign might seem excessive for such a short war; concentrating airpower on the front in Kuwait might have enabled everyone to go home sooner. However, since the Coalition's mandate extended only to the liberation of Kuwait, the strategic bombing campaign was a good opportunity to cripple Iraqi power in the case of any future aggressive ambitions.

By mid-February coalition aircraft were beginning to run short of targets. On the 13th, U.S. aircraft bombed a supposed "command and control center" in Baghdad, which was really an air-raid shelter, and hundreds of Iraqi kids, women and elderly died. This event put a damper on the strategic bombing campaign, and it was thought that airpower could now be better used against the Iraqi armored forces in Kuwait that the coalition would eventually have to attack. The only exception was the continued Scud-hunting in the west of Iraq in order to keep the Israelis out of the affair.

During the months of build-up in the theater over 230 U.S. soldiers died of illness or accidents. This was not an outrageous figure for a swarming "city" of troops, all of whom were handling weapons or heavy equipment, but some days were worse than others. On February 18 the morning report showed a Huey helicopter crash, four deaths in vehicle accidents, a Navy dockworker drowned, three wounded in rifle misfires and an MP officer accidentally shooting himself in the head while demonstrating the safety on his .45. The air campaign had lasted long enough; and it was high time to get the war going.

By this time Coalition forces numbered up to three-quarters of a million, 550,000 of them American. This was more than the highest troop level reached in Vietnam, and as such served as a perfect manifestation of the Powell Doctrine. What if, in that prior war of incremental build-up and sprawling occupation, the United States had been able to assemble its entire force for one quick, decisive battle? Powell himself had not been enthusiastic for the war in Bush's early councils, but once the decision was made he worked with enormous energy to ensure its success. In fact, he made the most famous statement of the campaign at an early press conference when he described what was

about to take place. Upon being asked how the coalition would deal
with the Iraqi army, it was the utter calm with which he replied that
impressed the public, and which should have served as a warning to
Saddam Hussein. He said, "First we are going to cut it off. Then we
are going to kill it."

The American line-up not only bristled with heavy firepower but
resonated with history. Under XVIII Airborne Corps were the famous
82nd and 101st Airborne Divisions (the latter now "Air Assault"), the
24th ID that had overrun the Philippines and had been the first U.S.
division in Korea, and the 3rd Armored Cavalry Brigade. Combined
in VII Corps were the 1st Armored Division, the 1st Infantry (Big Red
One), the 3rd Armored (which in World War II had suffered the most
casualties of any U.S. armored division), the 1st Cavalry Division,
including George Custer's old command, and the 2nd Armored
Cavalry Brigade, which had originally been formed by Andrew
Jackson. On the right were the legendary 1st and 2nd U.S. Marine
Divisions and the "Tiger" Brigade, part of the 2nd Armored Division
that had spearheaded so many crucial battles in the ETO.

Attached to XVIII Corps was the French 6th Light Armored
Division, which included two regiments of Foreign Legionnaires, and
in VII Corps was the British 1st Armoured. The British regiments of
Lancers, Fusiliers and Hussars possessed lineages older than the
United States itself, while its 7th Armoured Brigade was the direct
descendant of World War II's "Desert Rats" who had vied with
Rommel.

Schwarzkopf's plan for the ground offensive had been fine-tuned into
a brilliant use of forces. His plan called for the U.S. Navy and Marines
to feint an amphibious invasion of the Kuwaiti coast. This turned into
a creative effort with SEALs sneaking ashore to set off explosions and
planting buoys in the water as if to mark invasion lanes. One officer
had the idea to commandeer thousands of empty water bottles and
float them to the beaches, each containing a leaflet showing fearsome
Marines emerging from the surf.

The Marines themselves were already in the desert, anchoring the
coalition right south of Kuwait City. They were flanked by a Saudi-
Kuwaiti task force meant to be first to enter the capital, and by an

Arab corps anchored by the Egyptian and Syrian divisions. To their left, facing Iraqi territory beyond the Kuwait border, was VII Corps, the most powerful formation ever assembled, led by General Fred Franks. Even farther left, up to 300 miles out in the desert, was the XVIII Airborne Corps commanded by General Gary Luck.

The offensive would begin with the Marines kicking in the Iraqi defenses south of Kuwait City while the XVIII Corps on the far left penetrated deep into Iraq to the Euphrates River. It was anticipated that the Iraqis wouldn't recognize the fast incursion to the west and that their main units, including their Republican Guard armored divisions, would rush south to repel the Marines. After 24 hours the powerful VII Corps, spearheaded by its 1,600 tanks, would kick off, charging north and then east to crush the main Iraqi forces in the flank. XVIII Corps far behind the Iraqi lines would help seal off their escape routes.

The ground attack was originally slated for February 21, but then the Marines decided to shift their positions. They'd identified a weak spot in the Iraqi front where forward trenches had been abandoned and the second line was still unfinished. The possibility that Saddam would use chemical weapons was still a worry, and coalition forces would only be vulnerable if they got stalled and bunched up before fixed defenses. Schwarzkopf switched G-Day to February 24.

At the last minute, Mikhail Gorbachev unleashed another peace initiative, in which he hoped to convince the Iraqis to voluntarily withdraw, thus avoiding a ground war. Schwarzkopf and his generals in the desert were all for it, but in the White House the Soviet interference was unwelcome. In fact, President Bush had only two major fears at the time: the first was that the upcoming offensive would turn into a Coalition bloodbath; the second was that Saddam would suddenly pull the rug out from under the gigantic effort through a withdrawal, maintaining his strength and his capacity for future aggression, while over 700,000 troops in the theater lost their mandate to fight after accomplishing nothing at all.

But Gorbachev and his peace initiative had to be respected. In a White House council, Colin Powell suggested that another deadline be set for noon on Saturday, February 23. If the Soviet Union could swing an unconditional, immediate Iraqi withdrawal from Kuwait in the next two days, it would be a mission accomplished. If, as expected, Saddam was only trying to obfuscate while playing for time, and relying on misguided doubts about American resolve, he could soon be corrected. Despite Gorbachev's best efforts, the deadline came and went with the Iraqi army still entrenched in Kuwait.

On the evening of February 24, 1991, President Bush appeared before the nation and announced, "The final phase of the liberation of Kuwait has begun."

It was four in the morning local time when the Marines kicked off. Their first task was to surmount the Iraqi minefields and trenches—some expected to be filled with burning oil—but their sappers had been sneaking into no-man's land for days to clear lanes. When the Marines charged into the first line of Iraqi resistance there was no opposition. When they reached the second line the Iraqi conscripts began surrendering in droves.

On the far left, the French 6th Light and the 82nd Airborne raced due north toward the Iraqi airbase at Al Safwan. The 101st Air Assault Division launched 300 helicopters—the largest attack of its kind in history—deep into enemy territory. The 101st then spread out and made further jumps to spread a nest of Screaming Eagles atop the enemy's right rear areas. The 200 tanks of the 24th Infantry Division crashed across the border, churning into Iraq against negligible resistance. Prior to the attack, Schwarzkopf had grown suspicious of why Iraq had not moved any units above the far-flung coalition left, wondering if Saddam Hussein was purposely keeping the area empty as a kill-zone for unconventional weapons. Now it turned out that the Iraqis had been unaware of XVIII Corps' deployment. This was a tribute to the cooperation Bush and Baker had gained from Moscow, because if they had chosen the Soviets could have supplied Saddam with satellite reconnaissance, just as the U.S. supplied the Iraqis in the 1980s to reveal Iranian dispositions.

By noon Schwarzkopf's situation map was showing huge advances on both his left and right, with hardly any casualties, while reports of feeble resistance and thousands of Iraqi surrenders were flooding in. Most worrisome was that the Marines were advancing so fast on the right they were showing an open flank to a potential Iraqi counterattack. He decided that instead of holding back VII Corps until the next morning he would launch it at three that afternoon, 15 hours earlier than planned.

General Fred Franks, commander of VII Corps, canvassed his divisional commanders and they were all willing to jump off. Unlike the Americans, Rupert Smith of the British 1st Armoured didn't overly tax himself with advance planning, figuring he would simply engage the enemy and fight the battle as it developed. At the last minute he decided to let his Desert Rats lead his 4th Armoured Brigade in the assault.

Day one of the offensive had seen dozens of Iraqi battalions crushed or dispersed, with hundreds of dead and 13,000 taken prisoner. XVIII Corps reported only one man wounded against 3,500 prisoners and unknown Iraqi dead. Marine fatalities amounted to one while they had only been slowed down by directing traffic for hordes of POWs. From President Bush on down, thousands of allied casualties had been anticipated at this point, and even more had been feared. Total Coalition casualties so far were eight dead and 27 wounded.

On day two of the offensive the Iraqis launched their 5th Mechanized Division against the Marines, who proceeded to crush it like a bug. While Marine M-60 tanks and TOW anti-tank missiles destroyed every vehicle within sight, Cobra helicopters and Navy fighter bombers wreaked havoc on the Iraqi artillery, infantry and supply columns. The Iraqis seemed to be firing blind while the Marines calmly brewed up enemy vehicles, gunning down infantry who showed fight. It was this event that persuaded Saddam Hussein to call for a withdrawal of his forces from Kuwait. Rather than launch a counteroffensive, his three heavy Republican Guard divisions remained north of the country to protect the general retreat. The Iraqis blew up the desalinization plant in Kuwait City and methodically continued destroying Kuwait's oil wells. This was partly to create some kind of protection against coalition air power, but also to leave as much ruin behind as they could.

That morning Schwarzkopf saw that while the Marines and XVIII Corps had advanced on either end through the night, VII Corps in the center had gone to sleep. In fact it looked like they'd made a retrograde movement during the night, some of their earlier reported advances being made by scouts, and not genuine seizures of territory.

Stormin' Norman blew up at VII Corps commander Franks, and ever since the war there has been a debate about whether Franks had been practical or timid. In retrospect one suspects that the corps formation was too large. It would have been better to split it up, perhaps putting half under British command.

During day two, the French had achieved their objective; the 82nd Airborne was deep into Iraq; and the 101st was at the Euphrates River, between the cities of Samawah and Nasiryiah. The heavy unit of XVIII Airborne Corps, the 24th Infantry Division, had driven through the night and gained 65 miles over rough ground. On the coalition's far right, the Marines were almost to Kuwait City and the Arab task force on the coast had made similar progress. The Egyptian-Syrian corps to the Marines' left had proceeded methodically at first, perhaps for political reasons, but were now fully underway. Schwarzkopf's ire was spent mainly on his VII Corps, which was meant to be the main hammer in the offensive. The Marines had only been intended to tie down the enemy but instead had overrun them and were making enormous gains. On the left, the airborne corps had gotten within 150 miles of Baghdad.

That day was marred by a lucky Scud hit on a U.S. barracks in Dhahran, on the coast of Saudi Arabia. Twenty-eight soldiers were killed, mainly National Guardsmen from western Pennsylvania, and nearly 100 wounded. These casualties far behind the front were worse than those suffered by any unit at the cutting edge of the offensive.

On day three, Tuesday in Iraq, VII Corps began to flow north with an unstoppable wave of firepower. In a tactic that would later be criticized, the 1st Infantry Division used armored bulldozers to help spearhead its attack. These were available in numbers in order to knock down sand berms or fill in ditches, but the Big Red One started using them as destructive weapons. Upon reaching a trench full of terrified Iraqis, APCs would spray machine-gun fire to keep the enemy down while the bulldozers would grind along the trenches burying them alive. Attacking an enemy resisting from below ground was considered legitimate after the U.S. experiences against the Japanese on Iwo Jima and Okinawa, and the Communists' tunnel complexes in Vietnam. But the Iraqis were not such die-hards and all over the battlefield proved entirely willing to surrender. These instant mass graves did not turn out to be a point of pride for the Americans, and bull-dozing enemy forces was later avoided.

Toward evening the 2nd Armored Cavalry Brigade, spearheading VII Corps, finally made contact with the westernmost unit of Saddam Hussein's elite Republican Guard, a brigade of the Tawalkana Division. Though the Guard tried to stand and slug it out, its training and equipment were no match for the U.S. unit. After darkness fell the battlefield was illuminated by over 200 burning Iraqi armored vehicles. The 2nd Cavalry had lost one man to enemy fire.

Indeed, such was the preponderance of Coalition firepower on the field that troops were almost in greater danger from friendly fire than shots from the enemy. That night the 1st Infantry continued its advance, losing six men and a number of vehicles, all to accidental fire from neighboring units. The worst incident happened to the British when two of their Warrior armored vehicles were mistaken by U.S. pilots for Iraqi APCs. They were destroyed at the cost of nine dead and eleven wounded.

Earlier that day Coalition airpower, which had been flying over 3,000 sorties a day since the offensive began, spotted a giant exodus of Iraqi vehicles from Kuwait City. These were not primarily tanks or APCs but cars, buses, pick-up trucks and every other sort of conveyance that could be piled high with Kuwaiti loot. Imagine the French Army's retreat from Moscow in 1812 spotted and destroyed from above on the first day. Route 8 north from Kuwait City to Basra became known as the "Highway of Death" as aircraft obliterated the miles-long column of vehicles. For the F-14s, F-15s, F-16s, Spectres, Tornados, Mirages, Cobras, Apaches and Warthogs that blasted the column it was actually easier than shooting fish in a barrel.

The Marines had taken Kuwait's international airport, but held off from the city itself so that Arab troops could liberate it. Only a few Special Forces troops accompanied the Kuwaiti, Saudi and other Arab troops that marched into the capital, where they were greeted by cheering crowds.

The next morning the 1st and 3rd U.S. Armored Divisions, attacking side by side, overran the remaining two brigades of the Tawalkana Division, leaving acres of smoldering junk in their wake. The next Republican Guard armored division in line, the Medina, had by now recognized the left hook and had reoriented to face west rather than south. The 2nd Brigade of the 1st Armored pulled up, and, taking advantage of the superior range of its Abrams tanks, calmly brewed up dozens of T-72s and scores of other armored vehicles. Aircraft zoomed in to blast the enemy artillery and supply train. The third heavy Republican Guard Division, the Hammurabai, retreated to the north without risking contact.

Above Kuwait City, the 2nd Armored's Tiger Brigade had gotten astride the Iraqi escape route, which was now an inferno of black smoke from oil fires, combined with fumes from burning wreckage on the ground and a great deal of human carnage. For its part in the offensive the brigade counted 329 destroyed or captured armored vehicles, 263 Iraqi dead and 4,051 prisoners. It had lost two men killed and five wounded. Across the battlefield the Iraqis were either attempting to flee or desperately waving white rags in surrender.

That evening, Schwarzkopf gave a briefing to the press in Riyadh in which he waxed esctatic, saying, "The gate is closed." He explained that while Kuwait had not been completely sealed off, heavy enemy units could no longer retreat intact. "We've accomplished our mission," he said, "and when the decision-makers come to a decision that there should be a cease-fire, nobody will be happier than me."

These words resonated in Washington, where Colin Powell had recognized the turkey shoot from the beginning and had already been thinking about how to end the slaughter. President Bush was still determined to avoid the Vietnam mistake of interfering tactically with his commanders, yet he too was not pleased by the Highway of Death. If the war went on much longer it would only create a brutal picture of the Coalition's enormous firepower killing Iraqis who were trying to flee. The mission had been to liberate Kuwait, and that task had obviously been accomplished. Any more splashes of death inflicted on the backs of retreating Iraqi conscripts would not endure to America's credit.

It was still early afternoon in the White House when the discussion focused on how to close down the war. Powell and Schwarzkopf had already discussed the matter, with the idea that a five-day war would trump the Israelis' six-day triumph of 1967. In the White House, nine in the evening was considered, but that would be five in the morning Kuwait time. It was finally decided to end it at midnight Washington time, which would leave a couple hours of daylight for coalition forces to survey the battlefield and make any necessary adjustments. An additional advantage with this timing, suggested by Bush's White House chief of staff John Sununu, was the catchphrase: the "Hundred Hours War."

The next morning in Kuwait, the fog of war lifted to reveal that VII Corps had not actually driven as far east as indicated on Schwarzkopf's situation maps. He had designated Safwan airfield, just inside Iraq, as a place to lay down terms to the enemy commanders, but now he saw it was still held by an Iraqi brigade headquarters with 15 tanks. Schwarzkopf blew his top again, this time at the 1st Infantry Division, which was supposed to have taken the place. The Big Red One solved the problem by surrounding the airstrip with 50 tanks and dozens of APCs while Apache helicopters hovered menacingly overhead. Given their cease-fire deadline the Americans had actually been forbidden to engage in combat, but the Iraqi commander could not be so sure, and when invited to retreat gracefully, he accepted.

Two days later the cease-fire was broken farther north. Barry McAffrey's 24th Infantry had made the farthest progress of any mechanized division, and at the time the 100 hours expired had been following the Euphrates east toward the Iraqi city of Basra. Around Basra the bridges had been blown and a huge jam of Iraqi men and vehicles had piled up trying to escape north. The Republican Guard armored division Hammurabai got tired of waiting and began to move west, inadvertently straight into the positions of the 24th Infantry Division. The fight was said to have begun with an Iraqi rocket-propelled grenade, which was answered by American artillery. Then the entire 24th Infantry was given permission to open fire and it obliterated about 600 Iraqi vehicles. The Hammurabai, which had avoided VII Corps' left hook during the battle, came a cropper a couple days later against the heavy division of XVIII Corps.

The next day Schwarzkopf and the other Coalition generals sat down across from Iraqi military commanders to dictate terms of the cease-fire. One priority was a prisoner exchange and Schwarzkopf demanded a count of Coalition personnel, mainly airmen, held by the Iraqis. The response was 17 Americans, 12 British, nine Saudis and two Italians. Then Iraq's General Ahmad asked for a count of Iraqi prisoners and he was informed that so far the count had reached 60,000. (It would eventually top 80,000.) According to Schwarzkopf, "His face went completely pale; he had had no concept of the magnitude of their defeat."

The American public had never seen such a decisive victory on such a scale. For four decades they had wondered how U.S. arms would fare against Soviet arms in a full-fledged confrontational armored battle. Well, now they knew. The U.S. had lost about 90 soldiers in the 100-hour ground offensive, over half of them from the combination of friendly fire and the lucky Scud hit in Dhahran. In the 43 days of Desert Storm the total of combat deaths was 148, along with 92 among the allies. In contrast, Iraqi deaths were in the tens of thousands, and every time an Iraqi unit had tried to stand against Coalition forces it had immediately been destroyed.

For a brief period, the end of the Cold War had seemed to present a green light for dictators such as Saddam Hussein. But America's initiative in establishing a new international order, and its willingness to place its strength behind the rule of law, quickly shut the door on the ambitions of Saddam or any other regional aggressor who might have been tempted to follow in his footsteps.

With one stroke Bush had replaced Vietnam syndrome with new respect for American military personnel. Norman Schwarzkopf had become a poster boy, the most dynamic U.S. field general since Patton. Colin Powell's positive ratings went through the roof. Though a military man he had contradicted the stereotype by discernibly stressing a humanitarian element in the use of destructive power. And speaking of stereotypes! America had been wracked by Civil Rights wars for 40 years, which in domestic terms had been concurrent with and just as unsettling as the Cold War. And now here was Powell, an African-American, who embodied every quality the public admired. If he ever entered presidential politics he would be a dynamo, confusing the left, right and center, with no part of the population able to withhold their respect. (As it turned out his wife, Alma, shot down the idea.)

While Powell and Schwarzkopf became heroes, James Baker basked in the achievement that had raised the war to an historic significance beyond the purely military level. The United States had not just flexed martial muscle, but had also assembled an unprecedented global coalition behind its leadership. During the last year of World War II, everyone from Turkey to Tobago had suddenly professed to be a U.S. ally. But this time the alliance was meaningful, with every significant nation in the world on board from the start, or as in the case of China, willing to go along. Dick Cheney at the Department of Defense, and Brent Scowcroft as National Security Adviser, played largely unsung roles in the affair, but their expertise had contributed significantly to what, in the aftermath of the Gulf War, very much looked like the emergence of a Pax Americana.

Of course the main accolades went to President Bush, the head of the team, and its only elected official. And how the public's confidence had been vindicated! Bush's approval ratings reached 90 percent, an unprecedented figure. The Democrats who had opposed him now resembled, to excuse the expression, wimps, and those who had had an eye on the presidency were forced to put their ambitions on hold. On the Republican right, the leading conservative critic Patrick Buchanan simply admitted he had been wrong.

Bush himself tempered his pride in the achievement. While the tank battles had raged in the desert he had reflected on the Vietnam syndrome that had dogged the country for two decades. "We're doing something decent, and we're doing something good," he recorded in his diary, "and Vietnam will soon be behind us." On the day after the guns fell quiet another entry in his diary read, "Everyone seems to be giving me great credit, and yet, I don't look at it that way. I think our team has been absolutely superb."

American troops came home with a victory in a major war for the first time since 1945. Nearly a million people attended a grand parade in Washington, DC, and even more thronged the "Canyon of Heroes" in New York as 25,000 soldiers from Desert Storm were showered with confetti thrown from skyscrapers. America was seized by a kind of patriotic euphoria that only older citizens could remember having experienced before. And the best thing was that the victory seemed to have marked a new creation: of a peaceful world, secure and hopeful, under the firm hand of American leadership.

5

THE FALL OF BUSH

The Gulf War not only provided Americans with a rare degree of martial pride but a sense of security they had not felt for half a century. The U.S.-led Coalition's performance in battle had been impressive enough, while its logistical achievement had been astonishing. On August 1, 1990, Saddam Hussein had stared at a vast expanse of desert defended by a few Kuwaiti gendarmes. By the following January he was faced with 10,000 armored vehicles, 2,700 modern aircraft and 750,000 men. And the vast bulk of these forces returned to their homelands immediately after their success.

It did not take long, however, for criticisms to arrive. America's fourth largest paper, Newsday, featuring a garish photo of the Highway of Death on its cover, complained that the ground phase of the war had gone on too long. Others complained that the air phase had been prolonged unnecessarily. The latter critics had a point in that strategic bombing had only a minor effect on the ground offensive; however, since the Coalition had no intention of exceeding its mandate to liberate Kuwait, the air campaign had provided a good opportunity to cripple Saddam's ability to launch other wars in the future. A third barrage of criticism, the most persistent, was that Saddam and most of his army had survived the war. This became apparent shortly after its conclusion when Iraq exploded into bloody ethnic battles.

Hardly anyone, from Washington, DC to the various capitals of the Mideast, expected Saddam Hussein to remain in power after his debacle in Kuwait. Iraq had suffered enormously during its pointless war with Iran, and now its army and infrastructure had been crushed anew after another of Saddam's miscaculcations. And the dire politi-co-economic circumstances that had led him to invade Kuwait had only been exacerbated, now with no end in sight.

In the south, an Iraqi tank column that had escaped the inferno pulled into the center of Basra. It stopped in front of the Baath party headquarters, next to which was a gigantic mural of Saddam. After shouting curses against the dictator to the surrounding crowd, the lead tank commander got back in his vehicle and its cannon began blasting apart the mural. This act triggered a revolt throughout the city as soldiers and mobs of civilians descended on Baath, police and other government installations. The rebellion spread like wildfire throughout the Shiite south.

In the north, the Kurds needed no further impetus and seized back their traditional capital, Irbil, as violence flared in oil-rich Kirkuk and down to the mixed city of Mosul. Baath party officials and secret police were seized and killed, sometimes strung up in public displays.

In the center, the Sunnis grew worried, and any restlessness against Saddam was replaced by alarm at the bloody uprisings on either side. The Iraqi army may not have been able to beat the American coalition, but it could still wreak havoc on its own people, and Saddam had held back at least 20 divisions for just such a contingency. The army moved to quell the rebellions with brutal force.

Norman Schwarzkopf has stated that he erred by giving the Iraqis permission to use helicopters in the south, since instead of using them for humanitarian reasons they employed them to crush the rebellion. But this factor has probably been overestimated, since Iraqi main-force divisions would have sooner or later accomplished the same task. American forces were in an awkward position as aerial recon-naissance revealed the extent of the violence and terrified Shiite civil-ians came fleeing into U.S. lines. But the troops were under orders not to interfere. In later years the administration was criticized for not having invaded Iraq after the liberation of Kuwait in order to force Saddam from power. But as Bush and Scowcroft explained in their joint memoir, "A World Transformed":

We would have been forced to occupy Baghdad and, in effect, rule Iraq. The coalition would instantly have collapsed, the

Arabs deserting it in anger and other allies pulling out as well. . . . We had been self-consciously trying to set a pattern for handling aggression in the post–Cold War world. Going in and occupying Iraq, thus unilaterally extending the United Nations' mandate, would have destroyed the precedent of international response to aggression that we hoped to establish. Had we gone the invasion route, the United States could conceivably still be an occupying power in a bitterly hostile land. It would have been a dramatically different—and perhaps barren—outcome.

In southern Iraq, Saddam's forces put down the rebellion. It had turned out to be too chaotic to succeed, and Shiite elements made a mistake by raising the banner of religious war, an act that caused many secular rebels to split off and a number of tribal leaders to switch back to Baghdad. This was also a factor that confirmed America's decision to stand aside, since neither Washington nor its Arab allies wanted Iraq to break apart like an Islamic Yugoslavia, resulting in endless bloodshed and unsettling the region for decades to come. A separate Shiite state in the south would have comprised an open invitation for an expansion of Iranian influence, while in the north a new Kurdistan would have been a magnet for Kurds in Iran, Syria and Turkey to violate their own political borders. And the Sunnis in the center would have retained no other goal than to reconstitute Iraq by force.

Baghdad's counterattack against the Kurds was just as vicious as its response in the south, and by now Kurdish villagers knew not to wait for Saddam's forces to line them up, separating the young men and marching them to oblivion. A massive civilian exodus surged north to the Turkish border.

A warm and fuzzy perception has risen around the Kurds, as if they were a pastoral people unused to violence. In fact, they were extremely tough mountain fighters, previously employed as enforcers for the Ottomans. They had bloodied government forces for decades, and man-to-man were probably superior to Baghdad's troops. When the Iraqis conquered the two main headquarters of the Kurdish independence parties in 1988, it wasn't considered a furtive operation but a great victory, celebrated in later years on its anniversary. But the Kurds had no means to stop main-force mechanized divisions in a concentrated effort.

Saddam's drive against the Kurds can be compared to Soviet efforts against the Tajik Mujahideen of northeast Afghanistan. Like the Tajiks under Ahmed Shah Massoud, the Kurd fighters were too tough to kill, so the system switched to what Louis Dupree called "migratory genocide," which meant rooting up the civilian population and forcing it out. However, while millions of Afghans were able to find refuge in Pakistan or Iran, none of Iraq's neighbors wanted to take in large numbers of Kurds, since they'd always had similar problems with their own Kurdish populations. Turkey was especially adamant at keeping them out and had sealed off its border. So at least half a million Kurdish civilians filled the hills of northern Iraq, uprooted from their homes, with nowhere to go and Saddam's forces bearing down on them.

U.S. Secretary of State James Baker, diverted from one of his diplomatic missions, set down in the region and saw at firsthand the humanitarian catastrophe. When Bush heard his report he reactivated the Coalition. U.S. Special Forces teams arrived in the hills to provide emergency healthcare and coordinate shipments of aid by air. They were joined by British, French, Italian and other allied forces. Most importantly, Saddam's men, who didn't dare risk armed conflict with the Coalition, were forced to back off, allowing the Kurds to return to their homes. In June the Coalition slapped a "no-fly" zone over northern Iraq down to the 36th parallel, and in the south another one over Shiite territory up to the 32nd parallel (just above the holy city of Najaf). American and British fighter bombers would patrol these no-fly zones for the next dozen years.

While Bush heartily wished that Saddam and his clique would be overthrown by the Iraqi people, he stopped short of assisting anarchic rebellions that looked liable to dissolve the Iraqi state. His idea was that the army, or more responsible political figures in Baghdad, would remove Saddam from power and thence put the country on a more moderate path. The tragic irony was that while Saddam may have hung by a thread immediately after his disaster in Kuwait, the rebellions on either side served to rally the Sunni population and the core of the army behind him. The mother of all battles had been lost, but now Saddam, with his overriding sense of self-preservation, re-positioned himself as a conquering leader, this time crushing the rebels among his own people.

The further tragedy was that Saddam, no longer able to manipulate his country into greatness through prosperity or military power, fell back on brutality to hold the parts together. The Shiites suffered the most, because while their short-lived rebellion had been bloody enough, Saddam responded with many times the force, resulting in wholesale massacres of young men who were later found buried by the thousand.

For domestic support in the years after the war, Saddam, like an Islamic Castro, clung to power on the platform that he had defied the United States and all its allies and survived. After the Gulf War, he gave up any further ideas of becoming the new Saladin, propelling Iraq into martial greatness and becoming a rallying point for the Arab people. Instead he fell back on his specialty, internal security, trying to perpetuate his personality cult with ever greater palaces, murals, paintings and monuments.

This was sensible enough because Anglo-American warplanes now roamed the skies over the north, providing more autonomy to the Kurds than they had seen since the Middle Ages. They also guarded the south, in a zone that was later extended to just below Baghdad. Two-thirds of the country was patrolled by fighter planes while the rest was monitored by U.S. satellite reconnaissance.

The arms embargo and economic sanctions first instituted after the invasion of Kuwait remained in effect, preventing Saddam from rebuilding his forces. In 1996 the strict policy was ameliorated by the UN into a program called "Oil for Food," in order to relieve the suffering of the Iraqi people. Corrupt elements in Saddam's government immediately descended on the renewed flow of petro dollars to divert funds or enrich themselves; however, the West could be assured that if the Iraqi people continued to suffer it was, as usual, Saddam's fault. (At this writing, after accusations of corruption on the part of Western suppliers and bankers, the Oil for Food program is under investigation by the UN.)

As a final seal on Saddam's defeat, United Nations weapons

inspectors crisscrossed Iraq, destroying the chemical munitions left over from the war with Iran and dismantling the remnants of Iraq's nuclear program. Saddam tried to obstruct the inspectors, some of whom were CIA agents who worked closely with Israeli intelligence, but it was only an effort to retain some pride, as if Iraq had not become a humbled nation. As a ludicrous gesture of revenge, Saddam had a portrait of George Bush sewn in a carpet and laid down in the lobby of the Rashid Hotel in Baghdad, so that anyone coming through the doors would have to step on it.

In truth, all Saddam had left was bravado, and his own desperate need to cling to power.

A positive result of the Gulf War was the first peace conference between Israel and its Arab opponents. Earlier, James Baker had undertaken exhaustive shuttle missions to arrange for a permanent peace in Palestine. But he had only met with frustration on all sides. The Israelis, in particular, were in no mood to deal because they were expecting hundreds of thousands of immigrants from the Soviet Republics, and Housing Minister Ariel Sharon had enacted a crash program to build permanent Jewish settlements in the West Bank.

The neutralization of Iraq, however, together with America's new status in the region and the decline of Cold War militarization, redrew the playing field. On October 30, 1991, leaders from Israel, Egypt, Syria, Jordan, Lebanon and the Palestine Liberation Organization sat down at a conference table in Madrid. It was a first for the region, and also just a first step. But the next year Yitzhak Shamir was replaced as Israeli prime minister by Yitzhak Rabin, and in 1993 the historic Oslo Accords were achieved, setting the Palestinians on a path to autonomy. Unfortunately, Rabin was later assassinated by a Jewish settler, and to this day Oslo remains the apex of Israeli-Palestinian amity.

The eventful year of 1991 climaxed on Christmas Day when Mikhail Gorbachev phoned President Bush to inform him that he was dissolving the Soviet Union. Its constituent republics were free to go their own way, no longer controlled by the Communist Party in Moscow. That the Cold War, after so many years, ended with a warm, appreciative conversation between the leaders of the Soviet Union and the United States was a Christmas miracle in itself.

As the year 1992 dawned, it was apparent that, along with a noxious dictator in Panama, Iraqi armed aggression, the impasse in the Middle East, and the Cold War, President Bush had eliminated one other thing: the American public's concern with foreign policy.

Since the Soviets had erected the Iron Curtain across Europe, the United States had either been embroiled in limited wars or prepared to fight a total one, all the way up to the nightmare scenario of nuclear holocaust. During the Cold War, the Republicans had been considered the "Dads" in U.S. politics while the Democrats were the "Moms." When an intruder was at the door the public had turned to Republican presidents; when no immediate threat was evident and kids were sick inside the house, the public turned to Democrats, who in turn were expected to at least talk as toughly as the Republicans.

In 1991 Bush wiped foreign policy off the political drawing board. And aside from relieving the anxieties of the public he had also erased a great deal of apprehension in the armed services. For decades, weapons designers, military planners and service chiefs had wondered how they would fare in full confrontational warfare against their Soviet counterparts. The Israeli wars and Vietnam had sent conflicting signals. But in the Gulf War the American military was finally able to match its latest weapons, doctrine and training against a Soviet-model military in full confrontational battle. And the result had been spectacular.

The only caveat was the desert factor, which had provided the ideal environment for armored or tactical air operations. In World War II, the North African desert had presented the only "clean" aspect of a conflict that turned ugly in every other theater, where cities, civilians, mountains, forests and caves required indiscriminate firepower. War waged in a sandbox was preferable, and in fact the only German general to emerge with a high reputation in WWII was Rommel, the "Desert Fox." He would probably not have been lauded as a great general by Churchill and others if he had been assigned instead to the reduction of Leningrad.

Another factor that mitigated against premature euphoria was the military skill of the Arabs. The small state of Israel had been thrashing them for years in conventional battles—though had in turn been beleaguered by unconventional tactics—and it was hardly a surprise that the U.S. military could do the same. With a literacy rate near 50 percent at best, a tribal, ethnic and religious composition unconducive to unified national purpose, and only a recent emergence from foreign subjugation, the Arabs may not have been the ultimate test of the combined power of the Western coalition.

Still, any advantages in desert terrain or in the relative sophistication of the troops might well have accrued to the other side. The desert, after all, was the Iraqis' homeground. And there have been many examples in history where less educated soldiers have been more formidable than wealthier, less hardy opponents. Bush had led America into the Gulf War not fully knowing what to expect—and indeed, expectations were far worse than the results. But his courage was vindicated by a new sense of national confidence.

To a population that had once trained its little kids in air-raid drills, and which after Vietnam had worried about the capability of its battlefield forces, the Gulf War provided a huge sigh of relief. Suddenly there were no other threats around. We had not only won the Cold War but our military had quashed the most aggressive petty dictator in sight. Unfortunately for Bush, his strategic acumen, innate grasp of U.S. power, and unmatched success in aligning great nations from every continent behind American leadership spelled doom for his presidency. The American public no longer had to look outward, and could finally focus inward. And one could say that after so many years of life-threatening issues abroad, a period of concern for matters at home was long overdue.

President Bush had inadventently stripped the country of its main rationale for maintaining him as president, yet he still fought to convince the public that he was capable of handling domestic policies as well as foreign ones. In these efforts he was completely unsuccessful. His legendary flub has gone down on record as his retreat on an earlier campaign promise: "Read my lips; no new taxes." This unsavory vow, which in a way revealed a certain weakness since it was unrepresentative of his character, boomeranged against him heavily. Bush, who can be considered the very model of moderation in domestic policy, felt it necessary to feed red meat to the Reaganite conservatives, with their devotion to downsize the government. And taxes had replaced Communism as their new evil.

As President, however, Bush was pragmatic, and when faced with a Democratic Congress that threatened to shut down the government just as American troops were on their way to the Perseian Gulf, he compromised. He agreed to raise the top tax rate from 28 to 31.5 percent, and compromised on other issues, while cutting elsewhere in the budget and counterattacking as best he could. The result was that the Republican right went haywire. They had suspected all along that Bush was not a true Reaganite and now they had proof.

Just like Carter, whose most vicious attacks had come in from the Democratic left led by Ted Kennedy, Bush found his most formidable assailants coming from the Republican right, which was theoretically his base. By now the Goldwater-Reagan right formed the core of the Republican constiuency, and the movement had only increased with popular evangelical preachers forming political movements, and due to the skill of an ambitious Georgian congressman, Newt Gingrich. Nixon had been able to fend off the beginnings of this rightward trend in order to pursue a hard-nosed center, but Bush was not quite as capable. And previously, Nixon, Johnson and others had been able to keep control of the money-center of politics, not having to deal with billionaires such as Ross Perot, who emerged from Reagan's age of greed perfectly able to fund their own movements. George Wallace had been a pain enough to Nixon, but at least the Alabamian's support had been grass-roots democratic (with a small "d"). Perot, who owed his fortune to an innovation in computer services, built his movement on the airwaves rather than in Baptist churches or meeting halls.

The last years of the Bush presidency were marked by domestic dissatisfaction, while his astonishing approval rating after the Gulf War sank like a stone. The economy was in a lull, the government's deficit had grown to monstrous proportions, and in early 1992 the Los Angeles race riots looked to many like the sign of another great social unraveling as in the 1960s. The increasing dynamism of the Republican right peeled off into support for Perot, for evangelist Pat Robertson, or for conservative activist Pat Buchanan.

Another phenomenon occurred as the 1990s got underway: all-news cable TV channels and radio stations. These were ravenous for up-to-the-minute stories, and capable of ballooning the most minor events into huge national crises.

An enormous media focus attended one of the domestic acts of the Bush presidency: the nomination of a black jurist, Clarence Thomas, to the Supreme Court. Bush had thought about Thomas before, but at the time he was slightly inexperienced so Bush had instead chosen David Souter from New Hampshire. Souter, largely becauase no one could figure out the blank slate of his record, had sailed through Congress. But now that the only black member of the court, Thurgood Marshall, had retired, Bush settled on Thomas as his new nominee.

The nomination turned into a fiasco. Suddenly the vastly expanded news media, with 24-hour cable channels voracious for hot topics, had no war or other drama to fill air-time. Instead their lasers zeroed in on how Thomas had allegedly tried to go out with a demurely beautiful young woman, Anita Hill, who had worked for him. Damning evidence piled up, including verbatim reports of Thomas's clumsy pick-up lines and an allegation that he had once hung a Playboy centerfold in his kitchen. Conservatives rallied behind the nominee while liberals flocked to Hill, who like Thomas had been single at the time.

Thomas himself finally put a stop to the frenzy by appearing before a Senate panel. He was not a very good looking fellow, and unlike other prominent African Americans, for example Colin Powell or Ms. Hill, was about as black as one could be. He described his pillorying as "a high-tech lynching," and his clear anger and hurt shamed the entire public into backing off. The Senate confirmed his nomination to the Supreme Court, where he has since served as a thoughtful, if quiet, jurist.

Overall, these vicious, specific attacks by the Democrats on date-making would come back to haunt them. A Pandora's Box, once opened, is difficult to close, and it was not the gentleman George Bush, who simply stayed loyal to his nominee, but the growing Republican right-wing that took careful note of the Democrats' tactics. And they would soon have their revenge.

Bush's 1992 campaign for re-election was as much a comedy of errors as his 1988 campaign had been a triumph of tactics. It was difficult to perceive that he had his heart in it, and he was at a loss to match his opponent's message to average Americans, "I feel your pain." Bush had always dealt with broader, global issues, and evidently didn't understand why the richest nation in history needed to feel pain at all. He went to a supermarket and expressed astonishment at the new scanning technology used by cashiers. This showed that he was out of touch. His advisers implored him to demonstrate that he cared about the plight of ordinary Americans, and to deliver a message that would reassure them. So Bush opened up his next campaign speech with the most inelegant pronouncement in U.S. political history: "Message: I care." At least he included a pronoun, which was something he usually avoided.

Things only got worse during one of the nationally televised debates when the cameras caught him looking at his watch. In a subsequent town hall-style debate, he fielded a query from a sincere young woman who wondered how the national debt affected him personally. Bush thought for a second, and then said he didn't understand the question.

The real disaster occurred at the Republican convention where, in return for his support, Pat Buchanan had been given opening night for a speech. Lowering his voice and narrowing his eyes in a manner that only seemed to be missing a secret handshake, Buchanan declared the existence of a "culture war," and a "religious war," and ended with the battle cry, "Take back our country!" The convention crowd exploded in cheers, while a chill went up nearly everyone else's spine, including George Bush's. Was this still the GOP?

The 1992 election was lost by Bush, 43 percent to 37, with Ross Perot getting about 19 percent. One can attribute Bush's defeat to the Perot factor, but the truth is that if Bush had shown as much enthusiasm for delving into domestic special interests as he did for aligning the interests of the world community he would have won a second term. And by this time the United States no longer had a problem with the world. Bush had already solved those problems with courage, imagination, and a steady hand. When it came to domestic minutiae he didn't have the stomach for it.

It was an unusual twist that after Bush was turned out of office, his approval ratings shot up in the polls. He was like the star first baseman who could no longer handle the high fastball, and who the fans had clamored to step aside. But once he was gone they viewed him only through the prism of the championships he had won for them in the past.

GEORGE H.W. BUSH AS A MILITARY LEADER

Any assessment of American presidents as military leaders is necessarily speculative, since all have faced different circumstances, enemies, and widely divergent resources at their disposal. There is also the fact that some presidents displayed their greatest military skill before they took office. George Washington can be esteemed above all others as a commander, but once he became president his only challenge was putting down the Whiskey Rebellion. Once they had moved into the White House, Grant and Eisenhower also left their most admirable military achievements behind them.

As for wartime presidents, Abraham Lincoln holds the palm in many quarters for winning the Civil War; however, his strategic good sense was countered for four years by Jefferson Davis, who was dealt a far poorer hand but played it superbly. Davis would have preferred an appointment as a field general rather than president of the short-lived Confederacy, but the politically incorrect fact remains that if he had had a semblance of the demographic and industrial superiority that Lincoln enjoyed during the Civil War, half our population would now be singing "Dixie" before its ballgames.

Lincoln's brilliance was manifested in two major moves: First, at the height of the war he changed the national cause from preserving the Union—a principle that was beginning to wear thin under a torrent of bloodshed and was legally questionable anyway—to liberating the slaves, an exalting moral purpose that forestalled European interventon and gave fresh impetus to Northern support.

His second move, which he struggled for years to achieve, was assembling an array of operational talent that could match what Davis had found in the South. Lincoln had excellent judgment and eventually solved his problem by drawing commanders from his native west to the east. In late March 1865 he received informal updates from Ulysess S. Grant, William T. Sherman and Admiral David Porter aboard a steamer on the James River, while General Philip Sheridan's cavalry closed in on the enemy nearby and General Henry Halleck served as chief of staff in the capital. Lincoln himself died two weeks later, but by then he knew that the victory he had sought had already been achieved.

Woodrow Wilson proved exceptional in terms of both military leadership and a greater international vision, of which warfare should only be an enabling component. His problem was that he didn't have the strength to overcome domestic opposition, and America did not then have the influence to override the traditional nationalist animosities of Europe.

Perhaps the most esteemed of our wartime presidents was Franklin Delano Roosevelt, who elegantly guided the United States to victory in World War II. America entered that conflagration later than other combatants, and had the advantage of choosing where to counterattack the Axis Powers rather than taking the full brunt of their aggressions. The exception occurred in December 1941 with the Japanese attacks on Pearl Harbor and the Philippines, and thus the bulk of literature critical of FDR focuses on his inability to foresee those attacks. As the war progressed, Roosevelt coordinated closely with Winston Churchill and Josef Stalin to achieve success in history's greatest war.

If there were a complaint to be voiced about Roosevelt it would concern his laissez faire attitude toward the Holocaust, which by 1944 had become known to Allied intelligence. Anglo-American airpower by then owned the skies over Europe and the Nazis' death camp network could easily have been disrupted. There were valid reasons not to do so, most vociferously voiced by the bomber chiefs who preferred a quicker end to the war rather than a diversion of resources. It may only be with hindsight that one realizes that continuing to stir the rubble in Berlin did less for the greater cause than one show of force above Auschwitz would have accomplished. Stellar as FDR's leadership in World War II undoubtedly was, it was also unmarked by humanitarian concerns.

Harry Truman turned out to be a surprisingly good military leader, given his utter lack of prior foreign policy experience. Not hesitating to invoke America's possession of the atomic bomb, he put a seal on the Communist rush into Europe that once threatened to fill the vacuum left by Fascism. His policy of containment forced the Soviets to consolidate the gains they had earned from the Third Reich rather than attempting any new ones at the expense of the West. Just as important, when faced with a dire battlefield crisis in Korea, he rejected further use of the atomic bomb, establishing an international concordance that has lasted to this day. His fatal flaw was conceding too much authority to his commander in Korea, Douglas MacArthur, and thus both he and the general were surprised when the Chinese enlarged that conflict with a surprise 300,000-man counteroffensive.

Any assessment of John F. Kennedy as a military leader must necessarily be incomplete, and his successor, Lyndon B. Johnson, may well have been the worst ever, even if he only failed while trying to live up to Kennedy's rhetoric.

Nixon was a more decisive war leader than Johnson; however, he faced a much more difficult task getting America out of Vietnam than his predecessors had getting us into it. The option to cut and run, offered by George McGovern in the 1972 presidential election, was rejected by the American public 49 states to one (Massachusetts), a fact that did not save Nixon from becoming the most openly vilified man in history once he had finally slogged his way to a face-saving withdrawal.

Carter and Reagan, as we have seen, had no innate talent for military operations and were generally unsuccessful, though both were handicapped by the consequences of Vietnam. In broader strategic terms, Reagan was highly successful in rebuilding the U.S. military establishment and infusing it with a new sense of confidence.

As for Bush senior as military leader, history will record that he did not encounter the enormous challenges faced by Lincoln or FDR, or even Truman and Nixon. Yet he dealt with his own military crises so well that one suspects the Republic would have been in good hands had he been forced to take on larger problems.

Part of the expertise he brought to the presidency consisted of "moral courage." This term first gained currency during the Civil War, when it became apparent that some generals were willing to commit their troops to battle and others were not. The clearest contrast was between the Union's George McClellan and the Confederacy's Robert E. Lee, who vied with each other in 1862. McClellan was an impressive general, expert at building up his forces, and much beloved by his troops. But when it came time to commit his command to the carnage and chaos of battle, he blanched. On the other side was Lee, also beloved by his troops, who looked for opportunities to win victories for his cause.

Their differences in moral courage came to a head at Antietam Creek that September, when Lee with some 40,000 men faced McClellan's 80,000 in the bloodiest day in American history. McClellan held back much of his force while Lee's lieutenants, Stonewall Jackson, James Longstreet, Jeb Stuart and John Bell Hood, put every man into the line until, late in the afternoon when the Confederate line was about to crack, A.P. Hill came rushing onto the field with about 5,000 more men. And the next day, it was Lee who continued to hold the field, daring McClellan to use the last of his fresh forces to attack again.

Bush did not face such dire circumstances. But prior to his invasion of Panama, and far more so prior to the Gulf War, he was faced with projections of thousands of U.S. casualties, all of which would occur as a result of his command. The task, then, was to measure his belief in his country's cause against the risk that military action would entail. The decisions were difficult. But in the end he assessed his own forces, the enemy's strength, and not least the justice of his cause, to summon the requisite moral courage. And in the ensuing campaigns he turned out to be correct.

To revisit Antietam, it should be noted that Lee himself didn't fight the battle, but relied on an exceptional group of subordinates. In fact, throughout military history it can be seen that great commanders are nearly always supported by other talented individuals, often accidental confluences of a few great men all present on one side at the same time. Examples range from Alexander's army and Hannibal's in ancient times, to the First Crusade and Genghis Khan's Mongols in the medieval period, to the modern era where we have seen Napoleon's marshals, the Army of Northern Virginia, Hitler's generals in 1940 and the Israeli ones in 1967 and 1973. The single exception of a great commander who won all his battles personally was Julius Caesar; then again, what we know of his campaigns comes primarily through his own memoir.

The inner foreign policy circle of the Bush presidency—James Baker, Brent Scowcroft, Colin Powell, and Dick Cheney—ranks as one of the best balanced, most skillful braintrusts we have seen in the modern era. All, save Cheney, were veterans, whose experience stretched from Bush's plight as a young aviator in the flak-filled skies over Chichi Jima to Powell's slogs through the hot jungles of Vietnam. In today's world, veterans may become ever fewer in public office, and it cannot be said how much the military experience of the Bush team influenced its later decisions. What we do know is that the individuals meshed together superbly, in a proper order of influence, under the guidance of a hands-on president who was careful and expert in his judgments.

Bush's expertise was manifested first in tactical skill, knowing exactly what U.S. forces were capable of achieving; and second in strategic skill, assessing which battles were essential to fight. A third dimension was evidenced by the manner in which the Cold War ended, with a phone call placed by the leader of the Soviet Union to the president of the United States. This conflict, the most dangerous of them all, ended without fighting, and with the United States not trying to press its advantage. Though possessing the moral courage to commit U.S. troops to combat, Bush sensed that America's greatest strength resided in its principles, with the ensuing friendships and alliances that would extend the New World's example. Considering all the conflicts in which Bush engaged, it turned out that he had a "vision thing" all along, which was to create a cooperative framework for world peace under American leadership.

History deals every president a different hand, and those who presided during times of our greatest crises are justifiably most respected as military leaders. But the possibility exists that during the brief period 1989 to 1993, the United States under George H.W. Bush benefited from the most surehanded military leadership in its history.

6

THE CLINTON
INTERREGNUM

In January 1993, Bill Clinton succeeded George H.W. Bush as president. Clinton had been the governor of Arkansas, an office not normally considered a launching pad to the White House, but he had suddenly burst upon the public as a brilliant politician, some say the best in living memory, and he had picked his spot very well.

He first appeared on the national stage with a prime-time speech at the 1988 Democratic convention. He was tall and strikingly handsome in a boyish way, and was a terrific speaker, obviously well informed on a wide range of issues. He seemed like an impressive newcomer, and the only problem was that his speech went on a bit long. Before it was through half the nation had already turned to Odd Couple reruns while the other half had dozed off, half-expecting to see Clinton still on their TV sets in the morning. According to eyewitness reports, the speech eventually ended at some point before dawn. But it had been apparent that this young man had a lot on his mind.

Clinton saw his opportunity for the presidency just after the 1991 Gulf War, because by then hardly anyone else was willing to run against Bush. Most of the Democrats in the Senate had wrecked their foreign policy credentials by opposing the war, and the rest were intimidated by Bush's approval ratings. As governor of Arkansas, Clinton hadn't needed to take a stand on the issue, and when pressed on the matter had hedged his bets.

Recognizing how Dukakis in 1988 had been drawn and quartered by the Republicans as a "liberal," Clinton prepared for the race by forging his way to the political center, becoming head of the

Democratic Leadership Council, a group that contemplated pragmatic solutions to old Great Society problems. When he emerged in the 1992 race it was as a five-tool player: he was personally brilliant, could both speak and listen, he looked good, and he had a real knack for connecting with voters. His only weakness was that he apparently had a roving eye, and as early as the New Hampshire primary was dogged by sexual scandals. The press loved these things, and in prior years had zeroed in on alleged affairs to destroy other politicians, most notably Gary Hart in 1988, who had been caught with a girl on his lap on a cruise boat called the "Monkey Business." The press similarly got the goods on Clinton via reports and tape recordings of a lounge singer named Gennifer Flowers, who confessed to having had a long-standing affair with him. On the verge of ruin amidst the New Hampshire cold, his candidacy in jeopardy, Clinton pulled out his secret weapon: his wife, Hillary.

On the evening of the 1992 Superbowl, with half the country watching, Clinton and his wife sat down for an interview. The enduring impression is of the six-foot-two Clinton looking as apprehensive as a schoolboy in the principal's office, fidgeting slightly under interrogation while humbly professing all best intentions. Beside him on the couch was an upright, clear-eyed individual whose pinkish pulchritude gave nothing away to floozies, and whose pretty blond hair neatly set off in a headband actually started a fashion trend. Hillary kept her arm around Clinton with body language as protective as it was affectionate, and her implicit message to the nation was clear: Lay off our personal life; this Bubba is my problem, not yours.

Most of the viewers shrugged their agreement. The problem with Gary Hart had not been so much his tootsie but the devastating effect the revelation of the affair seemed to have on his wife. Here was a wife who obviously had control of the situation, standing by her man, so to speak, and the public politely backed off. This is aside from the factor that many male voters, having seen a parade of pictures of Flowers in the tabloids, had simply said, "Well, hey."

For his vice president Clinton chose Senator Al Gore of Tennessee, one of the few Democrats who had voted for the Gulf War. Gore, whose father had also been a senator, had graduated from Harvard, served in Vietnam, and possessed all the Washington establishment credentials that Clinton lacked. In addition, he was just as big, young and handsome as Clinton, and had an equally accomplished wife. And while questions about Clinton's character still bubbled in the press corps, Gore was as straight-arrow as they come. The two couples embarked on a bus tour, on which the youthful candidates could be seen tossing around a football during rest stops.

In contrast, Bush was still dragging along Dan Quayle, whom he had been more or less blackmailed into keeping by the vice president's chief of staff, William Kristol. After having compromised with the Democrats on taxes, the administration retained precious few connections to the Republican right wing, and without Quayle, Bush would have no firm base at all.

Since President Bush was all but invulnerable on foreign affairs, the Clinton campaign's internal guiding principle was "It's the economy, stupid." Nevertheless, in speeches and public policy statements Clinton took care to stake out responsible, centrist positions on foreign policy, America's role in the world, and matters having to do with the armed forces.

It thus came as a shock when Clinton assumed the presidency and revealed to the nation his true top priority: "Gays in the military."

This was only the first salvo of a decade-long barrage of events that would push America to the edge of the bizarro world. For Clinton's presidency, it was like the motel roof caved in on the first night of the honeymoon. The initiative was all the more startling because Clinton's political guru, James Carville, would never have allowed the candidate to prioritize "gays in the military" during the campaign; now that he was president, however, it was as if Clinton had thrown off his mask to say, "Ha! Ya'll knew I was a child of the sixties, right?" What would come next—teaching masturbation in grade school? (Whoops.) The second that Clinton took office it seemed as if all his genius had been purely political, while his governance blew caution to the winds. The Republican right, which had suspected as much, grabbed their battleaxes.

Not that there was anything wrong with gays in the military. Even though every branch of the armed services opposed gays serving openly in their ranks, the service chiefs were modern guys and knew that the issue was coming down the pike sooner or later. But for the new administration to slam it down their throats as its first military priority caused dismay. The idea of gay people clamoring to join the U.S. armed forces sounded odd enough to those who remembered Vietnam, when half the draft-age population, including Clinton himself, was scrambling to avoid military service. But now that George Bush had fairly eliminated the prospect of warfare from America's future, everyone felt entitled to sign up. It was a civil rights issue, after all.

The armed forces had in fact become a lucrative civil service, less dangerous than a number of other jobs, and not only gays but women were now trying to enlist in great numbers. All that remained was for the U.S. Army to become handicap accessible, with special ramps into helicopters or barracks, so that even physically disadvantaged people could join. Training manuals in braille were only a step away.

As it turned out, the battle between the Clinton administration and the service chiefs was resolved with a policy called "Don't ask, don't tell," which meant that if gay servicemen stayed in the closet they would be fine, and if straight servicemen didn't look into those closets it would be better. This may have been the inspiration for Donald Rumsfeld's later concept of "known knowns, known unknowns, and unknown unknowns." And in fairness, it was probably the same system long practiced by NFL football teams.

Meanwhile, the influx of women into the services was less easy to gloss over, and though many young women proved to be outstanding military professionals, there were also, over time, disturbing statistics. A full 25 percent of women air force cadets reported being raped, while on Navy ships the pregnancy rate among enlisted women was 30 percent while on duty. (Due to some stray strand of reason, women were still barred from submarines.) In today's Operation Iraqi Freedom, over 110 women have reported being raped or assaulted by their fellow soldiers. Experts believe that those who come forward represent about a quarter of the total. That the influx of women into the services coincided with a period of extensive army deployments to Muslim countries, where native women are off limits, may have accentuated the problem.

Social engineering aside, Clinton eventually deferred to the Joint Chiefs more than most presidents, and made sure to keep them fully funded. Vice President Gore, who was not as shy around uniforms as

Clinton, undertook a project to "Reinvent the Government," with a ground-up view of the various bureacuracies, cutting waste as necessary. But Gore, as the main hawk in the administration and the one who held the most responsible worldview, also refrained from weakening America's military establishment in any manner.

The important thing is that during the Clinton years the U.S. military had no reason to fight, or if there was a good reason just didn't. The world still boiled with bloody conflicts in faraway places, but fortunately none of these involved national security. Bush had already solved the essentials. So instead the choices became how to continue to project American leadership in conflicts that offered risk but precious little gain. Clinton was somewhat handicapped by his personal history, which involved dodging Vietnam, so as commander in chief he was extremely loath to order other U.S. citizens to die in causes overseas. His position was not without honor, and was at least unhypocritical. But unfortunately, under his watch, America relinquished the ring of preeminence it had briefly grasped, and settled instead into a self-absorbed era during which it lost international stature.

The military engaged in three major campaigns during the Clinton administration, all in accordance with allies and all for good causes. And though minor conflicts in the long scheme of things, each set important precedents, for better or worse, for the future.

SOMALIA

During the last months of the Bush administration, CNN had taken the lead in flooding the airwaves with heartbreaking scenes from Somalia, where countless civilians were dying of starvation. Under UN auspices, the United States and other countries rushed aid to the region, but by the fall of 1992 it was apparent that most of the food was being held up by a chaotic political situation. Bush had already lost the election but felt compelled to solve the problem rather than leave it to his successor. He even hoped to take care of it by the time of Clinton's inauguration, but was informed that due to logistics it would have to carry over into the spring of 1993.

The Bush team designed Somalia, or Operation Restore Hope, as a straightforward mission to relieve the terrible famine—or in practical terms, to place American power behind the relief effort in order to get all those tear-jerking scenes of dying little kids off U.S. TV screens.

America was singularly positioned to solve the humanitarian crisis. First, it was the richest country in the world, with by far the strongest military and the best air transport capacity, and it had such an abundance of food that domestic alarms were being sounded that the entire nation was becoming obese.

Second, the Gulf War had established the United States as not only the military but moral leader of the world. This was due largely to the fact that America had projected its enormous power to the Mideast and won a crushing victory, yet had withdrawn again just as quickly in concert with the voice of the United Nations and the will of its coalition partners. Prior to the Gulf War there had been much fear that America had secret imperial designs, and that after the liberation of Kuwait it would go on to further conquests while establishing a military stranglehold on the region. Instead, after leading the broadest world coalition in history to victory, the United States kept confidence with its allies, renouncing any new schemes cooked up among its own intelligentsia to violate the trust of the world community by seeking to expand its hegemony.

The Gulf War had not only pleased the American public, but the publics of every other nation whose troops had stood alongside the United States to achieve the victory. It was the New World's selflessness that struck a chord with older cultures. This could not have been said during the Cold War, when the U.S. supported every anti-Communist thug in sight. But now that America was the world's only superpower it could tangibly be perceived that the United States was genuinely different from the Soviets, colonial Europe or the martial empires of the deeper past. The Americans, for some reason, resisted exerting their own great power unless it was connected to justice, human rights, or to roll back unscrupulous foreign aggressions. In the 1950s, driven by church movements, many families had "adopted" Korean orphans. An entire generation had been persuaded into the Clean Plate Club with the refrain, "Children in India are starving." When the scenes of Somali innocents dying en masse appeared in the United States, it was more difficult for the Bush administration to ignore the problem than to act.

Condoleezza Rice has recently sneered at the notion that great power actions are only legitimate when not in their own self-interest. Metternich, Talleyrand and Molotov would certainly have agreed. But the greatest pride most Americans could feel was in their country being a positive force in the world. The United States has always been able to take care of its own self-defense. When projecting power, the point has been for America to have a positive influence, projecting its example as well as its strength. As far as strategic self-interest, America has never lagged behind other great powers in reinforcing its imperatives. One need only look to 1989, when the United States unilaterally resecured the integrity of the Panama Canal. This was the same conduit that in the 1940s had allowed the United States to fight Nazi Germany and Imperial Japan simultaneously. And it served as an optimal example that when America fought for its own self interest, it was also in the interest of other peoples who aspired to someday be governed by systems based on human rights, political freedom, and respect for individuals. Modern history has provided only one New World, unfettered by ancient hatreds and free to follow its own idealistic principles. And while America's uniqueness is generally felt at home, it is sensed even more acutely abroad that Americans should not relinquish their special opportunity.

In Somalia, the food crisis was resolved in early 1993, thanks to gigantic U.S. cargo planes delivering enough meals to feed the country for a year, and 30,000 troops who cooperated with various allies and the UN to ensure distribution to the countryside. By that time, although the Bush administration had been out of office for a few months, the mission had been accomplished. But then came the mission-creep.

Bush had envisioned the United States solving the immediate crisis and then handing over its infrastructure to the UN. But more complicated factors than the images of starving kids had entered the equation. It became apparent that the famine had been partly artificial, caused by warring factions who vied for the food supply in order to purposely starve their enemies. The influx of so much free food also disrupted the local economy, rendering farmers' produce worthless. In previous years Somalia, in a waltz with its hostile neighbor, Ethiopia, had switched sides more than once in the Cold War, with the effect that "Kalashnikovization" had fully taken root. The country was flooded with arms, and since the fall of the last legitimate government had splintered into militia fiefdoms run by warlords.

The Clinton administration assessed that providing lentils to Somalia did not solve its larger problems, and once the purely humanitarian mission had been accomplished it sought to impose greater social stability. A more caustic view of the turn of events was taken by Colin Powell, who after temporarily retiring from the government opined to historian Herbert S. Parmet: "The Clinton administration decided that, 'Gee, we've never had a nice little colonial country like this one before.' . . . Multilateral assertiveness, and all kinds of fuzzy liberal ideas, and it was a disaster. And then, when it blew up in their face, they ran."

As per the original schedule the humanitarian mission concluded in May and command was thence handed over to the UN. By that time the U.S. Marines had been withdrawn, and the hard-nut coaltiion force, originally consisting of U.S., Australian, French, Canadian, Italian and other troops, now consisted of about 30 national contingents, many of them feeble and even inferior in combat ability to the Somali warlords. The U.S. 10th Mountain Division, which was really a light infantry division, remained as a quick reaction force. The operation gradually shifted from famine relief to an attempt to impose social order. In June 1993, Pakistani troops were ambushed in Mogadishu, suffering 24 dead and dozens wounded. A number of the dead were gruesomely mutilated. The most powerful warlord in the area was Mohammed Farah Aidid and U.S. aircraft retaliated, blowing up some of his munitions depots and killing a number of his followers. Four journalists who arrived on the scene after this attack were murdered by an outraged mob.

At this point, American commanders in Somalia asked for armored vehicles to be sent from the States, but their request was denied by Secretary of Defense Les Aspin. Later that summer the administration agreed to send a large Special Forces contingent, Task Force Ranger, consisting of over 400 Army Rangers plus elite Delta counterterrorist troops. The SpecOps forces executed several daring missions against Aidid. They provided the hard edge to the entire UN effort. But then, in one operation, they overreached.

On October 3 the mission called for Delta and Rangers to swoop into the center of Mogadishu, fast-roping from helicopters, to capture a group of Aidid's top aides who were holding a meeting. A truck convoy of Rangers would meet them, bundle up the prisoners, and take everyone back to the U.S. base at the airport outside the city. The operation was scheduled for the middle of the afternoon.

Delta succeeded in surprising Aidid's men, and the vehicles arrived on schedule. But then a Black Hawk helicopter was hit by a rocket-propelled grenade and crashed to the street a couple blocks away. Hundreds of armed Somalis had converged on the scene and surrounded the force, which was now tasked with fighting its way through to the downed helicopter. A full-scale battle erupted in the streets, and then a mile away another Black Hawk went down. It was impossible to get a large force to rescue the crewmen of the second helicopter, and two Delta operators asked to be inserted in order to defend the three crewmen. They were able to hold off the horde for a short while before they were overrun and killed. The pilot of the Black Hawk was taken prisoner.

Back at the first crash site and the original point of attack, Rangers and Delta troopers had to hold out through the night, after a thin-skinned relief column failed to reach them, turning back to the airport with heavy casualties. During the dark hours, Night Stalker helicopters sought to sweep the surrounding rooftops clean of enemy fighters with their 1,600-round-a-minute chain guns. In the morning U.S. troops finally fought their way through and extricated the force.

As the only truly desperate fight U.S. troops engaged in during a stretch of 30 years, the "Black Hawk Down" battle (known as such from journalist Mark Bowden's book) gained much attention. The Americans had suffered 18 dead, as opposed to an estimated 500 Somalis. But for the first time in years, American forces had been seen to flee from a battlefield. And a devastating photo appeared on the world's front pages of a naked U.S. soldier being dragged through Mogadishu's streets by an exultant mob.

Clinton promptly reinforced U.S. strength in Somalia, but like Nixon's blows in Vietnam, the move was only meant to disguise a general retreat. Five months later, all U.S. forces had pulled out, leaving Somalia as an anarchic, failed state, which it still is today.

BOSNIA

The Communist nation of Yugoslavia, which had stayed quiet for decades, standing aside from the Cold War, suddenly became the biggest problem once the East-West stand-off disappeared. While the Bush administration had superbly cushioned the collapse of an entire superpower without armed conflict, the Soviet Union's mini-me, Yugoslavia, disintegrated into a maelstrom of armed clashes, border warfare and a new term, ethnic cleansing, which was meant to replace the more incendiary term, genocide. The Serbs, the largest group, were rampaging on all fronts.

When the troubles began, Secretary of State James Baker reflected the views of just about every American by saying, "We don't have a dog in that fight." It looked like a pure civil war along ethnic lines, and to the degree that tragedies unfolded it was only because of the Yugoslavians themselves. At the same time, Europe had begun to flex its muscles, progressing toward a common union and currency, so that it was anticipated that they could take care of their own backyard.

A complicating factor was Germany, which fresh after its reunification exercised its diplomatic muscle to recognize the independence of Slovenia and then Croatia, triggering the collapse of the Yugoslav federation. Both these peoples had been German allies against the Serbs in World War II, and their example encouraged the Muslim Bosnians (also former allies of the Third Reich) to declare independence.

In the spring of 1941 Germany had conquered all of Yugoslavia in three weeks; but 50 years later its military was still on probation, likely to have an incendiary effect wherever it stepped foot outside its borders. The Soviet Union had disappeared and pro-Serbian Russia had problems of its own. This left the British and French, operating under NATO auspices, as well as the United Nations, to take the lead in solving the problem.

During the 1992 campaign, Clinton had criticized Bush for not doing more in Bosnia, but now that he was president he was unable to devise a policy. Colin Powell was the only Bush holdover in Clinton's foreign policy councils, since his term as Chairman of the Joint Chiefs wasn't up until the following September, and at one point said he almost had an aneurysm when Clinton's UN ambassador, Madeleine Albright, demanded, "What's the point of having this superb military that you're always talking about if we can't use it?" Powell, who kept his Vietnam experience very much in mind, believed that a clear political policy goal should come first, and then the military would achieve it. Thrusting the military into the center of a foreign culture, fighting on all sides with no discernible end in sight, was not advisable.

Meanwhile, the war in the Balkans turned more vicious than anyone had expected. Under Communist rule, internecine fighting had disappeared, a great deal of intermarriage had taken place, and Yugoslavia had evolved into an attractive destination for tourists. But now, like a Chernyobyl spewing ancient hatreds, the entire population was at each other's throats. The Slovenians fought the Serbs while the Serbs and Croatians ganged up on the Muslims. Then the Croatians turned on the Serbs, while the latter cracked down on the Albanians. The Serbs were the largest group and held the geographic center, including Belgrade. Their strength stemmed in part from ad hoc militias formed in the provinces outside of Serbia proper, and partly from the formidable, well-equipped Yugoslavian national army, once it had been purged of other groups and had become, in effect, a Serbian army. During the fighting against the quickly formed Bosnian Muslim, Slovenian and Croatian forces, the Serb militias were not so subtly supported by the Yugoslav national army.

The result was that the world witnessed a level of brutality in Europe not seen since the Nazi era. Civilians were ruthlessly massacred and emaciated prisoners clutched the barbed wire of filthy death pens. No quarter was given in battle and in mass graves soldiers were as liable to be found with slit throats as bullet wounds. It began to amount to a disgrace to Western civilization; yet the West was unsure what to do. Rather than ship arms into the conflagration, it was decided to slap down an embargo in the hope that the Balkan fire would burn itself out. But this policy left the Serbs in a commanding position to act as ruthlessly as they wished.

No one had wanted the Muslims in Bosnia-Herzogovina to split off, thus forming the first independent Islamic state in Europe. But once they had done so the human tragedy began to take place mainly at their expense. Due to the arms embargo, their only support came from other Islamic nations or groups, yet this was still not enough to prevent the Serbs from committing ghastly massacres of their population. The centerpiece of the war became the Bosnian Muslim capital of Sarajevo, which was ringed by Serbian artillery firing into the streets, much as ten years earlier Israeli heavy artillery had surrounded and fired into Beirut.

In February 1994 dozens of women in the Sarajevo marketplace were wiped out by a Serbian artillery blast. There is reason to believe that if Bush the elder had still been president at this point, he'd have held a meeting in the Oval Office and concluded, "Enough is enough." But Clinton managed to outlast the outcry while not making a decision. The fact is that when he queried the Pentagon he found no enthusiasm for an intervention, while the Republican right was rallying against the idea, decrying "nation-building" as a useless waste of American strength. During the 1990s, U.S. politics turned topsy turvy as liberals argued for the use of military power while conservatives resisted. It cannot be said, however, that Bosnia was ever a huge concern to the American public, which was physically unthreatened, in the midst of a huge economic boom, and which had become thoroughly obsessed with the OJ Simpson trial.

The UN tried to halt the bloodletting by inserting peacekeepers. But placing blue-helmeted Fijians in among Serbian armored vehicles was like assigning bunnies to watch wildebeests. When NATO tried to influence the situation with air strikes, the Serbs responded by taking UN peacekeepers hostage, in one case chaining a group of them to a fence next to an ammunition dump. The UN was nevertheless able to organize some "safe areas" in eastern Bosnia where Muslim civilians could gather without fear of being massacred.

It became apparent that neither Europe nor the UN could solve the problem without the United States providing leadership. According to some estimates, 300,000 people had already died, and reports of depredations against civilians—including mass rape used as a weapon of humiliation, especially against Muslims—had become horrifying. Finally, in the summer of 1995, two events prompted America to act. First, the Croatians launched a two-pronged offensive against Serbian forces on their territory, winning quick, decisive victories. So the Serbs weren't as formidable as thought. Second, on the rebound from their defeats in Croatia, the Serbs refocused on Bosnia and their paramilitary forces seized the UN safe area around Srebrenica. There the Serbs finally went too far, slaughtering about 7,000 Bosnian Muslims in cold blood, while defying a Dutch peacekeeping force that had been meant to protect them. The Dutch thought both sides were thuggish, had no means of stopping the massacre, and were out of their element in the first place. It was the worst slaughter in Europe since World War II; and America could not stand back any longer.

The first step was to withdraw the UN peacekeeping troops. A British-French force with heavy weapons arrived in Bosnia to occupy strategic ground. Then, at the end of August 1995, from carriers in the Adriatic and bases in Italy, U.S. airpower was finally unleashed. American bombing and missiles, combined with British-French fire on the ground, forced an amazingly quick decision. A bitter war that had lasted for four years was suddenly over in two weeks. All sides subsequently attended a conference in Dayton, Ohio, and in November agreed on a division of territory to be enforced by NATO troops.

The campaign in Bosnia was waged without a single American casualty; however, one pilot, Scott O'Grady, was shot down and had to hide for a few days before he was rescued by helicopters. This was enough inspiration for Hollywood to produce "Behind Enemy Lines," a Gene Hackman film that took the O'Grady experience and embellished it slightly, portraying a downed U.S. flier stumbling upon mass graves and thence pursued by cold-eyed Serbian assassins. The film concluded with a spectacular battle scene, in which a phalanx of rocket-firing Marine helicopters faced off against a battalion of Serbian tanks and infantry. Following the traditional Hollywood convention, that when enemy troops spot enormous American firepower their first instinct is to run straight for it, the movie depicted the United States winning a great victory on the field.

KOSOVO

In 1991, Yugoslavia's southernmost region had declared independence, calling itself Macedonia. This move was opposed primarily by the Greeks, who heatedly pointed out that the territory did not correspond to ancient Macedonia, the land of Alexander the Great. The new state was only the site of some barbaric hill tribes that Alexander had once gone up to conquer. In any case, Macedonia kept its name, and the fuss was just more evidence that ancient claims in the region ran deep.

Nowhere was this more true than in Yugoslavia's next most southern province, Kosovo, which had been the site of the greatest battle in Serbian history, fought in 1389 against invading Turks. Notwithstanding that the Serbs lost that battle, and then another one 50 years later, Kosovo was considered a sacred part of their traditional territory. The complication was that the province was now 90 percent populated by Albanians.

In the late 1990s Serbian leader Slobodan Milosevic, rebuffed in all his other attempts to create a Greater Serbia, focused on Kosovo. He tried to eradicate Albanian culture and language and sent in military forces to consolidate Serb rule. With great quickness, Albanian insurgents formed a Kosovo Liberation Army (KLA) to combat the Serbs. The KLA's efforts only prompted a massive Serbian effort to uproot Albanian towns and villages to drive the people out of the country.

NATO had anticipated a conflict in Kosovo and this time the hand-wringing lasted only for a year. In 1999, when the new humanitarian crisis appeared to reach a height, NATO forces, led by American General Wesley Clark, prepared to act.

President Clinton, however, handicapped the effort from the beginning by announcing that the U.S. would not employ ground troops. This statement was designed to ensure domestic support, while neglecting the fact that presidents are supposed to make the case for military action to the public, not slip wars beneath the radar screen as if they are painless exercises. He tied Clark's hands from the beginning, and in Kosovo his announcement came as good news only to the Serbs.

General Clark had the difficult task of negotiating between the British-French desire to quickly insert ground troops, and his own government's orders to fight strictly from the air. In his memoir of the campaign, "Waging Modern War," he reflected on the European willingness to go charging in: "Was this the European way of war, then, to begin without assurance of decisive force, hoping to break the enemy's will, and then pick your way toward success at a cost of increased time and casualties?" Vietnam was still a factor in Clark's thinking, and he was not entirely sold on the European impulses. Upon receiving a target list for the upcoming air campaign, he observed: "This was the American way of war: strategic, heavy firepower."

The air assault kicked off on March 24, 1999, with the expectation that the Serbs would again cave in after a couple of weeks. Instead, the Serbs' reaction was to accelerate their ethnic cleansing of Kosovo. They closed with the Albanian population more ruthlessly than before, not just driving people out of the territory but murdering hundreds, burning villages, and renewing their tactic of mass rape. By now there were well over a million refugees. While American pilots were ordered to stay above 10,000 feet in order to avoid casualties, the depredations on the ground became worse than ever.

In addition, since the United States had ruled out using ground forces, the Serbian army had no need to deploy at fixed positions and could just scatter its armor and depots in the woods to avoid bombs. Part of the air campaign was devoted to strategic targets, in Belgrade and other places in Serbia proper, but these attacks had no effect on the troops at the front. U.S. airpower had gotten amazingly good at hitting inanimate objects, but was fairly useless against enemy soldiers who mixed with their opponents on the ground, in this case stalking through Albanian villages, herding some people away while killing others.

Clark managed the air campaign—negotiating with NATO allies who, having had experience on the receiving end of strategic bombing, were less enthusiastic about it than the Americans—while he continued to agitate for a ground option. He especially wanted squadrons of Apache helicopters, which could confront and blast apart Serbian armor directly. His requests were refused by both the Pentagon and the White House because, first, the Apaches were expensive, costing $15 million apiece; second, it was suspected they would need a support network, which would be equivalent to ground troops; and third, if one of them was shot down it would mean U.S. casualties.

In Belgrade the bombing knocked out electricity, bridges and government buildings and the United States began to run short of targets.

On May 7, U.S. bombers erred by bombing the Chinese Embassy, which caused a huge uproar and had the effect of curtailing the strategic end of the campaign. The pilots switched their focus to the woods of Kosovo where they attacked Serb tanks and armored vehicles, claiming great success.

After nearly two months the campaign was going on far longer than expected, and on the 18th Clinton announced that "all options were on the table." This meant a ground campaign, and Clark initiated such a high-profile flurry of planning at NATO headquarters that Serbian intelligence couldn't help but notice. At the same time, the Serbian population had grown tired of Milosovic pitting them alone against the rest of the world, and support for his program in Kosovo began to slip. In early June, Serbia sued for a cease-fire, to be enforced in Kosovo by NATO troops. Clark's verdict was that "Milosevic hadn't gone all out in the conflict with NATO; his most basic objective was to preserve his own power and authority."

There was a last-minute splash of drama when a Russian battalion suddenly swept into Kosovo's strategic Pristina airfield ahead of the NATO forces. Clark tried to persuade British commander Michael Rose, who led the only ground troops in the area, to pre-empt the Russians but Rose argued, "I'm not going to start World War III for you!" The Russians and Serbs had historically been allies, and the upshot of the affair was that just as NATO moved in to claim its victory, Russia decided to throw a pie in NATO's face.

The Kosovo campaign highlighted the decades-old argument about the efficacy of strategic airpower. There was not a soldier in the U.S. Army who didn't appreciate tactical air support, meaning aircraft supporting ground operations. But there was also not a soldier in the Army who didn't believe strategic airpower had always been overrated. From World War II to the Gulf War, air chiefs had claimed that their bomber forces could achieve victory by themselves, but they had never been able to do so. Once ground troops moved in they had always found that the airmens' claims were exaggerated. Even in World War II, the heyday of strategic airpower when entire cities were targeted, the churned-up rubble of Frankfurt had had little to do with the battles First Army had been forced to wage in Normandy, the Bulge, or on the Westwall. German armaments output actually increased in tandem with the strategic bombing campaign, while the massacres of urban civilians from the air contributed significantly to the anything-goes moral environment that enabled the Holocaust.

Once indiscriminate carpet bombing had been ruled out after World War II, due to the advent of nuclear weapons during the Cold War and the realization that everyone was at risk under such a concept, airpower was harnessed back into tactical strikes on justifiable targets. And even there the claims of the pilots—the only eyewitnesses to their deliveries of explosives—had proven to be exaggerated. The reason was simple. While it cost many millions of dollars to build, arm and train pilots for each modern jet aircraft, enemy soldiers could negate their effectiveness for free—by hiding. When NATO ground troops finally moved into Kosovo they found only three destroyed Serbian armored vehicles, while pilots had claimed 223. The Serbs had constructed decoys to attract their stand-off antagonists, while they had hidden their real vehicles in woods or at close-quarters in Albanian towns, often with engines turned off so as not to reveal heat signatures. Troops on the ground had far more incentive to escape bombs than pilots at 10,000 feet had in delivering them. And if opposing pilots claimed great success in devastating a target, this was all to the advantage of those on the ground, who could thence expect the next day's air strikes to aim elsewhere.

In theory, complete control of the air meant victory; in practice, a determined people would never allow itself to be conquered by invisible specks in the sky, without once seeing its opponents face to face.

Nevertheless, Kosovo turned out to be the first clear-cut victory for the airpower enthusiasts, who ever since Billy Mitchell in the 1930s had been claiming that bombing alone could bring America's enemies to their knees. And though the U.S. Army had not been eager to fight in the Balkans, it was a slight embarrassment that the Serbs had been defeated by airpower alone. Military historians wondered if they had seen a new turn in the history of warfare. Perhaps ground troops had become obsolete. Wesley Clark, it should be noted, thought that it was the highly visible NATO preparations for a ground offensive that persuaded the Serbs to cut their losses in advance. The Serbs, aside from Milosevic and his circle, hadn't been all that rabid about fighting for Kosovo in the first place, and aside from the inconvenience of having their infrastructure bombed, didn't appreciate being pitted by themselves against the rest of the Western world. Whether airpower had proven to be the ultimate solution in warfare or whether the Serbs simply didn't have a great enough reason to fight can still be debated.

In any case, the United States had passed through its second straight war without suffering a single casualty.

Other foreign policy problems during the Clinton administration resembled annoyances more than crises, and not infrequently ended up as embarrassments.

In 1990, two centuries after launching history's only successful slave revolt, the people of Haiti held their first democratic election, electing Jean-Bertrand Aristide, a somewhat erratic former priest. Aristide was soon overthrown in a military coup, however, and a flow of boat people headed for the United States to flee the brutal new regime. During the 1992 campaign, Clinton criticized Bush's policy on Haiti, especially the part that refused to accept Haitian refugees; but in the now-familiar pattern he was unable to arrive at a better policy. In October 1993, just a week after the Rangers' battle in Somalia, a U.S. ship packed with soldiers was turned away from Port au Prince by a stone-throwing mob. It turned out that the Haitians, too, had seen photos of the U.S. failure in Mogadishu, and the new sight that was presented to the world—of a U.S. Navy ship retreating before a rowdy mob—was even more humiliating.

By the following year the situation in Haiti had deteriorated and the refugee flow had increased to the point where Clinton ordered an invasion along the lines of Bush's 1989 operation in Panama. Former president Jimmy Carter asked to be given a chance to negotiate first, and along with Senator Sam Nunn and Colin Powell, was able to persuade the military junta to step down at the very last second. Planes carrying paratroopers of the 82nd Airborne Division were already in the air when the agreement was reached. American troops subsequently entered the country peacefully and Special Forces troops together with the 10th Mountain Division undertook civic reconstruction efforts.

The decade's worst disaster occurred during the spring and summer of 1994 in the central African nation of Rwanda. The Hutu tribe had launched a campaign of genocide against the minority Tutsi tribe, creating a scale of carnage that made the Balkans look like a hillbilly feud. There were so many bodies, mainly killed at close-quarters with machetes, that churches turned into morgues and the rivers became clogged.

Americans witnessed the slaughter like so many neighbors of Kitty Genovese, unable to call the police because they were the police. And for once, in the wake of the debacle in Somalia, Clinton enjoyed total bipartisan agreement on his policy: No intervention in Rwanda. Among those who recommended staying out of the fray was future president George W. Bush, though he must have considered the Hutus evil. Relief finally arrived in the form of a Tutsi counteroffensive that defeated the Hutu death squads and stopped the massacre.

While President Clinton was able to project American military power without loss, the uncomfortable flip side was that throughout the 1990s Islamic forces projected their own power against America, inflicting dozens of fatalities. Each attack came as a surprise, and after each one it was difficult to mount a decisive response.

In 1993 a huge car bomb exploded in the parking garage of the World Trade Center in New York, causing six deaths and hundreds of injuries, mostly to people's lungs due to the smoke. In the year of the Oslo Accords, which established peace between Israel and Palestine, the attack was considered a one-off by fanatics, and in fact, the FBI was able to hunt down the perpetrators. It had been an Islamic group based in New Jersey and its leader was tracked down in Pakistan. And, as the U.S. public noted with satisfaction, the World Trade Center had easily withstood the Islamics' best attempt.

In late 1995 terrorists blew up five U.S. soldiers in Riyadh, Saudi Arabia, and in 1996 a larger bomb destroyed an American military barracks at the Khobar Towers in Dhahran, killing 19. After investigation the United States determined that the latter attack had been launched by a Shiite group with ties to Iran.

In August 1998 the American embassies in the capitals of Kenya and Tanzania were simultaneously destroyed by gigantic explosions, killing over 200 people and wounding several thousand. This time it was determined to be the work of the Saudi terrorist leader Osama bin

Laden, who had been based in Sudan until 1996 and had since moved to Afghanistan. Clinton responded with a barrage of cruise missiles, destroying a factory in Khartoum, Sudan, that was thought to be producing chemical weapons, and a training complex in Afghanistan run by bin Laden's Al Qaeda organization. The Sudanese claimed that their factory had only produced pharmaceuticals, while the 70 tons of explosives unleashed on Afghanistan missed the terrorist leader.

By now Clinton was beleaguered, almost bending under an incredibly fierce chorus of condemnation from the Republicans. In fact, the entire nation seemed to have turned on him and it was unclear if he could even hang on to his presidency. The issue had nothing to do with foreign policy of course. Evidence had come to light that he had fooled around with a White House intern.

MONICA

In some ways, the Clinton administration was one of the most successful in American history. In regard to foreign policy, between his two Secretaries of State, two National Security Advisers, and three Defense Secretaries, he had endeavored to steer a responsible course while not sending American soldiers to their deaths. Though America's global military leadership slipped on his watch, Clinton was never faced with the urgent challenges faced by either his predecessor Bush or his successor. Clinton had meanwhile pursued the elder Bush's concept of enhancing American strength through global alliances, and achieving stability abroad through spreading international contact with America's free-market economy and its political example. He may have been congenitally unqualified as a true military leader, but then again there had been no roaring dragons to slay while he held office.

The public had elected Clinton, and then re-elected him resoundingly, to focus on domestic policy, and this he did very well. During the 1990s, the United States enjoyed the longest unbroken period of prosperity in its history. The Los Angeles race riots, which had so disturbed Bush's last year, became a distant memory under Clinton. Urban crime rates fell to 1950s' levels, the scourge of drugs came under control, and Clinton's 1996 reforms cut the welfare rolls almost in half. His only serious domestic policy failure came with Hillary's tactical missteps, or perhaps naïvety, in trying to achieve universal health care, but there had been nothing dishonorable in the attempt. Meanwhile, the gigantic Federal deficit that Reagan had blithely ignored and which had burdened Bush, disappeared during the Clinton presidency. The government was running a budget surplus, inflation and interest rates were low, and without any particular tax favoritism for the upper end, business was booming.

Before mounting Clinton on Mt. Rushmore, however, it should be noted that during his presidency the United States saw an economic perfect storm, when peace and prosperity met a tidal wave of technological innovation driven by the computer industry. Advances in computers not only tasked consumers with upgrading their systems every six months but compelled older businesses to transform while it spurred the creation of new ones. The entertainment industry found a newly fertile field in the video game, while digital electronics compelled the reinvention of everything from jet aircraft to refrigerators. A revitalized telecommunications industry burst upon the scene, as did the internet, each creating a wealth of new opportunities for entrepreneurs.

In addition, during the 1990s the auto industry reinvented itself, though this development can best be attributed to George Bush's triumph in the Gulf War. After the Arab boycott of the 1970s the auto industry had shifted toward smaller, fuel-efficient cars, relying heavily on styles from Japan and Europe. The shift also promised positive effects for the environment. But after the United States had formed its own coalition that included Saudi Arabia and a dozen other Islamic nations, and had crushed the only serious Arab power in the Mideast, the auto industry threw off its restraints. Fuel efficiency went out the window, and even small suburban families began driving huge SUVs through a government loophole that officially considered them trucks. The present-day governor of California, Arnold Schwarzenegger, jumpstarted a new trend by purchasing an Army Humvee after the Gulf War, so that the hottest selling vehicle in the United States became a massive, box-like object indistinguishable from a Brinks Armored Car. By Clinton's second term, SUVs accounted for half of all vehicle sales, contributing further to the robust economy.

After Clinton easily won reelection over Senator Bob Dole in 1996, the Republican right realized it had a problem. They criticized him for deploying military forces in too many places and for nation-building, but Clinton managed to avoid any U.S. casualties. They couldn't get him on the economy because their own portfolios were expanding due to a Dow that some predicted would soon reach 15,000. There were few openings on social policy because America's cities were in the process of regeneration, "white flight" having been thrown in reverse and replaced by a less serious problem, "gentrification."

The GOP's solution was to maintain an offensive against Clinton's personal character, in the hope that they could eventually make a breakthrough. For this reason they dogged him about a money-losing real estate transaction, dubbed Whitewater, that he had engaged in a decade earlier, and put their support behind a woman, Paula Jones, who said Clinton had come on to her while he was governor of Arkansas. Jones had evidently rejected Clinton's advances but had dedicated her life to suing him ever since. Thanks to the leadership of Representative Newt Gingrich, Republicans in Congress were able to arrange a special prosecutor named Kenneth Starr, who with unlimited government funds was able to spend year after year searching for the slightest chink in Clinton's defenses.

And then, in January 1998, the dam broke loose. A woman named Linda Tripp had secretly tape-recorded the conversations of one of her friends, a 24-year-old White House intern named Monica Lewinsky, who said she had gotten romantic, in a way, with Clinton in the White House. When Tripp's information met Starr's ears, the heavens fell in.

Nixon's rueful statement, "I gave them a sword," was now degraded by Clinton to, "I gave them fellatio." Every newscast, tabloid, and water cooler in the country headlined the development. People from Beijing to Botswana murmured about the allegations. More people probably missed the moon landing than the reports that Clinton had finally been caught red-handed.

It was probably the most ludicrous thing that had ever happened in American presidential politics. JFK would have guffawed while Nixon could only have shaken his head. Clinton, of course, denied any involvement with "that woman, Ms. Lewinsky," and he was believed by several people, including his wife. But then DNA scientists, funded by Starr's organization, got to work and gradually ascertained that the president had indeed spilled some seed.

In the midst of the scandal, Hillary-in-denial had blurted out on the Today Show that she thought her husband was the victim of "a vast, right-wing conspiracy." She was more or less correct, but only to the same degree that Clarence Thomas had previously fallen victim to a prurient feeding frenzy from the left. And Thomas hadn't even gotten a date. After Thomas had been persecuted on the national stage for his lame attempts to go out with Anita Hill, who could blame the right wing for climbing all over Clinton, who had turned out to be much more of a smoothie?

All of this would still not seem so serious except that the public had nothing better to think about at the time, and it was truly interesting to see a President squirm. The nadir of the scandal came when Clinton, obviously more fearful of his wife than anyone else, mumbled before a grand jury, "It depends on what the meaning of the word 'is' is." The tumult finally collapsed when Republican prosecutor Starr released a written transcript of hours of grand jury testimony that revealed all the most intimate details of the affair. No one had asked him to do so, and the public basically said "Yuck." Clinton had striven mightily to preserve a semblance of public respect for his office and family, while Starr, like some modern-day Cotton Mather intent on a public dunking, had insisted on violating it. The revelation of every detail had not been bargained for by the soap opera-loving public, which among themselves had a 50 percent divorce rate, and who were barraged by an ever-increasing glorification of promiscuity on TV. Seeing Clinton in a fix was one thing; humiliating him through private confessions was another. In December 1988 Clinton was impeached by the Congress. Two months later he was cleared of all the petty charges by the Senate.

The remaining curiosity was whether he would still be able to govern. In 1998, Hollywood, formerly a Clinton bastion, took advantage of his troubles by releasing "Wag the Dog," a movie that depicted a scandalized president who solved his problems by inventing an overseas war in order to rally the public around him. The movie did not become a huge box-office hit, but resonated enough with the intelligentsia that henceforth every military move Clinton made roused suspicion that he was trying to divert public attention from his personal problems. His attacks in Sudan and Afghanistan in response to the African embassy bombings were derided by Republicans as attempts to divert attention from the Lewinsky scandal. The hooting from the Right increased when, on the eve of his impeachment, he launched a three-day bombing campaign against Iraq after Saddam Hussein had obstructed UN weapons inspectors.

It's interesting that the concept of "Wag the Dog" could not have been thought of until the end of the first Bush administration, when the Cold War had ended and America had proven its overwhelming battlefield strength. But once the United States had become the only remaining superpower, able to pick its spots abroad without any particular sense of national urgency, it was seen to contain a hint of possibility. In fact it still does, to the degree that foreign wars are the very best elixirs for troubled presidencies, especially if they are claimed to be waged in self defense.

As for "l'affaire Lewinsky," though Americans had eagerly rubber-necked the debacle with reactions ranging from glee to grief and everything in between, a general sense of national embarrassment set in Incredibly, the Republicans kept their special prosecutor's office going, though by now the public viewed it as a kind of malevolent Energizer Bunny obsessed with gnawing at Clinton's ankles. And there were still some serious foreign policy issues to be dealt with.

As the sands ran out, Clinton undertook a full-fledged effort to negotiate peace between the Israelis and Palestinians, in an attempt to solve the conflict that was the very wellspring of Islamic hostility toward the West. Between Palestinian leader Yasir Arafat and Israeli prime minister Ehud Barak, he hammered out a deal that would have released approximately 95 percent of the West Bank back to the Palestinians. But the devil is in the details, and Arafat, who had never seen such Israeli flexibility before, and was suddenly faced with a sign-it-or-not dilemma, backed off. It is possible, after all, to give 95 percent of New York State back to the Indians, as long as New York City, Albany, Buffalo, Syracuse, and a few other select points, together with their road networks, water supply and other resources remain under outside authority. It was also obvious that Clinton would not be able to enforce an agreement, and neither would Barak. Just after Arafat shuffled home after the intense talks, former Israeli general Ariel Sharon decided to visit the Dome of the Rock in Jerusalem, the place where Muhammed had ascended to heaven. He and his huge security detail bulling their way to the most precious Arab shrine in Jerusalem set off Intifada II, a general uprising against Israeli occupation of the West Bank and Gaza.

Clinton's attempt to stamp his presidency with a truly valuable foreign policy success had come too late. Everyone involved was a lame duck, including Arafat, whose headquarters would soon be surrounded by Israeli tanks.

If those old chums, JFK and Nixon, were still able to hold debates in heaven or elsewhere, their observations on the Clinton presidency would be worth noting. Kennedy would lambast Clinton for having micro-managed the government, instead of conveying a broader sense of American potential and purpose. The poor kid from Arkansas was too happy to be there, not realizing that America's future depended not on ju jitsu against domestic political opponents but on how to set in stone a peaceful Pax Americana.

Nixon would be more sympathetic, noting how a young man could easily get sucked up into the end of the Cold War, a technological revolution, and an apparently endless road to economic growth that every other president would have envied. However, Nixon would also point out that in his second term Clinton should have gotten a better handle on the world. The Israeli-Palestinian issue had urgently needed to be closed off, as did Kashmir. Yugoslavia should have been settled far more quickly, and the U.S. had the power and influence to do it. Clinton had the opportunity to become the best of presidents, but for lack of an imperative vision had finally stumbled into the mud of his own impulses. The kid with the tuba just hadn't realized how powerful he had become.

In October 2000, Arab suicide bombers on a speedboat blew apart the hull of the USS *Cole*, a destroyer that had stopped off in Yemen harbor, killing 17 sailors and wounding 39. By this time Clinton was fairly crawling away from the presidency, as the 2000 presidential race heated up between his vice president, Albert Gore, and President Bush's son, George W. Bush. Clinton's currency was no longer good, and it was left to him and his national security team to pass on to the new president the fact that Islamic fundamentalists had become a very significant danger to Americans abroad. It was thought that they could eventually comprise a threat to the American homeland itself.

7

BUSH 43

The 2000 presidential race between George W. Bush and Al Gore was such a near-run thing that it raised philosophical questions. One school of thought has always held that history is a wide river driven by economic or demographic factors, an inexorable flow that sweeps individuals out of the way. Another school, sometimes termed "the great man theory," holds that history is more of a pinball, lurching between the impact of exceptional individuals who are able to sway the fate of nations to their will. A subtext of this school is the "little man theory," which claims that great men often take credit for happenstance created by ordinary people. The best example that comes to mind is the Battle of Midway, where if the Japanese scout plane dispatched in the direction of the American fleet had reported back as planned, the American carrier force would have been obliterated instead of the Japanese one. But then, as the "great man" partisans would claim, Roosevelt and Churchill would simply have moved to a plan B. Or as the "mighty flow" crowd would claim, regardless how many battles America lost, it was inconceivable that it could not have defeated Japan in the long run.

This is not to reinforce anyone's aversion to philosophy, but only to state that the 2000 presidential race, which could have gone either way by the slightest hair, has had enormous consequences due to the fact that one individual became president rather than another. And this in an era when American presidents are more important than ever. But then again, what if our parents had never met?

In the year 2000 the political issues on the table just called for flipping a coin. This was a novel situation for those who remembered the stark battlelines between Nixon and McGovern, Carter and Reagan, or even Bush and Dukakis. Clinton's political genius had been devoted to closing the ideological gap between Democrats and Republicans (in other words, stealing the other side's issues) so that in an era when the most serious event was the OJ trial, it was the Clinton-Gore team that took credit for reducing crime, solving the budget deficit, cutting the welfare roles, and maintaining the peace.

For his part, Bush claimed to be a compassionate conservative, a "uniter, not a divider," interested foremost in education, bipartisan amity, and improving America's relationship with Mexico. If the Democrats could swipe traditional Republican issues, turnaround was fair play.

During the Cold War, the bulk of the public had remained sensibly centrist, firebrands like Goldwater or McGovern shot down in flames as soon as they appeared. But now the center had become a moving object, graspable by both sides. In 2000 both Gore and Bush had their respective party strongholds, but in the center it all came down to personalities—who seemed more likeable.

The election ended up so excruciatingly close that any number of things could have tipped the final outcome. The easiest to quantify was the third-party candidacy of Ralph Nader, who received 2.7 percent of the vote, most of it from the Democratic side. Without Nader, Gore would have won New Hampshire and Florida, either one of which would have given him the electoral college as well as the popular vote. Consider that in Florida Nader pulled over 97,000 votes, and then after all the recounts Gore lost it by 537.

But due to that same closeness any number of other factors might have swayed the election. Gore, who started out crippled in the Bible belt because of Clinton's sexual miscreance, failed to carry his own state of Tennessee. Bush was ambushed by an impudent young journalist who asked him to name the leaders of several foreign countries. In an embarrassing exchange he got only one right by venturing "Lee" for Taiwan, though everyone figured it was just a lucky guess.

At one point during the campaign, columnist Maureen Dowd caught wind of the fact that Bush brought his own pillow along on campaign trips. This was like handing a match to a pyromaniac, and thenceforth the New York Times Op-Ed contained twice-a-week depictions of Bush curled up in a fetal position, clutching his pillow and sobbing for his Father, or sometimes for Dick Cheney. Dowd also tried to resurrect the "wimp factor," pinning it on Bush the younger, though this seemed like a dangerous taunt to those who sensed that Bush was determined to distance himself from his father. Gore had meanwhile overdistanced himself from Clinton, denying himself a willing ally who could have swung key constituencies to his side.

For most Americans, however, the campaign is best remembered for, and was finally decided by, its nationally televised debates.

Gore went into these as such a heavy favorite that many people were prepared to wince, close their eyes, or flip to Channel 9 if the carnage got too ugly. Bush had no foreign policy experience, limited achievements, and it was not even clear if he could correctly pronounce two consecutive words over three syllables long. Gore, on the other hand, had graduated from Harvard as a deep thinker, had written a bestselling book on ecology, had been a foreign policy specialist in the Senate, and had been an activist vice president for eight years on a wide range of issues. Yet it was foremost through the debates that Bush won the presidency.

American political lore has it that if Nixon had only shaved before his first debate with Kennedy, he would have won the election. The new lore is that if Gore had only been more modest in his first debate with Bush he too would have won. (This brings us back to the original philosophical question, because if Nixon had won in 1960, the Vietnam issue would surely have been handled more decisively, but then without Vietnam, where would America have acquired its current foreign policy wisdom?) Gore was brilliant enough in the first debate but also insufferable, thoroughly slaughtered by Bush's natural, if well-deserved, modesty.

In the second debate, George Bush won more converts by stating his intention for a "humble" foreign policy. How likeable was he? And in that debate, Gore, chastened by criticism of his previous huffing and puffing, hardly showed personality at all. At one point, in an obviously scripted maneuver, he strode up to Bush while he was making a point, as if to accentuate his greater height. Bush just threw him a glance that said, "Later, pard." Gore finally featured an acceptable aspect of his personality in the third debate, but overall he had missed the opportunity to deliver a knock-out punch.

Once the national tallies were in, Gore won the popular vote by over half a million votes and was ahead in the electoral college. But in Florida the election had resulted in an effective tie, with thousands of mishandled ballots, and recounts were in process. Both parties sent in their proxy champions to duke it out. These were Clinton's first Secretary of State, Warren Christopher, and for the Republicans, Bush the first's foreign policy vizier, James Baker III. One can be forgiven for thinking the issue was over right there. As it turned out, a resolution in Florida, where Bush's brother happened to be governor, was beyond reach. The issue was thrown to the Supreme Court, where seven of the nine justices had been appointed by Bush's father, Reagan, Ford, and Nixon. The Court decided in favor of Bush the younger by a vote of five to four.

Al Gore, to his everlasting credit, accepted the results so as not to cause a Constitutional crisis. Ever since, he has stalked the land like a sort of phantom president, occasionally giving more brilliant extemporaneous speeches than Bush would be capable of, while at the same time waxing introspective about his own personal failings. Just one "Thank you, ma'am," or an "Aw shucks" would have gotten him in. But his biggest problem was really that he ran for president when the public had nothing serious on their minds.

To the surprise of many, Bush took his less-than-a-mandate and ran with it. So much for humbleness. After eight years of stewing under Clinton, the Republican party had a pent-up brew of policies that it wasn't going to hold back any longer. And meantime the public got a chance to examine their new president, the first in living memory to take office without so much as a plurality.

Most presidents are extremely high achievers with a combination of brains, drive and charisma that not only make them successful in normal life but draws a crowd of exceptional followers when they enter the presidential arena. Bill Clinton was probably the first person from Arkansas most Americans had heard of until his "war room" engineered a brilliant campaign to gain the presidency. Jimmy Carter performed a bigger miracle with his "Georgia mafia" in 1976. Ronald

Reagan was the idolized leader of an entire movement, expanding the Goldwater one of 1964, which stretched from grassroots to boardrooms. The first President Bush did not have insurgent characteristics but he commanded enough loyalty from moderate Republicans that he was able to give Reagan a creditable challenge in 1980. As vice president, he made clear that his role was to provide loyalty and support to the Gipper; however, throughout the 1980s, much to the chagrin of the Republican right, it was evident that "Bush people" fairly permeated the government. Bush the elder had a subtle sort of charisma, based on selflessness, an insatiable intellect, and steady convictions down the center of U.S. interests. And though he has still never said an untoward word about Reagan, suffice to say that once he became president, he changed over the entire Republican cabinet.

George W. Bush did not seem like such a dynamic achiever for most of his life. A legacy admittance to Yale, he didn't excel in studies, showed no passion for 1960s' political issues, and made his mark mainly through the presidency of a jock fraternity and membership in Skull and Bones. He served in the Texas Air National Guard during Vietnam and learned to fly F-102 fighter jets. This was a more ambitious than usual role in the Guard (and he was joined there by Lloyd Bentsen's son, when both their fathers were vying for the Senate); but once Vietnam waned there appeared wide gaps in his attendance records. His last year was waived so that he could earn an MBA at Harvard.

In business in Texas Bush had the great advantage of being the son of the vice president of the United States, and though not greatly successful he was able to leverage several deals. The highpoint of his business career came when he was named managing partner for a group of investors in the Texas Rangers baseball team. It was not only a fun job but a fruitful one; when the Rangers were sold for a huge profit it earned Bush a solid nest egg for his family. He had failed in one race for Congress, but in 1994 ran for governor and won against the caustically colorful incumbent, Ann Richards. Bush's backslapping good nature went over well in Austin during the prosperous 1990s, and he was re-elected in 1998.

In personal terms, Bush had emerged from college fond of beer, and a number of his business deals had subsequently been consummated over suds. But at age 40, reportedly pressed by his wife Laura, Bush completely gave up drinking. Instead he turned to exercise, drew upon a latent lode of self-discipline, and devoted himself far more to his religious faith than he had done in the past. The result was that while George and Barbara Bush had considered their younger son Jeb the best political prospect in the family, their eldest shaped up considerably and surprised them. On the surface, being governor of the country's third largest state was qualification enough for the White House; and Bush had the enormous advantage of being his father's son, with all the name recognition and access to the Republican establishment that pedigree entailed.

During the 2000 Republican primaries, Bush had been challenged by the formidable son of another prominent family, John McCain. Bush stumbled badly in the early going, losing New Hampshire, and his supporters set up a firewall in South Carolina where they prepared to chop McCain off at the knees. Most notorious among the dirt thrown on McCain was the allegation that he had fathered a black child out of wedlock. The Christian Conservatives found a natural affinity with Bush, while McCain made the mistake of criticizing their worldview. Bush beat McCain so handily in South Carolina that the momentum carried him all the way to the nomination. It wasn't until later that the source of the rumor about McCain's out of wedlock child was widely realized—his family had adopted an orphan from Bangladesh.

Like Gore, Gary Hart, Joe Biden, and now Howard Dean, McCain has become one of those people who were tripped up or stumbled in their run for the presidency, but whose candor, insights and energy continue to be of great value to the republic. In McCain's case he performs a particular service—because of lingering animosity or not—by being the only member of the Republican Party who is willing to stand up to the president.

A mystifing aspect of the Bush-Gore debates was how Bush had persisted in citing "leadership" as his best quality. At the time he did not appear to be especially articulate, informed, or experienced; yet he continued to drive home "leadership" as if it was a characteristic divorced from knowledge or other skills. Once he became president, if not immediately validating the concept, Bush at least demonstrated what he had meant. He was the first MBA president, schooled in management, and he saw his own task as making decisions based on information provided by others. He considered his own skills to be decisiveness, moral clarity, and self-confidence—interrelated characteristics all buttressed by his religious faith.

While his father had named the lightweight Dan Quayle as his vice president, the younger Bush named Dick Cheney, a true heavyweight who had been Ford's chief of staff, a Republican whip in Congress, the first Bush's defense secretary, and more recently the chairman of Halliburton, an oil industry services conglomerate that also provided infrastructure to the military. Cheney left Halliburton with a $16 million compensation package when he became vice president. He was thus not only more experienced than Bush, he was a lot richer. On assuming office, Cheney assembled the largest vice presidential staff in history, and many assumed that he would be the de facto president.

After Cheney, and in keeping with a tacit promise to the public, Colin Powell became Bush's Secretary of State. In fact, Powell's imminent ascension to the top of Foggy Bottom was one of the factors that allowed Bush to squeeze past Gore in the election. Though the Clinton crowd had not taken to Powell, his popularity became greater than ever during the 1990s due to his bestselling book, "My American Journey." To moderate Republicans, and even some Democrats, the imminent return of Powell to the highest White House councils was considered good news.

Donald Rumsfeld was appointed Secretary of Defense, forming a neat bit of symmetry with Cheney. During the Ford administration, Rumsfeld had been chief of staff, but had plucked the then-unknown Cheney to take his place so that he could become the youngest-ever Secretary of Defense. Thirty-five years later, now that Cheney was vice president, he returned Rumsfeld to the Pentagon, so that at age 68 he also became the oldest ever.

The first Bush administration had kept its center of gravity at State, and the presence of Powell—whose starpower in some ways overshadowed the president's—seemed to indicate that the same would be true of Bush II. At the least, Powell, with his dynamic bull-of-a-man second at State, Richard Armitage, might have achieved a fair draw with the Cheney-Rumsfeld axis, including the prominent neoconservatives such as I. Lewis Libby, Paul Wolfowitz, and Douglas Feith who served as deputies to the vice president and secretary of defense. But then we come to one of the true exotics in American history, Bush's National Security Adviser, Condoleezza Rice.

Condi, as she is known, grew up in Birmingham, Alabama, where she was friends with one of the four girls killed in the church bombing that jumpstarted the Civil Rights movement. Her parents, who were of modest means, steered her toward academic excellence and also arranged for lessons so that she became a brilliant concert pianist. When the family relocated to Denver she also became an expert figure skater and developed a fascination with Russian/Soviet history. Upon entering the work world, Condi became the youngest provost in the history of Stanford University (also the first black and first female), and found time to serve on the board of Chevron, which named an oil tanker after her. She was not only professionally accomplished but athletic, attractive, with a beautiful voice, and considerable personal charm.

So in sum, she was just the average classical piano–playing, figure-skating, Russian-speaking black girl from the deep South with a Ph.D. in international affairs. At a conference on strategic arms policy she caught the attention of Brent Scowcroft, who brought her into the White House during the first Bush administration as his expert on Soviet policy. As the 2000 campaign got underway she bonded with George W. Bush, with whom she shared a devotion to religion, exercise, and pro football. And since he also needed a foreign policy tutor, she became his companion during the campaign and his National Security Adviser after the election, the first woman to hold that post.

As Secretary of State in the Bush administration, Colin Powell may hold claim to being the most powerful person of African descent in history. But Condi may already hold a greater distinction: the most powerful female of all time. The global influence of Queen Victoria, Catherine of Russia, and even Mrs. Thatcher, would in absolute terms pale before the influence Condi possesses with her voice near Bush's ear. Bush's administration consisted of a formidable array of high achievers. But in foreign policy he also needed a filter, someone who would negotiate the arguments, focus the options, and most importantly, always stand by him as an ally. Thus Condi, to the disappointment of Powell, and to the annoyance of Cheney and Rumsfeld, emerged as a third center of power in the administration via her singular loyalty to Bush.

Every American president has one person on whom he most relies. Kennedy's closest confidant was his brother Robert, who in a profound vindication of nepotism was named Attorney General, thence was invited into foreign policy and stood at the president's elbow throughout the Cuban Missile Crisis. Afterward, Robert McNamara at Defense eclipsed Dean Rusk at State as America marched blindly into the quicksand of Vietnam. Nixon, who was suspicious of Washington bureaucracy, formulated his most dynamic foreign policy initiatives from within the White House, relying foremost on his National Security Adviser, Henry Kissinger, a brilliant theorist and diplomat who would go on to be Ford's Secretary of State.

Carter continued the new tradition of powerful NSAs with Zbigniew Brzezinski, partly because he had scant support from the traditional Democratic establishment, at the time represented by the last hope of the Kennedy dynasty, Ted. In fact, Carter's only establishment "star" in his administration, Cyrus Vance, betrayed him by resigning after the failed 1980 attempt to rescue American hostages in Iran. Vance didn't object to the failure but the attempt, and in retrospect one suspects that Carter was never as attached to anyone in his administration as much as to his wife, Rosalynn, as well as to his own idealism.

When Reagan took over it was a pure free-for-all, with constant sumo matches between Caspar Weinberger at Defense and George Schultz at State, a situation that allowed for Reagan's own basement team to run amok with Iran-Contra. Aside from that Animal House fiasco, run by Colonel Oliver North under the jurisdiction of National Security Advisers Robert MacFarlane and John Poindexter, the Reagan administration actually achieved good foreign policy. This was largely due to vice president George Bush, a steady man who paid more attention to details than Reagan, had both global and Intelligence ties, and who had the good sense to be plausibly "out of the loop" when Iran-Contra blew up.

The first Bush administration, as we have seen, was a rarity in that the principals meshed in a manner rarely seen in history. It worked on all cylinders, moral courage paired with prudence, and an acute sense of American power matched with justice and diplomacy.

The second Bush administration shuffled the cards so that Cheney—formerly the runt of Bush I—was now the most powerful man in the government, with his mentor, Rumsfeld, at Defense. Powell had been brought back and even elevated at State, but he was primarily a political asset, not having near the influence that James Baker had held with his longtime friend, the first president Bush. Powell and George W. Bush did not have an easy camaraderie, and it was only in 2002 that Powell gained private chats with the president, which were always attended by Condi Rice. Condi and Powell had a natural affinity, but Powell may have gone too far by saying he considered her "like a daughter." It is still unknown how this patronizing statement was taken by Rice, who was entirely devoted to policy and the president, and who, unlike Bush, was not intimidated by Powell's career in the Army.

As for George W. Bush himself, it is to his credit that his administration was immediately stocked with the brilliant Rice, the prestigious Powell, and the rock-solid heavyweights, Cheney and Rumsfeld. This left him to pursue his concept of "leadership," providing moral direction while the rest of the government hashed out his options.

Nevertheless, eight months into his term, Bush was floundering. The dot-com bubble that provided the lucky coda to the Clinton years had burst, and now the economy was going south. His program to provide huge tax-cuts suddenly had to be rephrased: instead of giving the American people back a slice of the Clinton surplus, it was resdescribed as a means to regenerate the economy.

There was nothing to mention of foreign policy, except Rumsfeld's plan to build a huge, hi-tech missile shield along the lines of Reagan's "Star Wars." Somehow this plan seemed befitting for America's oldest Secretary of Defense, who had last served in the Pentagon during the 1970s and apparently hadn't been informed that the Cold War was over.

The missile shield was promoted on the fear that North Korea had come up with a nuclear bomb, and might someday assemble a missile that could get it to Seattle. Though it may sound absurd that the United States, after facing down the Soviet Union, would adopt a

Maginot mentality at the beginning of the 21st century toward a wretchedly poor Cold War leftover that would have to pour half its GDP into creating one rickety ICBM, the missile shield served as the centerpiece of Bush's defense policy.

In reality, though demonizing North Korea was a handy lever to gain public support, the administration's true concern was China. This was impolitic to state publicly, for the good reason that if China thought its nuclear deterrent was being negated it would simply double or triple its arsenal. And it already had the technology to do so, while no one knew if the missile shield would work. Another arms race would have started for no reason.

It was widely suspected that the missile shield, which would bring together 10 different programs under $150 billion of funding, was in fact a Trojan Horse for America to take the lead in militarizing space. This was the most dangerous idea of all because by 2000 the United States was unchallengeable on the nuclear playing field. To open the door to a new, potentially more deadly generation of technology would negate the non-proliferation treaty and invite new competition from states which had never been players in the nuclear stakes. Since the United States already possessed, far and away, the most destructive capability on earth, why would it wish to unlock the potential of space?

Of course, the most compelling argument for the missile shield was all the billion-dollar, long-term contracts it would provide to the defense industry. Research and development, in fact, was not an unsound idea. But deployment, which to gain public support would necessitate frightening the public by announcing threats where none existed, appeared unwise.

In order to get his feet wet in foreign policy, Bush traveled to Europe, where he met the new president of Russia, Vladimir Putin, who had succeeded Boris Yeltsin. Putin was a mysterious figure, younger than previous Kremlin leaders, a black belt in karate, a former top spy for the KGB, and a man intent on resurrecting Russia by filling in the cracks that Gorbachev had not anticipated. In photos, he looked like an awkward politician, as if he felt uncomfortable when not lurking behind dark street corners. It was only when he took off his tie and donned his favored black turtleneck to address the Russian people directly that a sense of his personal dynamism appeared.

After meeting with Putin in Vienna, Bush reported that he had "looked into his soul," and seen that he was a good man. While most of the American diplomatic corps groaned out loud, Bush came home confident that he had bonded with his Russian partner. At this writing it is still unknown what Putin thought when he took a look at Bush's soul, or if he even thought it was a priority.

As the summer drew to a close, even the conservatives who had hooted down Clinton had begun to wonder about Bush. They had received all the tax cuts they had desired, but the president was just floating, as if he had no ideas of his own. Underlying Bush's problems was the fact that Americans began to perceive that he was just as shallow and inarticulate as they had feared. His father had also fallen short of articulation, always short-cutting through the English language, but it had also been perceived that the father had a rare handle on the U.S. position in the world through his own contacts, experience, and intellect. Bush II seemed to have none of these things, only a slavish devotion to tax cuts and to his own leadership principle.

During the summer the news media embarked on one of their salacious frenzies, this time at the expense of a congressman named Gary Condit whose girlfriend had disappeared. Bush spent most of August at his ranch in Crawford, Texas. Back in the White House, on September 4 he was handed a plan to deal with the Muslim terrorist organization, Al Qaeda. The plan had first been handed to Condoleezza Rice back on January 25 by Clinton's counterterrorism chief, Richard Clarke, but had wallowed for months in committees. Bush himself disliked "swatting at flies," preferred to think in larger terms, and thought of the previous administration's concern with terrorism as a typical Clintonian example of micro-management.

On the morning of September 11 Bush was in Florida pursuing his goal to be "the education president." Powell was on a diplomatic mission to Peru. Cheney and Rumsfeld were at work in their offices. That day Rice was scheduled to deliver a major policy speech on the missile shield. In it she would cite the danger of a rogue state acquiring a nuclear weapon with which it would attack America. Little did any of them suspect that an attack had already begun, and it was entirely different from what any of them had anticipated.

SEPTEMBER 11, 2001

Bush was reading a book to a 2nd-grade class in Florida when the first plane hit the World Trade Center. For a few minutes people in New York considered it an inexplicable accident. Somehow an airliner flying low over Manhattan had crashed into the World Trade's north tower with tragic loss of life. Then a second plane came zooming in across the Hudson River from New Jersey, heading straight for the south tower. Its impact created another huge fireball that sent debris flying to the streets. Both the twin towers were now flaming near their tops. The realization set in that it hadn't been an accident; the United States was under attack.

Minutes later another jetliner crashed into the Pentagon in Washington; another passenger plane suddenly nosedived into the ground in Pennsylvania. A dozen more were on their way across the Atlantic; the FAA tried to land all planes over U.S. territory but some were still unaccounted for. Rumors hit the media that a car bomb had gone off near the State Department; the Secret Service reported threats against Air Force One.

In New York, thousands of people in the World Trade Center made their way down staircases, while hundreds of firemen and police rushed to the scene. Those who were at work above the points of impact could not get down the staircases but it was thought they could be rescued from the rooftops. Many had already died from the exploding planes and fuel, and now some on the upper floors began to jump to escape the torturous flames.

After being informed of the attacks by aides, Bush excused himself from the class and improvised a statement to the press. "This terrorism," he said, "will not stand." He had borrowed the declaration his father had made after Saddam Hussein's invasion of Kuwait, but this time it was not an apt phrase. Minutes later the 110-story Twin Towers collapsed into dust. If this terrorism would not stand, neither would New York's World Trade Center. Like a monstrous tidal wave, billows of smoke and debris raced through the canyons of Manhattan, chasing crowds of terrified people. Unknown thousands were already dead across 16 acres of devastation.

Bush then proceeded to charge to the rear, reaching Air Force One in a heavily escorted convoy and then flying to Barksdale Air Force Base in Louisiana. Vice President Cheney advised him to fly on to Olfutt airbase in Nebraska, where more command and control systems were in place. Bush dutifully complied, but soon began to chafe at being tossed around in the hinterland. Back at the burning Pentagon, Donald Rumsfeld and other employees were trying to cope with the fires and rescue the wounded. In New York the entire city was coping with the disaster. While hundreds of first responders had been killed in the sudden collapse of the Twin Towers, more were still rushing to the scene. With the tunnels closed off for train and subway traffic, hundreds of thousands of soot-covered people were trudging across the bridges from Manhattan, sometimes terrified by the low-level passes of U.S. fighter planes, which had now arrived above the city.

In Pennsylvania, Flight 93 smoldered in a field, all of its passengers dead. It was later found that the passengers had tried to seize back their aircraft from the hijackers after learning through cellphones of the attacks on the World Trade Center and the Pentagon. Led by a young man named Todd Beamer who yelled, "Let's roll," they grappled with the Arabs in the cockpit before the plane crashed into the ground.

By afternoon it was clear that the strikes had not been a harbinger of a general strategic assault on the United States or its government but a massive terrorist attack. Bush, who had spent the day in a state of frustration, even resentment at the ponderous security apparatus that had smothered him for eight hours, demanded to be flown back to Washington. He reached the White House and at seven in the evening addressed the shaken American public.

"Today our nation saw evil," he said. Solemnly, he recited the 23rd Psalm. "Though I walk through the valley of the shadow of death, I shall fear no evil, for You are with me." That night the nation saw a different George Bush from the one they thought they knew. There were no more non-sequiturs, stumbles, or verbal hesitations. In a grim voice, with barely concealed anger, he warned the world of the American response to come. "We will make no distinction," he said, "between the terrorists who committed these acts and those who harbor them."

The nation's feelings about Bush had been mixed, to say the least. But now it became hard to imagine that any other man should be president on this day, when America had suffered the most devastating attack in its history. Clinton's empathy would not have been enough at this juncture; and neither would his father's gentlemanly manner. Watching Bush it was possible to detect an element in his personality so direct it was almost primal. All he had previously offered to the country was his mysterious concept of "leadership," which many had viewed as a poor substitute for an in-depth grasp of policy. But immediately after the horrors of September 11, decisive leadership was what America needed most. Desperately desiring to trust their president, the public looked to George W. Bush for guidance.

It only took a day for American Intelligence agencies to identify the September 11 attackers as members of Al Qaeda. By the end of the week the FBI had identified 19 hijackers, and headshots even appeared in U.S. newspapers. Fifteen of them were from Saudi Arabia; the apparent ringleader, Mohammed Atta, was an Egyptian; the remainder were from other Arab states. The speed with which the attackers' identities were revealed, immediately after they had all gone to claim their 70 virgins as martyrs, raised questions among the public. If U.S. Intelligence had been so aware of these people, why had they been allowed to conduct their operation?

Richard Clarke, who had been the counterterrorism chief in Clinton's National Security Adviser's office, continuing with a somewhat diminished role under Condi Rice, reported that he was shocked when the FBI called him on September 12 to identify several of the hijackers as members of Al Qaeda. Clarke, along with another Clinton holdover, Director of Central Intelligence George Tenet, had considered Al Qaeda the most dangerous foreign threat to America. Yet here was the FBI tracking known Al Qaeda operatives in the United States without sharing its information with the NSA's office or the CIA. Like in a tactical military operation in which one attempts to hit the boundary between enemy units, Osama bin Laden's organization had hit a seam between the jurisdictions of U.S. Intelligence agencies. After the post-Vietnam scandals, the CIA had been restricted by law from domestic espionage. The FBI had meanwhile not been privy to the CIA's knowledge of foreign-based terrorists, and when Qaeda operatives gained residence in the United States they slipped into this crack. After initial reluctance, President Bush responded to Congressional pressure by creating the Department of Homeland Security to coordinate inter-agency intelligence in the future; but of course, the move was too late to save the 3,000 people who had died on September 11.

For two years after the attack the Bush administration resisted calls for an investigative commission until pressure from Congress, the public, and most forcefully the widows and family members of the victims, forced its hand. The administration first named Henry Kissinger as chairman, a choice that many found suspicious due to Kissinger's own history of secretiveness, but Kissinger turned down the post rather than reveal the client list of his private consulting firm. Former New Jersey governor Thomas Kean was appointed instead.

After grudgingly agreeing to the commission, and trying to insist that its findings be withheld until after the 2004 election, the Bush administration dragged its heels on supplying documents until it was threatened with subpoenas. Then it refused to allow Condi Rice to testify under oath until the political flak got too hot, and then only on the condition that no other White House personnel be summoned. Bush himself agreed to testify, oddly enough, on the condition that Vice President Cheney be at his side. Most recently the administration has been accused of withholding 8,000 pages of documents dating back to the Clinton administration.

All this recalcitrance was thrown into a particularly poor light when Richard Clarke began his public testimony by saying: "Your government failed you. Those entrusted to protecting you failed you. And I failed you. We tried hard. But that doesn't matter, because we failed. And for that failure, I would ask, once all the facts are out, for your understanding and for your forgiveness."

Notwithstanding that Clarke's assumption of responsibility for 9/11 sent his new book to the top of the bestseller list, his humility struck a chord that should have echoed in the White House. Hardly anyone in the public blamed the Bush administration for a catastrophe that had come as a shock to the entire world. And the commission had been created not as a forum for accusation but as a means of parsing the record so that similar events could not happen in the future.

Second-guessing being such an easy pasttime, however, both Bush and Clinton came under political sniper attack, in which they shared good historical company. A large body of literature has risen over the years claiming that Franklin D. Roosevelt should not have been surprised by Pearl Harbor—or, on a more sinister note, that he wasn't at all surprised. Stalin has likewise been criticized for being taken unawares by the German invasion of Russia. If the Nazis were still around, their self-flagellation over being surprised on D-Day would be continuous, though there is also much literature extolling the superb Allied deception effort. The fact is that surprise is the best force-multiplier in warfare, and in Al Qaeda's case it was their only advantage. Without sophisticated weapons or large numbers, they relied on utter secrecy, imagination, and audacity for their success.

As the American gotcha game unfolded, critics pointed to previous rumors of terrorists using aircraft in attacks. Clarke had already taken precautions against such an event at the Atlanta Olympics. The perpetrators of the 1993 World Trade Center truck bombing had been found with a plan on the drawing board to dive a plane into CIA headquarters. Earlier in the summer of 2001 the FBI had caught an Arab named Zacarias Moussaoui taking flying lessons in Minnesota, during which he insisted that he didn't need to learn how to take off or land. An FBI agent in Arizona also sounded warnings about Arabs enrolling in flight schools.

Fiction, of course, had already entertained airborne attacks. A 1970s disaster movie depicted a blimp aiming to wipe out the crowd at the Superbowl. Tom Clancy imagined an aircraft attacking a joint session of Congress. The infamous novel "The Turner Diaries" ended with its white supremacist protagonist flying an explosives-laden plane into the Pentagon.

A key thing to remember about 9/11 is that it wasn't the ramming of airplanes into buildings that caused the greatest shock and damage; it was the total collapse of the Twin Towers. And no one, from Aaron Spelling in his "Towering Inferno" days, to Osama bin Laden, to the hundreds of NYC firemen who had begun charging up the stairwells, had expected the skyscrapers to completely crumble. Bin Laden was later found on a videotape saying, "I was the most optimistic of all," going on to explain that he expected the towers to burn not only at their points of impact but all the way to their tops. Not even he and his fellow terrorists had imagined that the bottom 80 floors of both mighty skycrapers would collapse, thus creating the most visually spectacular feat of destruction of all time.

The United States was not only surprised by hijacked airliners turned into weapons; it, and the rest of the world, including the realm of engineers, was shocked by the effect that tons of burning jet airfuel had at the tops of skyscrapers. No one had ever tested this before. And to blame the Bush administration, or Clinton's, for the real disaster of 9/11, is to proceed down a fruitless dead end of recrimination.

Where the Bush administration could accept constructive criticism is in its dismissal of terrorism as a primary threat when it first took office. The Clinton administration had been somewhat younger, more flexible, and better attuned to global nuances. It was the Clinton holdovers, Tenet and Clarke, in fact, who continued to sound the greatest warnings about Al Qaeda after the 2000 election. The Bush people were more interested in traditional geopolitics, whether these involved relations with China, the missile shield, or finally settling scores with that old Bush family antagonist, Saddam Hussein.

In Bush's view, terrorism was a danger to U.S. citizens and an irritant to the country at large, but not a threat to its basic stability. And the disparate record of terrorist attacks over the past 15 years appeared to bear him out. Pan Am 103 in 1988 had been the work of Libyans. The World Trade truck bomb had been traced to an Islamic group in New Jersey led by a blind mullah. This group was so inept that the case was cracked when one of them tried to retrieve his rental deposit for the blown-up truck. The 1996 Dhahran attack turned out to be supported by Iran; the 1998 Embassy attacks were traced to bin Laden. At first it was not clear who had hit the USS Cole in 2000, but since the attack had been staged from Yemen, the Wild West of Arab radicalism, it could have been any number of groups.

Underlying much of the thinking about terrorism was the Oklahoma City bombing in 1995, which until 9/11 was the largest terrorist attack on U.S. soil. After 168 innocent civilians had been murdered, the public seethed with anger at Islam and the FBI began grabbing Muslims in midwestern airports. But then the terrorist was found to be a skinny, blond ex-GI from Buffalo. Timothy McVeigh's political cause, like his fellow traveler the Unabomber's, was so far out on the fringe that it was impossible to declare a War on Terror against such societal dregs. Any such conflict would have had to be called the War on Weirdos. Given the fact that terrorism had proven to be the last resort of the feeble or the demented, or a combination of the two, it was understandable that Bush preferred to concentrate on relations between nations rather than going on the defensive against ad hoc groups scheming away with homemade bombs in their basements.

But as we now know, Al Qaeda (in Arabic, "The Base") had emerged as a more formidable terrorist entity than any that had come before. Simultaneously forged through a victory against a superpower—the Soviet Union in Afghanistan—and the global economy during the information age, Al Qaeda members came from 43 countries and operated in over 60. The organization was well funded and enjoyed both dedicated, educated recruits, many of whom were combat veterans, and, through bin Laden, inspirational leadership. In its methods Al Qaeda resembled the Cult of the Assassins that had plagued the Middle East during the time of the Crusades, until it was finally wiped out by the Mongols in 1256. However, in the internet age the modern terrorists took care to keep their organization loosely knit and widely dispersed, both for broader effect and to avoid counterblows.

In retrospect, the spectacular destruction of two American embassies on the same morning in 1998, as well as the attack on a 550-foot, state-of-the-art U.S. warship, seem like classic Al Qaeda operations. But it was not until 9/11 that the organization fully rose from the ranks of other pinpricking terrorist groups to appear as a global menace. During the summer of 2001, U.S. Intelligence recorded a great deal of "chatter," mainly pointing to further attacks overseas, and much talk that claimed something big was about to happen. But until 9/11, who knew what "big" really meant?

The Bush administration was not prepared for the attack that finally occurred, which in its tactically small scale, insidious development, and startling destructive power, was unprecedented in history. Sadly, we are still due for a body of literature trying to assign responsibility for 9/11 to the American side—the airlines, New York City, the Bush or Clinton administrations, or to the architects or lease-holders of the World Trade Center. Much of this new chatter will be motivated by politics or lawsuits, while the bottom line is that a surprise attack is just that—a surprise. It could not have existed otherwise. The responsibility for 9/11 lies with Al Qaeda. And it was Al Qaeda and its allies who needed to pay the price for their havoc.

More important than recriminations over how the terrorists had slipped through our domestic security net was the question why they had attacked America in the first place. President Bush posed the question in his September 20 address to the nation: "Why do they hate us?" Unfortunately, the president gave the wrong answer to his own question by telling the public, "They hate us for our freedoms." This equation was received well by the public, which varied the concept into "They hate us because we love liberty," or, considering the Arabs' evil, "They hate us because we're good." Much was made of the medieval nature of "ragheads" such as bin Laden, who still dressed as if they were in the 12th century and held stern religious beliefs that predated the New World's regeneration of democracy.

There was, of course, some truth to the notion that radical Arabs hated American freedoms. This was not so much an animosity toward our electoral system. Nearly every country pays lip service to democracy, and the Middle East and Africa are full of dust-covered national constitutions guaranteeing human rights. An oddity of the Cold War was that every time a country went Communist it would immediately slap the word "People's" or "Democratic" onto its name. What fundamentalists such as bin Laden really hated about American freedom was its resultant cultural licentiousness, a trend that since the 1960s had steamrolled its way over nearly every safeguard of good taste. (Should bin Laden ever be captured, a good way to torture him without violating the Geneva Conventions would be to rig his cell with 24 hours a day of MTV.) But while bin Laden and his followers undeniably despise American freedoms, this is not to say that they object to our municipal, state, or federal elections, and neither is it to say that the 9/11 offensive was launched simply to put a damper on Snoop Dogg or Marilyn Manson.

Bin Laden's specific animus toward the United States stemmed not from hatred of our freedoms—after all, he could have attacked

Amsterdam—but from hatred of our overwhelming military power which had established, he thought, a new blanket of colonialism on the Arab people. On the receiving end of American power, it matters little how our presidents are elected or that our culture can be annoying. In the Middle East, America is represented by Apache helicopters hovering over Gaza City; guided missile cruisers on station in the Arabian Sea; and by squadrons of desert-based F-16s poised to protect the oil supply.

The ongoing Israeli-Palestinian conflict has put a tragically militaristic face on American influence, creating compound resentment among the Arabs year after year. While American neocolonialism in the Mideast may be a figment of bin Laden's paranoid imagination, the very real Israeli colonization of the West Bank and Gaza is a genuine embarrassment to America's claim to represent justice. In Pakistan, from which Al Qaeda draws many recruits, India's occupation of Muslim Kashmir is another bleeding sore, as is the Russian war over Chechnya. In Samuel Huntington's words, "Islam has bloody borders," and the Muslims have to face stronger powers on all fronts. Like a latter-day John Brown, Osama bin Laden may be a murderous fanatic, but the uncomfortable truth is that he represents arguments that need to be heard.

But not, of course, immediately after 9/11. The wanton murder of 3,000 civilians on American soil brooked no debate until the United States had responded with every means at its disposal. The question "why do they hate us" could wait until the first issue was settled on the battlefield.

On September 20, 2001, George W. Bush addressed a joint session of Congress. All across the United States people stopped what they were doing to gather together and listen to what he had to say. As if calmly looking every American in the eye Bush said, in part:

> Great harm has been done to us. We have suffered great loss. And in our grief and anger we have found our mission and our moment. Freedom and fear are at war. The advance of human freedom—the great achievement of our time, and the great hope of every time—now depends on us. Our nation—this generation—will lift a dark threat of violence from our people

and our future. We will rally the world to this cause, by our efforts and by our courage. We will not tire, we will not falter, and we will not fail.

Bush's speech instilled courage and confidence in a shaken public. It was one of the great moments in American history. And it was also the apex of his presidency.

8

THE WAR IN AFGHANISTAN

Al Qaeda was like no other enemy America had faced. Many terrorist organizations exist as furtive criminal networks, hidden from the reach of institutional law. Think of KKK chapters in the early 1960s or whoever sponsored the abortion clinic bombings of the 1990s. Other groups, such as the IRA, can become quasi-official public entities, keeping only their violent wings carefully concealed. Terrorist organizations that represent geopolitical causes, such as Hezbollah, can find state sponsorship; however the rule is that they must maintain several layers of plausible deniability between themselves and the official governments that give them support or refuge. This allows their sponsors to evade responsibility for terrorist actions while not preventing collusion in the event the terrorists provoke serious retribution and need to move elsewhere. For a time Al Qaeda fell into the latter category but then, as in other respects, it proved more brazen than any terrorist organization that had come before. Its leadership all but retained a mailing address, and it operated military training camps directly under the eyes of American satellites.

This was fortunate for the United States. Consider if Osama bin Laden had arranged the September 11 attacks while still based in Sudan. The Sudanese government would have immediately disowned him, or as in 1996 would have expelled him in a furtive rush from the country. In any case, the idea of the U.S. military pounding the wretched Sudanese as surrogates for bin Laden would have been ludicrous. Or imagine if the attacks had been arranged from Pakistan's Northwest Frontier Province, where at this writing bin Laden is thought to be hiding. Neither Pakistan nor the British before them have ever firmly controlled that mountainous tribal territory, and for that matter neither has anyone else. Since the United States could not have justifiably vented its wrath on the nation of Pakistan, the effort would have quickly devolved into police work on the detective or small-unit level. And 9/11 warranted far more.

Fortunately, by 2001 Osama bin Laden and hundreds of his Al Qaeda operatives resided in a country whose leaders were just as fanatic as he was and who defiantly refused to turn him over. For the United States this meant a target in plain sight; an entire nation on which to vent its just anger for the unprecedented crime of September 11. Problematically, however, this nation was Afghanistan—the fabled deathtrap for invading armies and the graveyard of empires past.

AFGHANISTAN

Once a geographic crossroads for great civilizations, Afghanistan was largely bypassed by the modern age. Landlocked, mountainous, and wretchedly poor, it is primarily noted today for its wealth of military history.

The earliest details of Afghanistan come from ancient Greek historians following the exploits of Alexander the Great. After conquering Greece, Egypt and the Persian Empire with spectacular victories, Alexander's men came to grief upon reaching the Hindu Kush. The climate and harsh topography of Afghanistan took Alexander by surprise, and then his army ran itself ragged fighting the fierce Scythian tribes in the province of Bactria and in Transoxiana, north of the Oxus River (today the Amu Darya). After two years of mobile warfare, during which time an entire 2,000-man Greek column was wiped out in an ambush, Alexander finally married a Bactrian princess and proceeded to his final conquest in India.

For the next thousand years Afghanistan served alternately as a prize and a transit route for invading armies from Persia, India and the northern steppe. The Greek kingdom of Bactria was overrun and destroyed by the Scythians, who, after being pushed off the steppe by Turkic hordes, flowed into the south and east of present-day Afghanistan. Today this swath of territory is known as the homeland of the world's largest remaining tribal group, the Pashtun.

In the 1st century a group called the Kushans came off the steppe to forge an empire that straddled the great cultures of India, China, Persia and Rome. A Kushan king, Kanishka, converted to Buddhism and became responsible for spreading the "Greater Vehicle," or image of Buddha, as far east as Japan. During this period the Silk Road from China began to take shape. The Kushans fell to a new Persian onslaught from the west, and then the Persian Sassanids fell to an invasion of White Huns from the north, who themselves were followed by Turks.

Toward the end of the 7th century, Arab armies penetrated the territory, brandishing not only weapons but new beliefs based on the Koran. In the centuries that followed, indigenous Afghan empires arose, based on the cities of Ghazni and Ghor. With the fierce zeal of the newly converted they launched predatory raids into India, extending the borders of Islam. Their conquests and the forcible conversions that followed eventually resulted in the partition of the subcontinent between India and Pakistan. Archaeologists later found that the staircase of the main mosque at Ghazni consisted of footworn Hindu idols.

By the early 13th century Afghanistan had been absorbed into a powerful new empire called Khwarezm, whose shah unwisely picked a fight with another new empire to the east: the Mongols. Led by Genghis Khan, the Mongols had just completed the conquest of northern China, and to the misfortune of millions, they headed west.

In 1221 the Mongols invaded southern Asia, establishing a record of ruin that would be unmatched until the 20th century. Welding the primitive hardiness of a nomadic people with ironclad discipline and superb command talent, Genghis Khan created an army that resembled an unstoppable force of nature. As the principal cities in Transoxiana fell, often with horrible massacres, the crown prince of Khwraezm, Jalal ad-Din, broke through a Mongol cordon and fled to Afghanistan. Arriving at Ghazni he raised an army and defeated an approaching Mongol force at Parwan. This was the only defeat suffered by the Mongols over the course of 80 years; but it was a pyrrhic victory for Afghanistan. Genghis Khan personally crossed the Hindu Kush, obliterating cities en route. After a two-week chase he caught and destroyed Jalal ad-Din's army on the Indus River.

During the next century a warrior known in the West as Tamerlane fought his way to the top of the Mongol empire of southern Asia, embarking on a career of rampage that exceeded even the original Mongols in wanton cruelty. In the early 16th century a noble named Babur, who had bloodlines to both Genghis Khan and Tamerlane, conquered Kabul and then Delhi, where he founded the Moghul Empire. By this time the nomads from the steppe had become fully ensconced in civilization, contributing to its grandeur, as witness the Taj Mahal.

But southern Asia was now declining in geopolitical importance. The process began in 1492 when with one stroke Christopher Columbus proved to Europe that the world was indeed a globe instead of a flat plane; he discovered an entire "new world" that would henceforth be the focus of much of the developed world's commercial energy; and he triggered the age of European colonialism made possible by seapower rather than by marching armies traversing continents. Afghanistan gradually became a neglected region, while the new empires projected might along the smoother, more easily passable lanes of the sea.

The Silk Road dried up as European seafarers instead directed the flow of commerce to ports. The Indian subcontinent was invaded by the French and British without either having to step foot on Afghan soil. Persian cities in the east, which had never quite recovered from the ravages of the Mongols, became arid waystations for the brigands who roamed Transoxiana, their mosques and monuments nearly outnumbering their people.

During this period the Afghan tribes emerged to ravage both India and Persia. Less touched by civilization than more urban cultures, the invention of firearms provided the tribesmen an equality they had lacked with the heavily armored warriors of the past. In 1757 a Pashtun named Ahmed Shah Durrani established a kingdom north and south of the Hindu Kush and as far west as Herat, thus establishing the rough outlines of the modern Afghan state.

In the early 1800s the British were able to subjugate India, a few thousand of their men able to achieve sovereignty over millions of natives. The elimination of Napoleon in 1815 left the British Empire and Tsarist Russia as the players of the "Great Game," a contest for southern Asia. While the British had arrived by sea and were quickly forging their way up through the subcontinent, Tsarist forces led by Cossack spearheads were chopping their way south.

All that stood between Tsarist power and the malleable resources of India was the difficult territory of Afghanistan. In 1838 the British became alarmed at news that a Tsarist agent had appeared in Kabul and that a Russian army was on its way across the steppe. The British assembled a huge force and invaded Afghanistan. For the next two years they held sovereignty over the country through a puppet monarch, Shah Shuja, and through cash payments to tribes. They also set up a vast cantonment, like a parallel city next to Kabul. British officers' families, as well as Indian families and servants were invited to add comfort to the occupation.

But it soon began to unravel. Shah Shuja, supported by British troops, began to levy taxes on tribal leaders, who were unaccustomed to such burdens and who were further beset by a sense of uselessness now that their king no longer relied on their military support. A new kind of opposition arose in religious fighters, called ghazis, who could not be bought or persuaded. Guided by Islam, the ghazis' only goal was to drive the Christian and Hindu infidels out of their country. The tribal chiefs couldn't control them, even as Islam became the glue that held the different anti-foreign factions together.

The revolt began in the fall of 1841 when an Afghan mob sacked the British Residency in Kabul, slaughtering its occupants. The British army in the cantonment sat idle during this five-hour battle, and then the cantonment itself became surrounded by thousands of Afghans. For weeks the British army fought back, while their isolated position became increasingly untenable. The final straw came when the British political leader, Envoy William Macnaughton, was murdered at a conference when ghazis suddenly overran the proceedings. Afterward the despondent British agreed to leave the country, having negotiated with the chiefs for safe passage during their retreat.

It turned into the most pitiful disaster of the colonial age. At the beginning of January 1842 nearly 17,000 people trudged out from Kabul, hoping to reach the British-held fortress town of Jellalabad, 80 miles away. The route wound through a number of shadowy passes, crisscrossed by ice-crusted streams. Darkness fell early, and from the first hour of the march Indian servants began to fall by the wayside, crippled by cold. The worst problem was that when the fugitives reached the passes they found that the heights on either side bristled with thousands of Pashtun tribesmen armed with their native muskets and long knives. When not performing relentless execution from above, the Afghans stole into the column, whetting their knives on the soft mass of Hindu camp followers. Soldiers were unable to quell the attacks, or the panic.

In mid-January the British force at Jellalabad was encouraged to see a member of the Kabul garrison approach their fortress. It was an assistant surgeon named William Brydon, who had stumbled out of the passes wounded in four places atop a dying pony. For days, the force at Jellalabad lit lanterns and blew bugles to guide in other British survivors, until they realized that Dr. Brydon was the only one. Left behind in the passes were nearly 17,000 bodies, frozen to death or killed by the Afghans.

By 1877 Victorian Britain had improved its situation in India considerably, thanks to the Suez Canal and the inventions of the steam engine and the repeating rifle. Alarmed at new Tsarist overtures to Afghanistan, the British invaded again, forcing the Afghan king to accept a 250-man British mission in Kabul. This mission was massacred by disgruntled Afghans a few months later, however, and the Second Anglo-Afghan War began in earnest. British forces led by General Frederick Roberts seized the capital, but Afghan resistance led by religious leaders quickly began to swarm around him. Just as during the first war, the army was forced into a camp outside the city where it was heavily outnumbered and surrounded by the enemy. This time, however, the British had a hard nut of an army instead of a civilian encumbered force, and Robert easily defeated a general assault.

Then news arrived that a British army in the south had been destroyed by an Afghan force at Maiwand. Roberts gathered his cavalry and Highlanders and marched 300 miles, whereupon he thrashed the Afghans at the battle of Kandahar. The British subsequently cleared out for good. On arriving back in England to find a debate about Afghanistan still raging, Roberts summarized his own view by stating: "I feel sure I am right when I say that the less the Afghans see of us the less they will dislike us."

The British left behind a ruler, Abdur Rahman, who became

known as the "Iron Emir" for his ruthlessness in hammering out a coherent state from what had always been a collection of quarreling tribes and ethnic groups. Still having India's protection in mind, the British kept their hand in with generous subsidies, in return for which they retained control of Afghanistan's foreign policy.

In 1893 a British survey team led by Sir Mortimer Durand drew Afghanistan's eastern border with India. Combining its task with hunting and birdwatching, Durand's party cut a nonchalant path through the center of the Pashtun ethnic group, making sure that the Khyber Pass and other strategic points, as well as important towns such as Peshawar and Quetta, were on the Indian side. This division of the Pashtun subsequently created problems for the British, and then more for Pakistan when it was created in 1947. Pakistan simply designated its westernmost mountain regions "tribal territories," and still calls the largest province there the Northwest Frontier.

Afghanistan made slim progress toward modernity during the 20th century. Every ruler who tried reforms met fierce resistance from the countryside, where people clung to their older ways and Islam, as well as to their traditional independence from a central government. The balance of gravity in the country, after so many centuries of invasion, existed in the hills rather in the cities, which had always been so easily overrun. Even today it cannot be said that the Pashtun in the mountains of Afghanistan have ever been conquered.

During the Cold War, Afghanistan briefly found itself courted by both the United States and the Soviet Union. The Americans built roads and irrigation systems in the south while the Soviets built roads and a huge tunnel atop the Salang Pass in the Hindu Kush to provide fast access to Kabul from the north. As the Vietnam War began to soak up American attention and resources, Afghanistan drew closer to the USSR. Its army was supplied with Soviet equipment and thousands of its officers received training at Soviet schools.

In April 1978 Communist elements in Afghanistan's Soviet-trained army revolted. They surrounded the government palace in Kabul, and by morning had killed the prime minister and his family. The new leaders of the Democratic Republic of Afghanistan (DRA) waited for the dust to settle before enacting revolutionary programs. In October they revealed their agenda: land reform, credit reform, new national languages in recognition of minorities, and compulsory education for women. They also pulled down the traditional green-and-white national flag and raised a new one: It was red.

Revolts began immediately as tribesmen in the countryside threw off government control. In March 1979 an Afghan army division revolted in Herat and 5,000 people died before order was restored. During the fighting, rebels had killed about 100 Soviet advisers and carried their heads around on poles. That fall, the Communist leader was murdered and his deputy, Hafizullah Amin, took control. Amin, who had been educated at Columbia University, proceeded to aggravate the situation further, proving so inept that the Russians feared he was a CIA agent.

Soviet leader Leonid Brezhnev pondered the dilemma. Earlier in the year, the Shah of Iran had fallen to Ayatollah Khomeini's Islamic revolutionaries, which meant that American power was no longer on Afghanistan's doorstep. However, evidence had appeared that the United States was fueling the counterrevolution in Afghanistan, perhaps to retrieve its position in southern Asia. And the new fear was that Islamic fundamentalism, if successful in both Iran and Afghanistan, would spread to the Soviet Union's southernmost, Muslim republics. Brezhnev decided to come to the rescue of the beleaguered Communist regime.

Afghanistan thus became the forum for the Soviet Union's only hot conflict during the Cold War. The Red Army invaded on Christmas Eve 1979, beginning with Spetznaz commandos and airborne troops flying into Kabul. They surrounded Amin's palace and by daybreak had killed him and his guard. At the same time, Soviet armored columns crossed the Amu Darya and spread down the ring road that surrounded the Hindu Kush. They did not goose-step into Afghan cities, but instead set up bases nearby, hoping to be as inconspicuous as possible. The invasion was executed superbly, with overwhelming strength, speed, decisiveness, and an impressive use of combined arms.

In the United States Jimmy Carter cancelled grain sales to the Soviet Union, further arms reduction talks, and American participation in the 1980 Moscow Olympics. However, to people in the rest of the world the invasion looked to be a Prague-like fait accompli. The only exception was the Afghan people, primarily those from the countryside, who had no intention of accepting conquest by a secular superpower. Across tribal and ethnic lines, the Afghans resisted, and their fighters became known as the Mujahideen, or Soldiers of God.

The first surprise encountered by the Soviets was that the DRA army they had intended to support began to fall apart the minute they entered the country. Thousands of tribesmen abandoned the government and deserted to their villages, taking their weapons with them. The Soviets found their troops and convoys ambushed from hidden positions every time they ventured from their base camps. At first this type of warfare was at a low level, as after the American invasion of Iraq in 2003, with casualties only about one a day. But the more vulnerable the Soviets appeared the greater the resistance grew.

The key international role was played by Pakistan, which after the invasion was faced by a hostile India on one side and a Soviet-occupied Afghanistan on the other. It was completely isolated, and President Zia al-Haq, who had previously been considered an international pariah for taking power in a military coup and hanging his predecessor, now saw an opportunity. By helping to resist the Soviet occupation of Afghanistan he could simultaneously become a hero to Islam and to the West. Pakistan did not wish to confront the Soviets directly, but could help to make their occupation untenable.

The first country that offered arms to the Mujahideen was China, which had a tacit alliance with Pakistan due to similar hostility towards both India and the Soviets. And the Chinese had a good sense how to fight a guerrilla war. The second was Saudi Arabia, which poured funds into the conflict in defense of Islam. The United States joined in, disguising its contributions by buying up Soviet armaments from Egypt, Israel and elsewhere. Pakistan's Inter-Service Intelligence agency (ISI) shepherded the flow of arms and helped to organize the resistance parties.

Among the heroes who rose in the Afghan resistance were Gulbuddin Hekmatyar, who led the largest group of fundamentalist Pashtun in the southeast; Ismail Khan, a Tajik, who led the resistance around Herat; and Abdul Haq, a Pashtun who operated around Kabul. The greatest Afghan champion, however, was Ahmed Shah Massoud, a Tajik who led the Mujahideen in the Panjshir Valley. Massoud was 26 years old at the time of the invasion, and the Panjshir was the one piece of territory outside the cities that was vital for the Soviets to control. From the Panjshir, Massoud could attack the Salang highway, Bagram airbase, Kabul, and Soviet bases in the north—all of which he frequently did. In return, the Soviets launched a number of offensives into the valley, using tanks, bombers, and helicopter-borne commandos. With each successive assault the Panjshir turned into more of a wasteland, but Massoud could not be defeated.

1984 was the bloodiest year of the war, as the Soviets lost 2,300 dead. The Afghan resistance was not nearly as formidable as the North Vietnamese Army the Americans had faced in Indochina, but it was clearly a notch above the Viet Cong. And it had a similar cross-border refuge and supply network, this time in Pakistan, where a multinational effort—consisting of both aid and volunteer fighters from throughout the Islamic world—was underway to support the Mujahideen. The Soviets responded by carpet bombing the Afghan countryside, destroying crops and herds as well as people in order to dry up the pool of resistance. The Afghans sprung hundreds of small-unit raids and ambushes, while the major battles resulted from full-scale Soviet efforts to wipe out resistance strongholds.

In 1985 the war turned when Mikhail Gorbachev became leader of the Soviet Union and Ronald Reagan, fresh after a landslide re-election, was finally convinced to divert his attention from Latin America. His hand was forced by Congressmen such as Charlie Wilson of Texas and Senator Gordon Humphrey of New Hampshire. That year, Gorbachev gave his generals one last chance to win the war, and the Soviets overran the primary Mujahideen tunnel complex near the Pakistani border. But by now American aid, previously dripped covertly through the CIA, was arriving in full force.

In 1986 the Mujahideen appeared with the U.S. heat-seeking Stinger missile, the most advanced, hand-held anti-aircraft weapon in the world. Over the next year 270 Soviet aircraft were shot out of the sky. Anyone following the current U.S. occupation of Iraq, where a helicopter goes down only every couple of weeks, can imagine the resultant impact. The Soviets had lost air superiority, their greatest advantage. Gorbachev could have increased the brutality of the conflict with high-level bombing, but instead began to seek a way out. In spring 1988 he pushed through a timetable for withdrawal, and on

February 15, 1989, the last Soviet combat troops left Afghanistan.

Once the Soviets were gone it was expected that the Mujahideen would quickly triumph. But their first combined effort, a siege of Jellalabad, turned into a disjointed failure, and the resistance parties separated. The DRA had prudently withdrawn into a network of cities and essential bases, so that even as the Soviet Union expired at the end of 1991, the Communist government of Afghanistan was able to hold out. As the Mujahideen reverted to their former guerrilla tactics, the focus of the war shifted. Whereas previously the Soviets had secured the cities and wreaked havoc in the countryside, now the reverse was true as the rebel parties surrounded urban centers, pouring in rocket and artillery fire, completing Afghanistan's utter devastation.

In 1992 Kabul finally came to the point of capitulation with Massoud attacking from the north and Hekmatyar leading a larger force from the south. With the help of the UN, the Mujahideen agreed on the shape of the government that would follow. But then Hekmatyar seized the initiative and tried to take over the capital himself. Massoud responded and his troops were able to force Hekmatyar's men to retreat. For the first time in centuries, forces from the north had wrested Kabul from the Pashtun. The result was all-out civil war among the Mujahideen.

Both Moscow and Washington had lost interest in Afghanistan by this time, while the rubblization of the country continued. Massoud controlled Kabul and part of the DRA's former base network, but in practice the country split up along party, tribal, or ethnic lines. With the central government fighting for its life rather than exerting control, local chiefs held sovereignty over their own domains just as in the time of Tamerlane. The ancient practice of exacting tolls for passage on roads resumed, as did the practice of warlords taxing villagers to support their private armies. There was no justice system outside the whims of local commanders, and neither was there an educational system, a social safety net, healthcare, or any public works.

The Afghans had the sole advantage at this juncture that they were well trained in logistics, extremely well armed, and unbothered by government. Thus the country became the world's primary source of opium. The farmers could grow poppies for profit while the former Mujahideen could guarantee delivery, through Pakistan or the former

Soviet republics to end users in the West. In an otherwise devastated country, Afghans managed to make money, while in most of the country the rule of warlords meant a lawless, frightening existence.

THE TALIBAN

The situation began to change in 1994, near Kandahar, with the emergence of a group called the Taliban, a word that meant students, or "seekers." Some girls had been raped by a warlord's men, and a local mullah, Muhammed Omar, was asked to provide assistance. Omar and his religious students avenged the crime. Thereafter they were called upon to provide justice elsewhere, and Mullah Omar found himself commanding a great body of volunteers. The Taliban began to erase the rule of warlords from southern Afghanistan, confiscating weapons and restoring the rule of law as written in the Koran. Pakistan, which had watched the devolution of Afghanistan with dismay, supported the Taliban from the start with arms and expertise.

As the Taliban flowed north they met setbacks at the hands of both Ismail Khan at Herat and Massoud at Kabul. But Pakistan's ISI continued the flow of students from madrasses on its territory, providing weapons and rudimentary military training. The Taliban surged again to Herat and this time forced Ismail Khan to flee. Moving north toward Kabul they overran Hekmatyar's forces, who like the Taliban were fundamentalist Pashtun. Hekmatyar suffered far more from defections than casualties.

During this period an Uzbek warlord, Abdul Rashid Dostum, who had formerly been on the Russian payroll and had dived in on all sides of the civil war, united with Massoud against the Taliban. The Hazaras—a Shiite people descended from the Mongols—emerged from the center of the Hindu Kush to join the assault on Kabul, but then switched sides to resist the Taliban.

Massoud was finally forced to retreat when the Taliban threatened to cut him off in Kabul. Facing isolation, the onset of winter, and thousands of disgruntled former enemies roaming the streets, Massoud retreated with his Tajik forces. The Taliban surged above the Hindu Kush, taking Mazar-i-Sharif, Kunduz, and other cities, while Massoud tenaciously held on to a corner of territory. He was now the military leader of a group called the Northern Alliance, which basically consisted of every ethnic group in Afghanistan save the Pashtun.

To the rest of the world, the Taliban onslaught did not seem unwelcome, though there was a science-fiction element about it. The black-turbaned fighters seemed to have sprung from the ground, replacing chaos with order and anarchy with law. However, it soon became apparent that their notion of law had a fearsome, medieval aspect. They barred women from schools, medical care, or even from appearing in public unless covered from head to toe and escorted by a relative. Their justice was meted out with swords, and their idea of crime ranged from not growing a beard to flying a kite.

Interestingly, while the various splinters of Afghanistan had had no use for central government control, once the Taliban established a firm government, it had no use for international controls. When the Taliban seized Kabul in September 1996, their first act was to invade the UN compound where the last Communist leader was hiding. The Taliban castrated and hanged him, leaving his body to swing in a public display. For the next five years the Taliban regime would be recognized only by Pakistan, Saudi Arabia, and the United Arab Emirates, while the rest of the world gradually became aghast at its behavior.

In 2000 the Taliban banned poppy farming from Afghanistan, perhaps thereby contributing to its own downfall. Analysts have pointed out that the ban sent the price of opium through the roof, temporarily enriching the government and those who held stockpiles. But the average Pashtun farming community now stared at a bleak future, stripped of the only profitable trade it had known.

OSAMA BIN LADEN

In May 1996, Osama bin Laden returned to Afghanistan. He had first gone there as a 23-year-old at the behest of Saudi intelligence during the first year of the Soviet war. Setting up a base in Pakistan, he had helped carve out tunnels and fortifications in the Afghan mountains south of Jellalabad, drawing on the expertise of his family's billion-dollar construction business. He had also fought in the war, participating in at least two ambushes of Soviet forces.

In 1990 bin Laden became discouraged by the Mujahideen civil war and returned to Saudi Arabia, where he worked in the family business. Tall, with a deceptively placid visage, he was considered a Saudi national hero, the young millionaire who had given up wealth and privilege for jihad. Bin Laden fell out with the Saudi royal family over the Gulf War, however, arguing vehemently against allowing American forces into the country. A fanatically strict Muslim, he thought a U.S. presence in Arabia was as intolerable as the Soviet occupation of Afghanistan.

He moved to Sudan where he formed Al Qaeda from Arab and other veterans of the Soviet-Afghan War. Al Qaeda forged ties with other terrorist organizations such as the Muslim Brotherhood and Islamic Jihad, and soon had an international network of operatives. In 1994 the Saudis revoked bin Laden's citizenship and the Sudanese, under pressure, requested that he leave. The CIA set up a working group to follow his activities in 1996.

After his return to Afghanistan, bin Laden began to work closely with Mullah Omar. The Taliban, otherwise ostracized from the world, now had an ally with operatives in dozens of countries. In 1998 Al Qaeda destroyed the American embassies in Kenya and Tanzania. Stand-off American retaliation was ineffective. In 2000 Al Qaeda operatives blew up the USS *Cole* in Yemen, and this time there was no retaliation. Afghanistan had previously defeated a superpower that lay on its doorstep; and now that rugged, remote land appeared to be beyond America's reach. On September 9, 2001, Al Qaeda agents assassinated Ahmed Shah Massoud, the commander of the Northern Alliance. Two days later they launched the greatest terrorist attack of all time, against New York and Washington, DC.

While to the Bush administration it was fortunate that Al Qaeda hadn't dispersed or disappeared, and was instead sitting defiant, allied with the rulers of a large, identifiable nation, the previous military history of that nation caused some worry.

What U.S. military planners should also have realized is that since the days of the Persian Empire, Afghanistan has been a very easy country to invade. In fact, with the exception of Iraq, or perhaps Belgium in Europe, it has been the most commonly invaded country on earth. There's never been a problem breaking into the country; the only problem is staying there.

WASHINGTON, DC

Aside from his formal televised speeches, President Bush inspired the nation with smaller projections of confidence. These ranged from cowboy talk—referring to bin Laden as "Wanted: Dead or Alive"—to regaling a crowd of hardhats at Ground Zero in New York with the words, "I can hear you. The rest of the world hears you. And the people who knocked these buildings down will hear all of us soon!" Even his body language found new appreciation. An exercise aficionado, the president had a tendency to walk with his chest puffed out, his arms churning mechanically at his side like a rock'em-sock'em robot, as if his biceps were just too big to hold still. Such macho affectations now found favor.

Unfortunately, it turned out that the Pentagon had no contingency plans for a war in Afghanistan. And the American way of war—strategic, heavy firepower—was difficult to apply in a poor country that had already been destroyed several times over. A former Clinton official told the New York Times, "When we looked at Afghanistan before, the sense was we were going to bomb them *up* to the Stone Age." Bush himeslf mused, "What's the sense of sending $2 million missiles to hit a $10 tent?"

Nevertheless, the vast machinery of U.S. military power began to move. America already had a naval battle group built around the carrier *Enterprise* in the Arabian Sea; it was soon joined by another, led by the USS *Carl Vinson*, from the Persian Gulf. The huge nuclear carrier *Theodore Roosevelt*, with 70 strike aircraft, set sail from Virginia, and the *Kitty Hawk*, stripped for helicopters, departed from Japan. The U.S. already had 15,000 men in the theater: 10,000 in Saudi Arabia and Kuwait, with the rest stretched from Turkey to Diego Garcia. Fuel and munitions stocks were reinforced from Missouri to southern Asia. The Pentagon named the forthcoming operation "Infinite Justice."

Now granted that military codenames have been going downhill ever since "Autumn Mist," the German term for their huge surprise attack in the Battle of the Bulge; but "Infinite Justice" was going too far. It sounded more like a phrase Mullah Omar would use. Donald Rumsfeld reconsidered, and the operation's name was revised to

"Enduring Freedom." As this first American attack on an Islamic country approached, everyone was warned to stop using the word "crusade."

But the question was how to wage the war. After the 1990s the idea of using soldiers to fight had become so exotic that a new phrase had been invented to describe the phenomenon: "boots on the ground." In Bush's war councils, everyone instinctively looked to the safer option: "machines in the sky."

When Rumsfeld admitted that he still lacked a specific plan the CIA jumped in to take the initiative. The agency had retained connections in Afghanistan since the Soviet war, and since the 1998 embassy bombings had been newly funded to penetrate the territory. The agency had been covertly supporting the Northern Alliance and was familiar with its leaders. Here was an opportunity for the CIA to reclaim its pre-Vietnam glory days, like when it had toppled the government of Iran to install the Shah. According to Bob Woodward's inside look at the administration's deliberations, "Bush at War," CIA counterterrorism chief Cofer Black gave a power-point presentation to show what the agency could do. "When we're through with them," he concluded, "they will have flies walking across their eyeballs." Black estimated that once CIA paramilitary teams were on the ground the campaign would be over in weeks. Bush was sold.

The first 10-man CIA team was inserted into northern Afghanistan on September 26, followed over the next few weeks by three more. The agents brought bulging suitcases containing millions of dollars in cash.

The Pentagon's plans for a bombing campaign had meanwhile been held up by the lack of Combat Search and Rescue (CSAR) helicopters at nearby bases. A doctrine had taken root in the Air Force that operations could not get underway unless CSAR was available.

In wars such as Bosnia and Kosovo, where the United States chose to wave its hand over the water without getting its feet wet, CSAR was a superb idea. But in a case where America had just suffered 3,000 civilian casualties and needed to strike back with full force, the idea of holding back high-level, long-range bombers because there were no short-range CSAR helicopters available was open to question. CSAR personnel were among the best trained and most admired in the military; and during Vietnam, thousands of men had owed their lives to the search and rescue teams. But against an opponent with no air force and little anti-aircraft capacity, it was possible to be too cautious. During the Gulf War, after 20,000 sorties, CSAR had only rescued three airmen. In fact, one of the worst disasters occurred when while rushing to rescue an F-16 pilot, a rescue helicopter went down with the deaths of five crewmen, three others wounded and captured.

Woodward describes an interesting vignette when former infantry general Colin Powell is the only member of Bush's war council to ask, "Why do we need CSAR?" The Chairman of the Joint Chiefs, Air Force General Richard Myers, replies, "For the bombers and TAC air." Since Powell was a former Chairman of the Joint Chiefs himself, he knew good and well what the answer would be but apparently just felt like asking the question.

There had long been suspicion in the infantry that airmen tended to equate their own value with that of their expensive machines. On the other hand, there was no such thing as CSAR for a foot soldier who took a bullet in the head or was killed by mortar fire; and of course ground troops were also far more vulnerable to being captured.

In Bush's war council, Rumsfeld declared, "For this value of targets, I wouldn't go in without CSAR." According to Woodward, he meant, "To lose a pilot for these low-value fixed and mud-hut-type targets made no sense. For a really high-value target, yes." The former infantryman Powell must have seethed. An entire campaign could be held up to make sure an airman wasn't captured

Though Bush continually pressed for action, the American public displayed patience. The magnitude of 9/11 called for more than a reflexive jab or a hasty counterpunch. America was the most powerful country in the world, and in response to the most heinous surprise attack in history, the public expected to see overwhelming force. The build-up for the Gulf War had taken over five months; a few weeks of preparation for dealing with Al Qaeda and the Taliban was not a problem.

In early October the CSAR issue was solved when Uzbekistan agreed to allow the use of its bases. Pakistan's President Pervez Musharraf, deeply chagrined at the havoc his country's Taliban creation had wrought, had already allowed basing rights, and every necessary country had granted overflights. Despite entreaties from Pakistan, Mullah Omar refused to hand over Al Qaeda personnel. The UN, NATO, and nearly every country on earth stood behind America's response to the devastations of 9/11. On the 6th Bush announced, "Full warning has been given and time is running out."

ENDURING FREEDOM

On October 7, 2001, the war began with strikes by 15 land-based bombers, 25 Navy fighter bombers and 50 cruise missiles launched by American and British ships in the Arabian Sea.

The first priority was to knock out the enemy's air force, radar, and anti-aircraft installations, which in the Taliban's case was not difficult. In a country where nearly ever structure was made of mudbrick, damage assessment was a trickier task, and it appeared that many of the known military compounds had been abandoned prior to the attacks.

The first sign that the United States had not correctly calibrated its response came with news that the Air Force was dropping food on Afghanistan on the first night of the attack. It was the President's idea, but the prepackaged meals, along with bombs, appeared to send a mixed signal. While untold thousands of human body parts remained to be retrieved from the wreckage of the World Trade Center, U.S. airpower had sprung into action with nutrition. This did not exactly match the American response to Pearl Harbor, even as the 9/11 attacks had been more dastardly in every way than the Japanese attack on battleship row.

For all his cowboy rhetoric, Bush was appearing to be even shakier than Clinton in his grasp of the moral courage necessary to wage war. Imagine if Clinton had dropped food in response to the 1998 embassy bombings. What would come next—little bars of hotel soap and shampoos? As for the bombs, General Tommy Franks at CENTCOM was struggling to maintain a list of viable military targets. Bush could order the food dropped where he wished.

By mid-month, like an airborne contagion, war fever had spread both east and west of Afghanistan. In response to a deadly car bomb, Indian artillery had opened up on Pakistani lines in Kashmir. In

Palestine, after the assassination of an Israeli official, IDF aircraft were plastering the West Bank.

On the 16th the CIA sent in its second paramilitary team to hook up with the Uzbek warlord, Dostum. The military still hadn't been able to insert "boots on the ground," and that day in Bush's war council an argument erupted between Rumsfeld and the CIA. George Tenet had stressed that the CIA paramilitary teams would be subordinate to CENTCOM, led by General Tommy Franks. This was a war, not a spying operation, and the CIA only meant to provide assistance. But Rumsfeld felt that he didn't have control of the agency teams and denied his own responsibility. "You guys are in charge," he said. "You guys have the contacts. We're just following you in."

"I think what I'm hearing is FUBAR," said Richard Armitage, Powell's deputy at State. The term meant Fouled Up Beyond All Recognition. Bush indicated to Condi Rice to straighten out the confusion and she later took Rumsfeld aside. "Don," she said, "this is now a military operation and you really have to be in charge."

On the night of October 19 U.S. troops staged dual raids south of Kandahar. Special Forces A-teams broke into one of Mullah Omar's compounds, while Rangers made a low-level parachute drop to scout an airfield. The U.S. public was electrified by nightvision videotape of its soldiers in action. And it was a demonstration of exactly the sort of American capability that the enemy most feared. While the main front of the war was in the north, the U.S. had inserted troops into the Taliban's heartland in the south. It later developed that five Green Berets had been wounded by one of their own demolition blasts and a number of Rangers had been injured in the drop. In addition, a CSAR helicopter following up the operation crashed in Pakistan with the deaths of two crewmen. Discouraged by the accidents, the Pentagon refrained from launching similar operations.

More significantly, that night a Special Forces A-team was finally inserted into northern Afghanistan. After disembarking from two SpecOps helicopters loaded for bear, the Green Berets were cheerfully greeted by a CIA agent. The A-team, accompanied by an Air Force combat controller, was guided to the nearest Northern Alliance unit, providing it a direct connection to U.S. support.

In the air, the American effort in Afghanistan was beginning to look like a nearsighted version of Kosovo, with less than half the aircraft sorties but more than twice the number of accidental casualties. A UN compound was destroyed by mistake, some families were wiped out, and in one case a village was devastated with the deaths of dozens of women and children. The next day, while the villagers were holding a mass funeral, aircraft had come back and attacked them again.

The fault lay not with U.S. pilots but with the fact that Afghanistan was not a proper forum for strategic airpower. The Taliban had no industrial infrastructure, its men didn't even have uniforms, and from high in the sky every dusty compound looked the same. It was an excellent forum for tactical air, however, because Taliban fighters were manning clear front lines opposite the Northern Alliance.

Bush's dilemma was that he had agreed with Pakistan's Musharraf not to break the Taliban dam above Kabul, allowing the Northern Alliance to rush down to seize the capital. This would reignite the civil war that had devastated the country in the early 1990s. On the other hand, since Bush had decided to designate the Northern Alliance as America's "proxy" fighters after 9/11, nothing would happen unless they moved. After the death of Massoud, the main Northern Alliance forces were commanded by Muhammed Fahim, who was showing no eagerness to fight. And meanwhile, the Taliban lines above Kabul had been strengthened by thousands of reinforcements because U.S. aircraft were bombing everywhere else except at the front. After two weeks of bombing the enemy front lines had only gotten stronger.

On the evening of October 25, as recounted by Woodward, National Security Adviser Rice went to see President Bush and asked if he wanted to start looking at alternative strategies. "There is always the thought that you could use more Americans in this," she said.

Bush took umbrage at the thought, which sounded to him like "hand-wringing." He had settled on a strategy and desired to stay the course. The next morning he encountered Vice President Cheney and said, "Dick, do you have any—is there any qualms in your mind about this strategy we've developed? We've spent a lot of time on it."

Cheney answered, "No, Mr. President." Bush similarly queried the members of his war council at that day's meeting, and they all reaffirmed their confidence in the strategy: using the Northern Alliance as troops.

It can be mentioned at this point that any one American division would have outnumbered the entire Northern Alliance, while having more firepower at its disposal than the entire Taliban. One Marine MEU, in fact, could have driven from Kandahar to Mazar-i-Sharif and back without breaking a sweat. The elder President Bush's first option, the 82nd Airborne Division, sat idle for months after 9/11 as if it were obsolete, as did its Air Assault cousin, the 101st Screaming Eagles, with their 300 helicopters and thousands of light armored vehicles. While the administration tried to prod or bribe the Northern Alliance into action, U.S. troops after 9/11 would not have needed to be asked twice.

As the conflict stalled in late October, the Pentagon countered criticism in the press by revealing details of its latest munitions, the most deadly in the history of airpower. But instead of rousing admiration, to the rest of the world it began to look like a war waged by the Adams family, with Uncle Rumsfeld unveiling ever more ghastly stand-off weapons like the Predator robot drone, armed with Hellfire missiles, 15,000-pound Daisy Cutter bombs that could wipe out every living thing in half a square mile, or 5,000-pound Thermobaric bombs, which could similarly destroy with exploded gas underground chambers where soldiers and civilians might be hiding. Then there was the CIA's Thugsley, dispatching agents across the territory with bulging suitcases of cash, secretly buying off the Taliban and Northern Alliance alike. To America's many allies, this was not the sort of war remembered from 1991, when America had called for steady courage in a great confrontational battle. This was war on the sly, or from 30,000 feet up, and not even the United States was putting in troops.

Looking on, Osama bin Laden may have reflected that it was a good thing he had hit New York instead of London. The British did not possess a Predator, but Osama's days would have been numbered had British regiments, with their institutional memories of the Afghan plain, started coming after him. The American way of war seemed designed not to risk defeat, while the British, as Mrs. Thatcher had said, did not know the meaning of the word. Or as Tony Blair stated at the outset of hostilities, "This is a battle with only one outcome. Our victory, not theirs."

Depressed by its inability to get Muhammed Fahim to move, the approach of winter, the fact that strategic airpower was useless in Afghanistan, and by lack of public appreciation for its food drops, the Bush administration took care to prepare Americans for a long, hard war.

But the situation on the ground was rapidly changing. In the west, the famous Mujahideen leader Ismail Khan had returned to his old stomping grounds at Herat. Dostum had rallied his Uzbeks in the north, Khalid Khalili his Hazaras from the center of the Hindu Kush, and Mohammad Attah commanded a force of Tajiks in the northeast that was more dynamic than the forces led by Fahim. CIA teams with cash, and Special Forces teams with direct control of air support and supply had by now made contact with the warlords. These men would not have continued knocking their heads by themselves against the Taliban, but with American support they espied a path to victory.

In the last week of October, U.S. airpower switched to direct tactical strikes on Taliban positions. B-52s came in, armed with fifty 500-pound bombs apiece. And the Taliban began to collapse like a house of cards.

The first major city to fall was Mazar-i-Sharif, after Dostum's and Attah's forces—each accompanied by Green Beret advisers—had cut it off from the south and east. The breakthrough was made after a respectable amount of cash persuaded a Taliban commander and several hundred men to open a hole in the lines. The people of Mazar, who had chafed under Taliban rule, were ecstatic.

In Herat, 6,000 Taliban suddenly defected, allowing Ismail Khan to reclaim control. Taliqan in the northeast fell under similar circumstances, and then all eyes switched to the Shomali plains above Kabul, where the Taliban had maintained its most vital front. But then the front disappeared. The Taliban began to abandon the capital, as well as Jellalabad in the east, their former lifeline to Pakistan.

Bush attempted to keep his promise to Musharraf by holding back the Northern Alliance from seizing Kabul. "We will encourage our friends to head south across the Shomali Plains," he said, "but not into the city of Kabul itself." However, there was no stopping the exultant Tajik troops, who had been fighting for five years for this moment. On November 13, Northern Alliance forces entered Kabul, prudently entering the city through the Tajik quarter where they were greeted with jubilation. In fact, the whole city took on a festive mood as women threw off their burkhas and music blared in the streets for the first time in years.

In Washington it looked like the war had taken on a logic of its own. Either American airpower was more effective than anyone had thought, or the Afghans had taken over the war, using U.S. power for their own advantage. With the exception of the lamented Massoud, all the main players of the Afghan civil war were resuming their places, now calling in U.S. airstrikes anytime they wanted an opposing obstacle, or tribe, to be obliterated.

A confusing factor to U.S. observers was how the Taliban would surrender and then shake hands or wave so long to their Northern Alliance antagonists, even as USAF and Navy fighters roamed the skies looking for targets to kill.

But not all enemy fighters were so easily defeated. In the north a group of Pashtun Taliban with foreign volunteers and elements of Al Qaeda held out in the city of Kunduz. Dostum and Attah arrived to lay siege, and it was seen that when ordinary Taliban tried to surrender they were fired on by Al Qaeda diehards. U.S. aircraft plastered the enemy positions, while at night Pakistani planes slipped into Kunduz airport to bring out their nationals. At one point Dostum took over 1,000 prisoners. He separated some 400 foreigners—Arabs, Chechens, Pakistanis and others—and placed them in a huge fortress near Mazar called Qala Jangi. Kunduz finally fell on November 26, but by then a more devastating battle had broken out. The prisoners at Qala Jangi had revolted, taking over the fortress.

During the prisoner revolt, the United States suffered its first combat fatality, a CIA agent, and former Marine captain, Johnny Michael Spann. The agency normally kept its field operations out of the news, but in this case took the opportunity to gain some credit. Spann and another agent had been interviewing the prisoners, and it was their presence, in fact, that prompted the revolt. Fanatics among the prisoners had not realized they had surrendered to Americans.

Supported by U.S. Special Forces teams calling in air strikes, the Uzbeks surrounded the fort and soon drove the survivors into basements. The ground was littered with bodies. The Uzbeks poured oil into one of the basements and set it afire while positioning a tank out-

side the entrance to gun down survivors. They flooded another basement with water, and after several days a starving, bedraggled group
of 80 remaining Taliban emerged. And one turned out to be an
American: 20-year-old John Walker from California. He had converted to Islam as a teenager, gone to the Mideast to study the Koran and
found himself in a madrassa in Pakistan from where he was plucked
for jihad against the Northern Alliance.

The U.S. public exploded with its greatest outrage since 9/11 at
this Cat Stevens-like figure, as calls for his execution, or worse, rang
through the land. Of course since Walker—wounded, burned and
dehydrated—also appeared to be the only American who had fought
in the war, the anger at him may have been the result of subliminal
frustration. When handed over to the Marines he was stripped,
strapped, blindfolded, and placed in a casket-like metal box. However
a journalist was able to get through to him to ask whether, when he
had joined the Taliban, he had expected such an ordeal. Walker enfu-
riated the public even more when he replied, "It was exactly as I
expected."

President Bush, to his credit, declined to join the bloodlust against
Walker, just calling him "misguided." Bush's own kids were about the
same age, and as often occurred with the President, sometimes at dis-
concerting moments, he revealed an acute empathy for personal
frailty. Walker was subsequently sentenced to 16 years in prison,
though he had not raised a hand against American forces, and permanent exile from his homeland would have been enough.

At the end of November the 15th Marine Expeditionary Unit,
some 2,500 strong, had arrived in the country after the longest helicopter insertion in Marine history, from the carriers *Bataan* and *Pelilu*.
They set up a base called Camp Rhino on the airstrip the Rangers had
first explored, and they proceeded to dig in. By this time two-thirds of
Navy aircraft were returning with full bomb racks because they could-
n't identify targets.

It was not mysterious how the Taliban had collapsed in the north,
since there they had been surrounded by hostile ethnic groups. But it
was a bigger surprise how they fell apart in the Pashtun south, their
home territory. Before the United States could organize a Southern
Alliance, Kandahar fell to competing Pashtun tribes. Three days later

Taliban rule disappeared from the last of Afghanistan's provinces, though Mullah Omar and his top lieutenants escaped. The Marines, followed closely by the press, were still digging in.

On December 7, 200 U.S. Rangers arrived back at Fort Benning, Georgia, where they were greeted by their family members in a heart-warming scene. America's Rangers are considered the best light infantry in the world, trained in mountain, winter, and every other type of warfare. Individually, they are the elite of U.S. combat forces. The question was why they were returning home so soon.

The Taliban had only been a secondary objective of the war; the primary objective was Osama bin Laden and Al Qaeda. Regardless of the collapse of the Taliban, which had much to do with internal Afghan politics, America's primary antagonist remained Al Qaeda. Bin Laden may or may not have been surprised at the collapse of Mullah Omar's army, but his own hundreds of Al Qaeda volunteers could not be bribed, and would not surrender. U.S. Intelligence determined that bin Laden was in a mountain region called Tora Bora (Black Dust) south of Jellalabad near the Pakistan border. This was a region pocked by caves stocked with munitions that bin Laden had helped to create during the Soviet war. U.S. aircraft bombed the region but it was also necessary to send in troops.

The Americans were bribing local Afghans with money, clothing, and equipment to encourage them to serve as proxies, but this was not working out well. You can't kid a kidder, and the former Mujahideen, who had been been engaged in warfare for 20 years, had little interest in risking their lives on America's behalf. The Afghans obligingly went into the mountains and claimed many kills. They also said they were in contact with Al Qaeda, negotiating their surrender. This report turned out to be false as Al Qaeda used the time to vacate the area. When one of the former Mujahideen commanders came down from the freezing heights a reporter asked him about the whereabouts of bin Laden. The man replied, "God knows. I don't."

Rumsfeld, frustrated at the escape of the Taliban leadership and now Al Qaeda, announced on December 21 that American troops would henceforth be employed for pursuit. Five days later he changed his mind. As the lead headline in the New York Times summarized: "U.S. putting off plan to use G.I.s in Afghan Caves. Asks local forces to act. Reason given for turnabout include risks in Tora Bora and need for a big base." But the Afghans and Al Qaeda didn't have a big base, and were taking even greater risks. The U.S. offered a $25 million reward for bin Laden, but none of the tribesmen took them up on it. ($25,000 would have been better, a figure they could understand.)

The year ended with 200 Marines venturing out from Camp Rhino in the largest U.S. operation of the war. They were assigned to rummage through an abandoned Taliban compound, and then the entire MEU began to evacuate the country.

As the yellow ribbons and flags hanging outside American homes and offices turned somewhat the worse for wear during the winter of 2001–02, the country remained in denial that the bulk of U.S. forces after 9/11 had failed to engage. The Marine MEU had dug in south of Kandahar but hadn't been ordered to fight. Air Force and Navy pilots had performed magnificently, but against a country with no air or anti-aircraft capacity, their efforts had resembled a high-tempo training exercise. The U.S. military had suffered nearly 10 dead by the time Kabul fell, to accidents or friendly fire, but except for CIA agent Spann, no one had fallen to the Taliban or Al Qaeda in battle. While Hollywood accelerated its production of war movies, on subjects from the Alamo to Ia Drang to Mogadishu, the uncomfortable fact remained that America had not really avenged September 11. In Afghanistan the only victors were the Northern Alliance.

Nevertheless a great deal of print made its way into U.S. newspapers extolling America's "revolutionary" form of warfare. The belief spread that the United States was now the strongest military power in the history of the world, so powerful that its troops didn't even have to fight. All that was necessary was to apply hi-tech explosive power behind rather more wretched indigenous peoples who would take care of the more dangerous situations on the ground. Like Cassius Clay standing over the addled Sonny Liston after the phantom punch, a large segment of the American public bellowed, "We are the greatest!"

Afghanistan, of course, had just done its usual rope-a-dope when confronted with a powerful invader. Around 100 B.C., a former steppe people called the Parthians, enriched by their conquest of Mesopotamia, rode into Afghanistan to confront their poorer

Scythian cousins who had taken over the territory. There were no great battles recorded during this conquest, and it likely saw the same exchange of cash, intimidation, and tribal self-interest that marked the American effort. And of course the Parthians, like the Greeks, Arabs, Mongols, British and Soviets, could not hold sway for long in the territory. Afghanistan has never been structured to resist an invader, but it has always been structured for civil war. It is only if intruders prove unassimilable or overstay their welcome that they eventually find the place untenable.

Having no internal unity of their own, the Afghan tribes and ethnic groups first look to see what they can gain from cooperating with a new power. In the modern era it was only the Soviet invasion that compelled the Afghans to instinctively unite from the beginning and thence fight as hard and as long as they had to. And that was because they knew that the Communist system threatened Islam.

As for the Taliban, who in the view of most of the country were akin to an outside invader, it would be a mistake to think that the incredibly strict mullah regime was any more palatable to the Afghans than to any other people. A fundamentalist Pashtun movement from the countryside, it had once been greeted by a majority of the country as a cure for total anarchy. But by 2001 Afghanistan's urban population, and the 60 percent of the population that was not Pashtun, were happy to be rid of Mullah Omar's fanatics. When the strength of that fabled New World democracy, the United States, suddenly appeared after 9/11, a great number of Afghans were willing to switch sides again. Like in "The Mouse that Roared," Afghans far preferred conquest by America to rule by their country-cousin Taliban, and had every expectation of receiving billions of dollars in aid—as well as far more freedom—once they had been conquered.

For his part, bin Laden benefited from Afghanistan's fearsome reputation. In 1812, during his retreat from Russia, Napoleon's ragged remnants of the Grande Armeé had encountered the Beresina River, a seemingly impassable stream, while three separate Russian columns converged on him. Each was stronger than Napoleon's entire force; yet the Russians mysteriously held back while French engineers constructed two rickety bridges to safety. Carl von Clausewitz judged that it was only Napoleon's reputation that saved him. The Russian commanders held back because "no one wanted to be defeated by him," and Napoleon was saved by "the capital he had built up long before."

Such was the case in late 2001, when bin Laden, Mullah Omar, and most of their lieutenants escaped because of the reputation Afghanistan had earned over the centuries. The Bush administration chose not to risk a losing battle, and while hesitating to engage, allowed America's greatest enemies to escape.

After the fall of the Taliban, U.S. troops began arriving in greater numbers, somewhat giving the lie to the notion that logistics had previously prevented them. On January 4 the United States suffered its first military fatality when a Special Forces soldier was killed, and his accompanying CIA agent wounded, by quarreling Pashtun tribes around Gardez. This event was highlighted the next month when the gruesome murder of Wall Street Journal reporter Danny Pearl was revealed. The press could not resist pointing out that since 9/11 ten journalists had been killed in action in the theater, as opposed to one U.S. soldier.

The U.S. committed and lost more men in the invasion of Panama, which was triggered by the abuse of a Navy lieutenant's wife, than it did in Afghanistan, which was triggered by the slaughter of 3,000 civilians on American soil. The Bush administration had not reacted appropriately to the 9/11 attack.

In January the 101st Airborne finally arrived in the country, replacing the Marines. They immediately launched a devastating attack on a compound known to be stockpiling weapons, killing 24 men and capturing 27. However, it turned out to be a mistake. Two months earlier the villagers may have been Taliban, but now they were collecting weapons as ordered by the new, American-supported government in Kabul. The Screaming Eagles had to cool their ardor, because the situation had changed.

In March 2003 the Americans finally launched a confrontational battle, against a nest of Al Qaeda and Taliban diehards in a mountain region called Shah-i-Kot. Eight U.S. soldiers were killed in fierce fighting atop the 10,000-foot mountainsides. The Pentagon reacted with a series of claims of enemy dead. While only 250 opposing fighters were originally thought to be in the area, Pentagon casualty estimates of the enemy reached 250, then 500, 700, and topped out at 800. Journalists following up the battle, however, could find only three enemy bodies. It was as though the Pentagon had falsified numbers. It was not necessary for them to do so, because the U.S. public had swelled with pride at the bravery of its troops who had finally taken on Al Qaeda face to face. Ambushed after helicopter insertions, the American soldiers had stood their ground against buzzsaws of enemy fire, and in the end had held the field.

Oddly, Shah-i-Kot stands as the only American battle of the war in Afghanistan. By that spring of 2002 the bagpipes had nearly stopped playing at the churches around New York—for the hundreds of firemen and police lost on 9/11—and the American public had accepted President Bush's claim that they had won a great victory.

Unfortunately, the ultimate winner of the conflict was Osama bin Laden. Going where no one had gone before, he projected force into the American homeland, killing thousands of people while creating the most spectacular feat of destruction in history. As Americans rushed to declare each of their victims "heroic,"covered their streets in red-white-and-blue, and mounted the most tepid, clinical military response imaginable, bin Laden simply dodged the counterblows. At this writing, 30 months after the World Trade Center was destroyed, the world has seen more terrorist attacks than it did in the same period before 9/11. And both bin Laden and Mullah Omar have had enough time to ensure that, should either of them ever be killed or captured, their work can be carried on by new volunteers.

There was something about the American war in Afghanistan that resembled the leverage of a good financial deal, or a C student claiming triumph from mediocrity, extolling his project so well that his professors failed to realize it was a hasty effort until the period of scrutiny had passed. In Woodward's account, George W. Bush appears gleeful at the end, happy to have waged the war with little effort and even smaller cost. He had defeated the Taliban, after all. The fact that Al Qaeda was still intact seems not to have fazed him.

The American effort in Afghanistan brings to mind Churchill's tribute to RAF fighter pilots after the Battle of Britain: "Never, in the course of human history, have so many owed so much to so few." Of course Churchill was referring to living people. It is still difficult to contemplate the thousands of American dead on 9/11 imagining in their last moments that the U.S. government would not avenge them with full force, committing only a few elites, and allowing Osama bin Laden to escape.

And now the sad task is to assess Afghanistan three years later. President Hamid Karzai is still alive, having narrowly evaded one assassination attempt, and he is now guarded by U.S. Special Forces. With his writ extending little further than Kabul, he has begun to resemble Shah Shuja, who held power in the 1800s only as long as the British army was there to support him.

In the meantime, as we have listened to George W. Bush stress the imperative of extending American-style "freedom," we have seen Afghan society exercise the principle by resuming its place as the world's primary source of heroin, unbothered by government edict. The drug trade not only enriches farmers and dealers but other segments of Afghan society, including appliance dealers, the construction industry, clothing stores, and every other part of the economy, now that there is an infusion of money. The last Afghan government that tried to stamp out the drug trade was the Taliban, and one need only look to how much popular support they retained in 2001.

George W. Bush did not distinguish himself as a military leader in the Afghan conflict. But as we now know, in his "first things first" administration, he had only considered Afghanistan a waystation on the route to achieving larger goals. Al Qaeda was never his primary concern. Despite all that had come before, what the younger Bush and a number of others on his team really wanted to do was conquer Iraq.

9

THE AXIS OF EVIL

In January 2002 George W. Bush delivered his State of the Union address to a joint session of Congress. Coming after the drama in Afghanistan had all but concluded, it served as a bookend to his September speech prior to the war. Both addresses were of historic importance. However, while the first instilled the public with much-needed confidence in the face of a terrible attack, the second opened the door to future violence, this time at America's option, and as such caused new worries.

Bush singled out North Korea, Iran and Iraq as dangerous regimes, stating that they constituted an "axis of evil." "By seeking weapons of mass destruction," he said, "these regimes pose a grave and growing danger." He vowed, "I will not stand by as peril draws closer and closer. The United States of America will not permit the world's most dangerous regimes to threaten us with the world's most destructive weapons."

The public could not realize it at the time, but Bush was giving clear warning about a war he already had in mind, even providing the rationale which over the next year he repeated so often that people couldn't help but believe him. But he wasn't going to attack North Korea or Iran; they were only included for window dressing. What he intended to do was invade Iraq.

Since the speech, it has been revealed by various insiders that the Bush administration was contemplating war with Iraq from its first days in office. Deputy of Secretary Defense Paul Wolfowitz, in fact, had been recommending it since 1992. A group of neo-conservatives, including Rumsfeld, Richard Perle, William Kristol and others, under the name Project for the New American Century, had written to Clinton in 1998, advising him to "Remove Saddam from Power." In the days after 9/11, Rumsfeld and Wolfowitz even suggested hitting Iraq before Afghanistan, since it was a much easier target. Bush, supported by Colin Powell, rejected the idea, but as Bob Woodward has revealed, on November 21, 2001, Bush secretly asked Rumsfeld for a plan of attack. Former White House counterterrorism chief Richard Clarke said that on the day after 9/11 he was pressed by Bush to find a connection between Iraq and the plane hijackings. Later, Clarke walked into a meeting that he assumed would focus on Al Qaeda. "Then I realized with almost a sharp physical pain," he wrote, "that Rumsfeld and Wolfowitz were going to try to take advantage of this national tragedy to promote their agenda about Iraq. Since the beginning of the administration, indeed well before, they had been pressing for a war with Iraq."

It was no secret that the Bush administration held a great deal of animosity toward Saddam Hussein—whether personal, political, or paranoiac. Cheney seemed to be gripped by the latter, always fearing a mushroom cloud, while the pro-Israel branch of the neocons were most fervent about attacking Iraq for geopolitical reasons.

It can be left for psychologists to assess the nature of Bush's personal motivation. On the surface it would seem that he wished to take revenge against Saddam for surviving his father in office, allegedly plotting to kill him (when the elder Bush visited Kuwait in 1993), and not least for that huge picture of his father's face on the floor of the lobby of the Rashid Hotel. But it can also be considered that the Gulf War was the first president Bush's greatest triumph. It was one of the most spectacular victories in American history, not just on the battlefield but in its enhancement of America's international stature. With Bush the younger's every insistence that Saddam was a rogue, a worldwide menace, and a growing threat, the implication was that his father's great victory in the Gulf had not been a victory at all. The real triumph still waited to be achieved by the son.

Where last we left Saddam he was 66 years old, sitting with his diminished army and rickety infrastructure under no-fly zones, acquiring cash by sneaking it from the UN Oil for Food program. He hadn't tried a foreign venture since the Gulf War, and of all Arab leaders he was probably the highest on the fanatical bin Laden's assassination list. However, during the course of 2002 Bush succeeded in elevating Saddam to the status of world-straddling evildoer, so threatening that even the United States had to cower beneath his wrath. Saddam had never been able to create such a powerful image by himself.

Iraq had one primary attraction to the neocons in the Bush administration. Though they argued that the country was dangerous, the truth was that it had the virtue of being the one member of the Axis of Evil that was easy to defeat. No one in his right mind wanted to take on the North Koreans again, and that country had nothing of value anyway (even to the South Koreans). Iran was almost triple the size of Iraq and most of its territory was mountainous where U.S. armor couldn't go.

In comparison, Iraq looked like a rotten apple hanging off a tree.

So President Bush, who, unlike his father and other recent presidents, was about to have the advantage of majorities of his party in both houses of Congress, was left only with the task of convincing the American people that an invasion of Iraq was necessary. While subliminally reminding the public of 9/11 at every turn, the stress would be put on how Iraq was a dangerous new threat.

The American people, dimwitted as always about foreign cultures and history, immediately signed on to Bush's concept. Forgotten was all the talk about Muslim fanaticism, and sheikhs and mullahs who wanted to turn back the clock to the medieval period. Now the U.S. would fight the closest thing to a secular regime the Arab world possessed, one that had liberated women, pursued industry and literacy, and had made enormous efforts to try to join the modern world.

A it turned out, a large majority of the U.S. public was perfectly willing to lump Islam's fanatic "ragheads" in with any other Arab regime in sight. A radio talk show host said, "I don't want to hear about this so-called difference between Saddam and Osama. They're all the same!"

A reverse perception in American terms would be if some huge foreign power had been outraged at an atrocity committed by rural rednecks in southern Alabama, and in retribution decided to hit back at Mafia bosses in Brooklyn. To the foreign power, they were all

Americans and thus equally culpable. And the irony is that Americans, whether attacked in Coney Island or Selma, would have subsequently united in defense. This does not mean they had anything to do with each other beforehand.

Saddam was a truly vile dictator, but that wasn't reason enough to invade his country. If Bush followed that logic, next thing you know the public would be insisting he ameliorate the genocide in Sudan, or solve the terrible bloodletting in Liberia. Saddam wasn't connected to 9/11, but on the other hand Bush could say that by bringing freedom to Iraq he would be preventing Saddam from planning a 9/11 in the future. That might pass. The best idea was to point out Saddam's use of unconventional weapons in the 1980s. If the entire administration put its full force behind warning the American public of Saddam's Weapons of Mass Destruction, how could support for an invasion be denied?

It is not precisely known how the September 11 hijackers were armed, since they and all the witnesses on the planes were incinerated during the attacks. Betty Ann Ong, a gallant flight attendant, provided a running commentary to American Airlines officials from Flight 11, the second plane to hit the World Trade Center. Over a phone in the back of the plane she reported, "Someone has been stabbed in business class," and that no one could breathe there, she thought because of Mace. Aboard the planes that hit the Pentagon and crashed in Pennsylvania, passengers with cellphones reported that stabbings had occurred in the front of their planes and then all passengers had been pushed to the back. In a preliminary report the 9/11 investigative commission headed by Thomas Kean, it was estimated that the hijackers' primary weapon was "four-inch blades," either box-cutters or pocket knives.

Al Qaeda thus armed its operatives with weapons that could be found in the back pockets or handbags of at least half the pedestrians encountered on any given day in Flatbush, Brooklyn. To the degree that technical sophistication played a part, it was only in the skill of the Arab operators who had learned how to fly airliners toward specific destinations. Most of the 19 terrorists were employed for "muscle," and three out of the four teams managed to maintain control of their cockpits. Flight 93 was missing a hijacker and was nearly seized back by its passengers.

The simplicity of the attacks was shortly forgotten by the American public, which was soon whipped into a frenzy by the Bush administration over the spectre of Weapons of Mass Destruction, or WMD. As if the 9/11 attacks hadn't been damaging enough, worse scenarios began to emanate from Washington. Now that the public realized it could suffer a devastating attack, the Bush administration racheted up the fear factor.

It was obvious that America's true vulnerability had been unveiled by the fact that 19 Arabs had been so passionate about their cause that they were willing to commit collective suicide to hit us. This uncomfortable truth caused a mini-tempest in the United States, when Bill Maher, the host of a late-night talk show, had the temerity to contradict the president's claim that the hijackers were cowards. He then rubbed the salt in a bit deeper by saying that waging war by pushing buttons to launch cruise missiles was more cowardly. He was forced to humbly apologize and then his show was abruptly cancelled. It had been called "Politically Incorrect."

But of course Maher had a point. The Arabs who participated in what bin Laden termed "a martyrdom operation" were anything but timid, and it was their self-sacrifice that resulted in such damage and a cascading sense of future vulnerability. The United States was in real trouble if there were more where they came from.

The subsequent miracle was that the Bush administration managed to sidestep the issue of Islamic passion and instead shift the issue to Arab technological prowess. While the American homeland suffered its most devastating attack to a small group that was barely armed at all, the focus now shifted to Weapons of Mass Destruction, a playing field where America was king.

WHAT IS A WMD?

One would think that a B-52 loaded with 25,000 pounds of precision-guided explosives would qualify as a Weapon of Mass Destruction. Or a 15,000-pound Daisy Cutter that could burn the lungs out of everyone within half a mile. But officially, WMD are considered unconventional weapons, such as nuclear, chemical, and biological. So far the latter two have proved more effective at creating mass panic than destruction because no one is sure what they can do outside of controlled conditions.

During the campaign for war, it was commonplace to hear Bush administration officials warn of deaths in the hundreds of thousands if Saddam's WMD were ever unleashed. Just a suitcase full of anthrax, it was claimed, could kill a million people.

It probably could, if the person with the suitcase was also able to put a million people in a room, spread the contents evenly and then make everyone take a simultaneous deep breath. But that's the hard part.

During the Iran-Iraq War, the Iraqi army helped to reprise World War I by using mustard gas and nerve agents on a largely static front. This was not a sign of its technological superiority as much as a response to the fact that Ayatollah Khomeini was also reprising World War I by launching massed infantry attacks. If the Iranians had possessed sufficent motorized armor or a decent air force, chemical weapons would have been useless against them. And if the Iranians had had huge stocks of chemical weapons themselves, the Iraqis would not have introduced them into the conflict.

The same equation holds for Iraq's use of chemical weapons on the Kurds, most famously at Halabja in March 1988. In that case the Iraqis used aircraft to crisscross the city, inundating it with deadly poisonous gas. This was only possible because the Kurds didn't have their own air force or significant anti-aircraft firepower. They were a static target with no retaliatory, or even defensive, capability, and so were easy targets for poison gas. By then the Iranians had also come up with chemical weapons, but as in other respects were more ostracized by the world community than Iraq and couldn't match Saddam's technical proficiency.

The essential point about Halabja, which had just been overrun by Iranian Revolutionary Guards, as well as other Kurdish towns that were in revolt, was that Saddam used poison gas in situations where he knew the enemy couldn't fight back in kind. Using such weapons revealed his ruthlessness, but by no means indicated that Iraq had come up with a novel sort of lethality. He'd just reverted to the methods of World War I, and if he was up against an opponent such as the United States, which stockpiled 40,000 tons of the most lethal chemical weapons scientists can devise, and moreover had unsurpassed means to deliver them, with the ability to turn all of Iraq into one huge Halabja, Saddam would not have ventured to introduce his own puny chemical weapons at all. In fact, this was borne out during the Gulf War, when Saddam was suddenly faced with direct conflict with the United States. While American troops were warned of chemical weapons, Saddam prudently decided not to even try.

To step back a bit about chemical weapons, the Germans introduced them in the Great War during their defensive phase on the Western Front after 1914. The British and French replied in kind, and after the war the major powers agreed to ban them. It was not that poison gas was especially deadly; in fact, it resulted in a far greater proportion of wounded to dead than other weapons. One could survive poison gas easier than a a machine-gun bullet or high-explosive shell, while the simple act of donning a gas mask would certainly not save you from the latter. The problem with gas was that for victims who were caught unawares or unprepared, it was a disgusting way to die, viscerally repelling both attackers and defenders. Gas was also a clumsy weapon, difficult to use on the offensive, and on the defensive subject to unpredictable wind conditions. Once both sides were able to set off equal clouds of poison, gas was seen as an unwelcome advent to warfare, only increasing the barbarity of a process that was bloody enough, and which with manned weapons still had a shred of honor.

Ironically, since World War I, the most famous proponent of gas warfare has been Winston Churchill, who as Secretary for the Air and Army in 1920, said, "I do not understand this squeamishness about the use of gas. I am strongly in favor of using poison gas against uncivilized tribes." Coincidentally, he was referring to the Iraqis, who had risen in revolt after Britain took over the country from the Ottomans.

It is well known that Churchill also planned to use gas on any German invasion forces that dared to cross the English Channel in 1940, an act that would have broken the taboo in the West. Recently another memo has come to light in which Churchill advocated using gas on the Germans in Normandy in 1944. His idea was based on the fact that the Germans were committed to hold an entirely static front, and by that time the Allies held full air superiority.

His views were rejected, as the Allies decided to rely on firepower instead. But it also indicates why the Germans breathed a sigh of relief when their V-weapons finally emerged. The V-1, a predecessor to the cruise missile, began firing at England just after D-Day. In August the first V-2s, a ballistic missile designed by Werhner von Braun that was unstoppable in the air, began dropping on London. Either of these weapons could easily have been filled with nerve agents instead of conventional explosives. It was fortunate that cooler heads had prevented Churchill from introducing poison gas into WWII, because the rule was that one shouldn't introduce it without clear technological superiority. His first idea was better, in that it should only be used against natives, as Mussolini did in Ethiopia. Saddam Hussein followed this formula by using poison gas against massed Iranian infantry attacks, and also against Kurdish communities that had no means to respond. At the time Saddam was still supported by the world community, as he was the veritable front-line against the fanatic Islamic fervor of Iran.

But later, when faced with the power of the United States, supported by Britain, France, the Saudis, and having earned fairly universal approbium for his invasion of Kuwait, Saddam had the good sense to put his chemical munitions aside. His army was crushed in Kuwait, but as Saddan well knew, it would have gone a lot worse for him if he had mistaken the U.S. and its coalition for defenseless Kurds or Iranian conscripts.

BIOLOGICAL WEAPONS

Biological warfare dates back to ancient times, yet today it is considered more insidious than its chemical cousin because no one has really tried it during the technological age. Consisting of the purposeful spread of disease, biological warfare is especially sinister because a target group would not know it had been attacked until the attack was already successful, and the weapon itself would be nearly invisible.

In past centuries, bio warfare was not so subtle. Besieging armies would use catapults to fling leprosy-ridden bodies over a city's walls, or drop rotting animals into an enemy's wells. In America, Colonists would leave smallpox-infected blankets for Indians to pick up, or sometimes bodies that they knew the Indians would dig up in order to scalp. Smallpox was a scourge of the English colonies in the New World, but many had developed an immunity while the Indians had no natural defenses against Old World diseases. Through biological means (not always intentional) much of the Iroquois Confederation was depopulated before it had to be confronted in battle.

The problem with biological warfare in the modern age was how to deliver, or control, it as a weapon. This was difficult enough with gas warfare, where an ill wind might blow the poison cloud back on one's own troops. The first time the Germans used gas in WWI, a number of their own men charged triumphantly into the poisoned French trenches. Disease was even more difficult to control, and first one had to immunize one's own side, or else deliver the germs from such a stand-off position that one's troops wouldn't be affected. Either way, this meant a great margin of technological superiority.

The biggest strides in bio warfare during the 20th century were made by Japan's infamous Unit 731, operating in Manchuria during World War II. This group performed ghastly experiments on both Chinese and Western prisoners, killing thousands, and then it tried to go operational against the Chinese population. The Japanese dropped bombs filled with fleas infected by the bubonic plague, but the fleas worked better when mounted on rats, so hordes of these were let loose on the ground. In these and other attempts the results were disappointing, and other Japanese units had better success just shooting at the enemy. Unit 731 had a core strength of 3,000 personnel who worked in a vast complex in Manchuria, as well as control of 20,000 troops elsewhere in China. This is worth noting in view of later U.S. accusations that Iraq's bio warfare program was taking place in a few tractor trailers, or as they were more frighteningly termed, "mobile bio-weapons labs."

For all of Japan's insidious failed efforts, a far greater strategic effect occurred when the United States closed in to establish full air superiority over the Japanese homeland. Japan, an island nation, should have been the last to initiate bio weapons, since it was susceptible to a genocidal quarantine in response. But a B-29 Superfortress turned out to be a more effective weapon than a flea circus, and at the end the United States came up with a far better WMD of its own. Instead of expending clumsy efforts to try to make people fall sick, the U.S. had come up with an atomic bomb that, with no muss, no fuss, could wipe out entire cities in one blinding flash.

As for Unit 731, its activities caused an uproar when they became known after the war. This was mainly in the form of U.S. scientists trying to get hold of its files and top personnel. The commander of the unit, General Shiro Ishii, was flown to Washington, where in exchange for immunity he provided extensive debriefs. He eventually died of cancer back in Japan.

After the war, both the Soviets and Americans started elaborate bio-weapons programs. When smallpox was finally eradicated from world populations in 1980, the only remaining samples were in Soviet and U.S. bio-weapons labs, where scientists tried to engineer new, unstoppable variants. More importantly they tried to anticipate what the other side was coming up with in order to provide new vaccines. Fortunately, just as with chemical and nuclear technology, the two superpowers never triggered their inventions in total war.

Both biological and chemical weapons are sometimes called the poor man's nuke, in that they can be created without all the trouble and expense of building nuclear reactors, acquiring fissile material, and avoiding IAEA inspectors (not to mention Israeli F-16s). But the truth is that in warfare, like life, the rich get richer, while the poor find it difficult to compete. The key is in the delivery systems, which remain in the hands of the most sophisticated nations. And if a country has ICBMs, nuclear submarines, and inter-continental bombers, there is no reason why it needs to fool around with bio-chem weapons. To the degree these are a poor man's nuke it's because they are only useful against even poorer opponents, preferably tribesmen without aircraft, or 13-year-old Iranian infantry conscripts.

Since World War II the only serious terror attack using bio-chem weapons occurred in Japan, of all places. A religious cult called Aum Shinrikyo (think of the James Jones Kool-Aid cult except with top university graduates and unlimited funds) launched at least nine biological attacks during the mid-1990s, but they all failed. Even worse, most people didn't even know they were being attacked, though some got sick and an elderly person or two died. Switching to sarin gas, the cult did somewhat better, claiming seven deaths in one assault. The cult finally found the perfect venue in a packed Tokyo subway on a Monday morning rush hour. Five separate canisters began spitting out sarin after being poked with umbrellas, resulting in 12 dead and 5,000 injured. Eighty percent of the injuries were caused by the ensuing panic rather than the gas, and the death toll was surprisingly low. In February 2004, Chechens placed a conventional bomb in a Moscow subway, killing 39. The next month an Arab group blew up 10 trains in Madrid, killing almost 200 and wounding 1,700 more. Explosives are easier to handle, easier to deliver, have a longer shelf-life, and kill more people than gas weapons. If TNT were only now being invented it would be considered a WMD.

In the United States in the autumn of 2001, a person or group (still unknown) dispatched military-grade anthrax to various media offices and the U.S. Senate. Their delivery system was the U.S. Mail, the deadly powder sprinkled into letters. Two postal workers died, plus several others, including an old lady in Connecticut. Though it caused much alarm, the anthrax delivery system left much to be desired, and the following year the Washington sniper killed twice as many people using a rifle. The problem for the anthrax assailant was that he had made, or had access to, a potentially deadly weapon, but he needed far greater technology to get it to his victims.

In February 2003 Colin Powell dramatically held up a little vial before the UN General Assembly. He said that such a tiny amount of anthrax was enough to shut down the U.S. Senate, and he went on to say that Saddam Hussein had 8,500 liters of the stuff. This conjured up the image of Saddam and his henchmen busy licking envelopes in the mother of all mass mailings.

NUCLEAR WEAPONS

Like every other nouveau riche dictatorship in the 1970s, Iraq considered nuclear power a true status symbol, even more so if it could secretly be used to come up with an atomic bomb. Israel caught wind of Iraq's secret weapons program, however, and in June 1981 a flight of F-16s swooped in to destroy the reactor. Israel was widely lambasted for this attack, which clearly broke international law, but the criticism was muted 10 years later when the rest of the world found itself at war with Saddam.

One effect of the Israeli attack was to disperse the Iraqi effort and drive it further underground so that over the next decade no one was sure how much progress Saddam was making. Iraq had every incentive to accelerate its nuke program during those years, not because of the Jewish state but because it was locked in a total war with Iran. In 1985 the Islamic Revolutionary regime in Iran restarted the Shah's nuclear program. Thus, while Iran protested Iraq's illegal use of chemical munitions on the battlefront, the Ayatollah was trying to come up with an equally illegal nuke with which he could have finished off Saddam once and for all.

Fortunately neither side was able to produce a weapon before the conflict was called off in 1988. But after the 1991 Gulf War, when Saddam was forced to allow UN weapons inspectors on his territory, they were surprised at how close he had gotten. The inspectors immediately began dismantling his program, and a strict arms embargo coupled with oil export controls ensured that Saddam would find it extremely difficult to start it up again. If Iraq could not create a bomb during the 1980s, when it was receiving billions of dollars in Arab aid and arms and technical advice from the Soviets, Europeans and the United States in its role as the front-line state against revolutionary Iran, how was it to come up with a bomb in the 1990s when it became wretchedly poor, ostracized by the world, with UN inspectors on its ground and U.S. and British aircraft patrolling its skies?

The question also arises: if Saddam had managed to make a nuclear weapon, what could he have done with it? To have fixed it to a missile capable of reaching America would have required a leap in technology equivalent to making the bomb itself. Mounting it on an aircraft or a Scud would have provided range enough to hit Israel, but that would have resulted in the utter destruction of Iraq at the hands of Israel's own sophisticated, easily deliverable arsenal. Blackmailing weaker neighbors is often considered to be one of the prime threats of a rogue state with a nuke, but following the Gulf War, when Iraq found itself at odds with the world's sole remaining superpower and its allies, such petty regional games were no longer possible.

The only use for an Iraqi bomb would have been defensive, as a means to prevent itself from being attacked. Or in other words, the same kind of deterrence that North Korea has achieved, while the Bush administration pursued its obsession with Iraq.

The near-zero likelihood that Iraq was close to producing a nuclear weapon, as well as the even lesser possibility that it would use one, jerrymangled, untested invention to go on a rampage against the United States and its 10,000 nuclear warheads, did nothing to stop the Bush administration from spooking the American public about the prospect throughout 2002. A favorite stump phrase used by the Bush administration was, "We don't want the smokng gun to be a mushroom cloud."

Part of the fear-mongering was achieved by Bush continually describing Saddam as a "madman." Yet the CIA, among others, had been profiling Saddam for years and had determined he was rational—brutal in his own self-interest but not suicidal. His two aggressions, against Iran and Kuwait, had both been miscalculations, and in the latter case his big mistake was that he didn't think the United States would respond with force. And since that 1991 debacle he hadn't attacked anyone outside his borders.

When it comes to nuclear weapons, however, one cannot be too careful, and Saddam's 1998 expulsion of UN inspectors was cause for concern. For this reason, Bush's efforts in the Fall of 2002 to gain both Congressional and UN approval to use force if Saddam did not comply with a new inspections regime was useful. Cowed by the threat that the U.S. might attack, Saddam allowed the inspectors to return with greater intrusive power than before. Hans Blix and his team set about with great energy and eventually reported that Iraq's WMD programs, including its nuclear one, appeared to have long been dismantled. With inspectors remaining on his territory, he could not have reconstituted any of the programs.

Much to Saddam's chagrin, and to the dismay of most of the rest of the world, however, the United States attacked him anyway.

THE VALUE OF FEAR ITSELF

During the run-up to the Iraq War, an alarming note came from British

Intelligence, which reported that Iraq was capable of launching its Weapons of Mass Destruction on 45 minutes' notice.

What was this supposed to mean? That ill-paid Iraqi conscripts could suddenly grab old mustard-gas shells to put into their mortars? Even old Soviet mortars could reach up to five miles. If there were gas-filled artillery shells that hadn't yet expired they could go up to 12 miles with some accuracy. The Iraqi air force had effectively ceased to exist, and if some remnant had taken to the air it would only have caused joy to the Anglo-American fighter pilots who already covered 70 percent of Iraq in "no-fly" zones. The opportunity for a dogfight would have been welcome to those youngbloods who had trained to fight, not just overlook sand.

But then it was reported that Saddam might have UAVs—unmanned aerial vehicles—which could deliver the poison gas that was already obsolete in Western warfare since 1918. The Israeli Air Force probably would have quaked in its boots had its radar spotted a propellor-driven Iraqi drone heading their way. But after the 2003 invasion it turned out that these UAVs didn't exist, or at least that the Iraqis didn't have big enough rubber bands to fly them.

This 45-minute warning, as with every aspect of the fear mongering that led up to the invasion of Iraq, turned out to be nonsense. The Iraqis had never possessed an inter-continental missile, and had no merchant fleet to speak of on their miniscule coastline at the head of a Persian Gulf otherwise bristling with U.S. ships. It had six territorial neighbors, all of whom it had offended at one time or another. The only possible exception was Jordan, which had supported Saddam in 1991, paid a steep price for it, and was in any case now under the very attentive eye of the Israelis.

If Saddam had suddenly said, "OK men, let's man our Weapons of Mass Destruction," the worst that could have happened was a brief cloud burst along the Iraqi border, hopefully under the right wind conditions so it wouldn't blow back against the troops. And that is only assuming that Iraq still had its 1980s stockpiles.

So far we have tried to examine the WMD question from a pre-war perspective, to make the point that the hubbub was all hogwash from the beginning. But of course the invasion of Iraq is now a year old and we know the most surprising fact of all. Iraq not only failed to possess WMD that posed a threat to the United States, it didn't have any at all. Even the most doubtful observer expected that we would find some old mustard gas stocks from the Iran-Iraq War. Or perhaps some persistent pip of the former nuclear program. But it had all been destroyed years before. The smoking gun turned out to be all smoke.

For months the administration tried to claim otherwise, grasping at each barrel of fertilizer as if it were a hopeful sign of WMD. The most ridiculous convolutions came when one of the so-called mobile bio-weapons labs was found. Unlike the sleek, sporty schematic Colin Powell had held up at the UN, the vehicle turned out to be a rusty derelict. Further, inspectors determined that it was unsuitable as a bio lab and had probably been used to fill weather balloons with hydrogen. The Pentagon took this as proof of even greater perfidy, because the Iraqis may have purposely made them unsuitable for bio weapons, just so the U.S. wouldn't suspect they were really for . . . bio weapons! Unfortunately the controversy only attracted greater scrutiny of the hulks, and the final word came down that they were harmless.

The WMD story came to a close at the end of January 2004 when the CIA's chief weapons inspector, David Kay, reported to the Senate. When Hans Blix had been appointed to lead the UN team prior to the war many had complained that the erudite Swede would not be rigorous enough and that a no-nonsense U.S. straight-talker like Kay would be preferable. After the invasion Kay was indeed sent in at the head of a huge team and nine months later reported, "It turns out we were all wrong." In a considerate nod to the administration, since he had quit early after scouring only 85 percent of the country, he added the word "probably."

Much as Kay tried to shield Bush from personal blame for the fiasco, it was difficult not to recall all the scare-talk about mushroom clouds and massive poison gas attacks. This fear-mongering had come not from the CIA, but from Bush, Cheney, and the unfortunate Powell who had been shanghaied into reciting the longest list of flimsy evidence ever voiced by an American official at the UN. The administration was properly embarrassed, and the next week Bush announced the formation of a bipartisan panel to investigate U.S. Intelligence. The implication was that Bush, Cheney, Rumsfeld, Wolfowitz, Perle, Rice and others who had clamored for the invasion had simply been misled. The risk for Bush was that blaming the CIA had the potential to rouse all the analysts whose reports and cautions had been ignored during the hellbent rush to war. CIA director George Tenet appeared to have the most secure job in Washington at this time because the administration needed to keep him on the team. Fired officials tend to write brutally frank memoirs, and as additional insurance, Bush directed that the conclusions of the investigative panel be withheld until after the 2004 election.

The larger issue is how Bush the younger employed pure fear to enable a war. In 1991 his father had taken an opposite approach, calling upon American courage. The father never claimed that Pittsburgh was about to suffer a nuclear attack, even though in 1990 Iraq's WMD programs were at their apex. The father correctly pointed to the 1988 chemical attack on Halabja as evidence of Saddam's brutal nature, and prepared U.S. troops in 1990–91 accordingly. The fact that Bush the son continually said that Saddam "gassed his own people," referring to that same 1988 event in order to justify a 2003 invasion, was bizarre.

The son trafficked in fear, pumping paranoia into the population, all with the safety net that his father had provided. The first President Bush didn't know for sure if American forces could decisively prevail in 1991 but they had done so. In 2003 George W. Bush knew that the Iraqis could easily be defeated. He just had to drum up a reason to stage a new attack.

Meanwhile, almost three years after 9/11, Osama bin Laden continued to look on from his base in southern Asia, while he and his followers continued to sharpen their pocket knives.

SADDAM'S LINKS TO TERRORISM

Part of President Bush's drumbeat to war was the accusation that Saddam Hussein supported terrorists. Though intended to invoke 9/11 in the public's mind, the only evidence consisted of Saddam's financial contributions to the families of Palestinians who died fighting or as suicide bombers against the Israeli occupations of the West Bank and Gaza.

Now regardless of how one views the Israeli-Palestinian conflict, if the United States wanted to invade every Muslim country that supported the Palestinians it would have to conquer all of them, beginning with Saudi Arabia. If it wished a war with every nation that gave the Palestinians moral support, it would have to take on nearly the entire world. In fact, the relative coalitions can be quantified in advance. In October 2003 the UN General Assembly held a vote on the Israeli barrier wall that had begun snaking into the West Bank, confiscating desirable farmland and water resources while ghettoizing Palestinian villages on behalf of protecting Israeli settlements. The UN vote was 144 to 4 against the wall, which indicates that if the United States wanted to respond militarily, on one side would be 144 nations—which we can consider the world community—and on the other would be the United States, Israel, Micronesia, and the Marshall Islands. The point is that the lending of moral or other support to the Palestinians is not a good reason to attack a country, unless of course you are the Israelis.

Part of the great WMD scare of 2002 was based on the theory that even if Saddam Hussein did not openly use illicit weapons, he could slip them to terrorist groups to use against America on his behalf. This theory ignored the true nature of our September 11 assailants, in keeping with Bush's half-hearted effort in Afghanistan and his allowing the Al Qaeda leadership to escape. It was as if one's house had been blasted by a gang's drive-by shooting, but instead of pursuing the gang one simply attacked a despised neighbor down the block. In this case Saddam Hussein, with his cigar-smoking, cognac-sipping ways, felt as comfortable with the Al Qaeda gang as did George W. Bush. His reputation for ruthlessness had been earned foremost by fighting the forces of Ayatollah Khomeini and by repressing religious conservatives in his own country, a task the United States has now assumed with a semblance of the same ruthlessness.

Iraq was vulnerable precisely because Saddam followed the secular model of Stalin far more than the teachings of the prophet Muhammed, an approach which left him bereft of the type of passionate support commanded by bin Laden. That he was nearly as ostracized by fellow Arabs as much as by the West is part of the reason his regime looked so "brittle" to Wolfowitz and other U.S. planners.

Unlike some of his neocon underlings, President Bush has stopped short of claiming that Iraq had a direct involvement with 9/11. But his entire drumbeat to war was pounded with the strings of 9/11 in the background. Everytime he conjured up a grave and gathering threat to America, he subliminally invoked images of the burning Twin Towers. Without them, he could not have roused support for a pre-emptive, or more realistically, unprovoked, attack on a sovereign nation. The fact that Iraq had nothing to do with 9/11, did not have WMD, and thus Bush created the cassus belli from whole cloth, stands as something of a propaganda miracle. And it appears that no one in the administration considered that removing Saddam's tightly held dictatorship would open Iraq for the first time to elements of radical Islam, vastly increasing the type of danger we confronted on 9/11.

Then again, Orwell mentioned long ago that "ignorance is strength." The U.S. public can always say mea culpa; but let's hope that the greatest ignorance this time wasn't our president's.

NORTH KOREA

One of the bizarre things about the long build-up to the Iraq invasion was the bravado of North Korea, which had been named a member of the "Axis of Evil" in Bush's 2002 State of the Union speech, and which, unlike Iraq and Iran, fully agreed with the assessment.

While Iraq continually protested that it didn't possess Weapons of Mass Destruction, had no ill intent for America, allowed UN inspectors to crisscross its territory, and basically did everything it could except surrender in advance of the U.S. invasion, North Korea was defiant. The picture emerged of America as a huge schoolyard bully threatening to beat up a helpless kid who already cowered beneath its might. But in a corner of that schoolyard stood a very tough kid with a toothpick hanging from his mouth and a cigarette on his shoulder, daring the bully to knock it off.

While Bush accused Iraq of having WMDs in 2002, the North Koreans cheerfully informed the world that they already had them. After being named to the Axis of Evil, apparently North Korea welcomed finally being a member of some kind of group. While Bush concentrated on Iraq and sent ominous signals to Iran, North Korea further announced that it was reactivating a secret nuclear plant. Having grown bored with reprocessing plutonium, they had decided to enrich uranium, to produce even more nuclear weapons than the CIA had deduced in 1994 that they already had. The NKs also test-fired a few missiles so the West could have few doubts about their long-range delivery systems.

While retaining its focus on Iraq, the Bush administration prudently announced that it would try to renew negotiations with North Korea. In fact, when North Korea confirmed the existence of its nuclear bombs in October 2002, the administration kept the news quiet for two weeks until after Congress had ratified the use of force against Iraq.

Bush's hesitance with North Korea, as opposed to his truculence with Iraq, may seem ludicrous in retropsect, or at least hypocritical, but it was founded on good reason.

The United States had fought the North Koreans once before and did not have a good time. The experience contrasted mightily with the previous Iraq war, which resulted in an utter collapse of the Iraqi front. To be plain about it, if America was determined to attack a member of the Axis of Evil, it was far better to choose Iraq again than to instigate a rematch against the NKs.

The 1950 Korean War had begun with a huge North Korean attack on the South, which was met by a United Nations response led by the United States. Soon the odd situation arose where the UN forces had more armor and artillery than the enemy, more manpower, and complete control of the air, yet it was the North Koreans who kept the UN cooped up on the defensive in the Pusan perimeter. They were simply very tough, aggressive fighters whose tactics, running contrary to every principle taught in Western military schools, threw the Americans for a loop. While U.S. doctrine stressed the sanctity of supply lines, a continuous front, and careful regard for flanks, the North Koreans were disruptors who strived to place unsupported units in their enemy's rear areas to create havoc. In the first summer of the war, when U.S. forces fell back before multi-pronged assaults, they would be ambushed on their retreat routes with tactics that generated panic and residual fear. There were certain units in the U.S. Army, like the airborne troops, who could execute this sort of infiltration warfare, but the entire North Korean army practiced it.

The original crisis was solved by Douglas McArthur's master-stroke at Inchon. The NKs lost their logistics and cohesion and scattered back to the north. But once the Chinese came in on their side the war could not be won.

After epic retreats, and with Seoul switching hands four times during the war's first year, the United States, UN and South Korea were able to fight their way back to the center of the peninsula against the Chinese and North Koreans, who were by then fully supported by the Soviets. In 1953 the war ended as a stalemate, less 36,000 American dead.

North Korean fighting prowess is not the main lesson of the story, or at least one that was learned at the time, since the U.S. returned to Asia a dozen years later to similarly butt heads with the North Vietnamese. (By now the U.S. has no doubt learned, after the Japanese, NKs, Chinese and NVA, that fighting Asians is entirely different from fighting Arabs.) What the United States really discovered in Korea was that there is nothing in the north of that peninsula worth fighting for. It consists of barren, cold, mountainous wastes, bereft of resources and on the veritable edge of the world. The Korean War was waged primarily as a test of wills between the Western and Communist blocs that had emerged from World War II. Since North Korea bordered both China and Russia and was halfway around the world from the West, it was an enormous achievement for America, backed by its UN allies, to hold its own there.

The Korean War can be seen as a defensive victory in that the NKs were prevented from occupying the southern half of the peninsula. In 1950 this was mainly farmland but today South Korea is an industrial juggernaut, fully enmeshed in global trade and with a democratic government to boot, after a series of dictatorships finally gave way to the growth of a powerful SK middle class. If a new war were to break out, the NKs would be overrunning Hyundai factories, not rice paddies. And a dangerous thing about the North Koreans is that they still appear to have very little to lose.

Once a powerful limb of Ronald Reagan's "Evil Empire," since the collapse of the Soviet Union and the liberalization of China, North Korea has resumed its historic insignificance. It has only recently been upgraded to one of only three members of George Bush's "Axis of Evil," notwithstanding that "evil," perhaps a functional term for describing psychopathic individuals, is a ridiculous word to use in describing a nation of millions of people.

The truth is that North Korea is an anachronism in today's world, like one of those decrepit remnants of Tamerlane's empire that persisted into the 19th century, completely unaware of the how the rest of the world had evolved. Like Cuba, it's a small puddle left over from the Cold War, generating its national purpose precisely from its isolation, as totalitarian propaganda convinces its people they are under siege. Far from achieving the Communist ideal that Gorbachev, for one, decided was impractical, these states achieve a certain martial formidability through totalitarianism, while in reality relying on nationalism and leadership cults that are inseparable from the practices of ancient tribes.

With Cuba, the United States has finally gotten within sight of its traditional policy goal: "Wait for Castro to die." With North Korea, the dear leader Kim Jong Il is not so old, so the U.S. will have to think of a different solution. The very worst idea is for the United States to take an aggressive, confrontational stance against Kim, who would have difficulty justifying his draconian rule without the perception that North Korea was in danger of attack. The United States should by no means repeat its Iraq formula in North Korea. Initiating a war there would only play to the one strength that North Korea possesses: its ability to wreak havoc.

The North has nothing to defend because no one has a need for its meager resources. The United States, an ocean away, has no need to attack it. And the South Koreans, many of whom would personally love to reconnect with their cousins from the north, are wary of reunification. The West Germans had problems enough in reuniting with their East. By now the South Koreans have progressed so far ahead of the state to their north that unification would only disrupt their prosperity. Imagine the United States suddenly having to absorb the population of Mexico into its Social Security, Medicare and unemployment systems. Of all the regional powers the Bush administration has summoned to deal with North Korea—China, Japan, Russia, and South Korea—it is South Korea that is most sanguine, advising calm.

The American public, whatever its travails in Iraq, should remain grateful that the U.S. didn't go to war against North Korea. The NKs would have taken a high toll of our forces, devastated the South, perhaps used nukes for the first time since Nagasaki, and the United States would have gained nothing by occupation of their territory.

George W. Bush is on record as saying that he "despises" Kim Jong Il. Well that's all very good except that there are many millions of people involved, and an impetuous mano-on-mano is the least of the desired outcomes. The South Koreans are the best authorities on the situation, and the pecking order then runs through the Japanese, the Chinese, and the Russians. As the richest country in history, America should be able to influence the situation without rattling its sabre. But while some grim satisfaction can be found from seeing the tiny but tough state of North Korea puncture Bush's bellicosity, transforming a John Wayne president into a Jimmy Stewart chamber of commerce leader, the fact remains that North Korea's nukes are intolerable in the long-run, and they must eventually be dealt with.

To take a long view of the logic of non-proliferation, there are both political and cultural forces at work that must be considered. First, after the United States perfected the first bomb, it was incumbent on the Soviet Union to rush to invent their own. (Nature abhors a vacuum and we now realize how dangerous the world can be when one nation alone has overwhelming military power.) The British, French and Chinese were not slow to follow, the latter as much from fear of the Soviets as the West. This made all five veto-capable members of the current UN Security Council.

Thereafter India, as the second-largest nation on earth, could not be denied, which lent some urgency to Pakistan's secret program. India and Pakistan have fought three major wars since the Indian partition in 1947, but there have been no all-out clashes since nukes arrived in the sub-continent. In spring 2002, Indian and Pakistani artillery opened fire on each other's positions in Kashmir but both sides stopped short of war. Who can say that the balancing arsenals of nukes have not actually saved lives on the subcontinent?

White South Africa developed nuclear weapons in tandem with Israel in the late 1960s, but it was truly a rogue program since none of Pretoria's potential enemies had anything near its level of technology, so that the use of nukes could only have meant gigantic civilian massacres. To its enduring credit, and as a victory for the non-proliferation concept, the black government that assumed control of South Africa quickly dismantled the entire program.

Israel's nuclear arsenal, which may now be larger than that of France or Britain, is still not counterbalanced, which is why several Arab countries, even dinky ones like Libya, have had furtive programs going on for decades. None of them have succeeded, and the full strength of non-proliferation enforcement should continue to be applied. Iraq has been considered the most dangerous case, not only because Saddam Hussein imagined himself a modern-day Saladin, but because Iraq had an additional incentive to counter Iran. Under the Shah, Iran began investigating nukes in the 1970s, and after he was overthrown the mullah regime restarted the program in 1985, smack in the center of the Iran-Iraq War. Iraq had likewise begun a program, but it was set back when Israeli jets destroyed its French-built nuclear reactor in 1981. By then Saddam, while mouthing the usual aggressive platitudes against Israel, had a far larger problem with Iran, which had his army in a death-grip along a 450-mile front and which Iraqi intelligence reported was trying to construct a nuclear bomb.

Saddam redoubled his efforts during the 1980s, until in 1988 Ayatollah Khomeini finally agreed to end the conflict. There was still an imperative for Iraq to claim leadership of the Arab world, in part by obtaining a nuke, and after the Gulf War Western inspectors found that Saddam had gotten fairly close. But the program was dismantled, starved by the subsequent embargos, and it generally atrophied until by the end of the 1990s there was nothing left but a hope and a dream.

This still left Israel with a considerable arsenal of nukes in the Mideast, against potential opponents who had none. It has recently been revealed that Golda Meir contemplated using them in the Yom Kippur War, when it seemed possible that Arab tank forces might get to Tel Aviv. This would have been a disastrous precedent, accomplishing nothing but the acceleration of nuclear programs around the globe, as well as a permanent stain upon Israel. President Nixon is often criticized for putting U.S. forces on a worldwide alert during the Yom Kippur War, as perhaps an overreaction to the Soviets' threat to send paratroopers to defend Cairo. But a large part of his thinking was to get Golda's hand away from the button, assuring her that the U.S. could handle matters if worse came to worst. And as it turned out, Israeli conventional forces were able to repel the Arab attacks, and then some.

Today it is still imperative to enforce the Non-Proliferation Treaty, and place the strictest scrutiny on those nations that haven't joined it. The Arab world should draw the world's closest attention due to the religious fanaticism afoot in that region, unstable monarchies, and personality-cult politics such as practiced by Saddam Hussein. This leaves the Iranian nuclear program, which has been continuous since the mid-1980s. In December 2003, Iran agreed with the French and Russians (their main technology suppliers) to allow unfettered inspections of their plants. This move may have partly resulted from the American invasion of Iraq, by way of demonstrating to the U.S. that reasonable people can come to amicable agreement. On the other hand, the neocon wing of the Bush administration trusts neither the French nor Russians, nor the UN, to enforce Iranian compliance-- instead it is expected that the insidious Iranians, the second member of the Axis of Evil, will still be up to no good.

And indeed, even as the Iranian people maneuver on their own toward democracy, mistrust reigns foremost. When the ancient Iranian city of Bam was flattened by an earthquake in December 2003, most of the victims poor and the survivors desitute, the Iranian government hesitated to accept U.S. aid, and would take none from Israel. One really couldn't blame them given Bush's stated designs on the region, his unprovoked invasion of their neighbor, and the fact that he has called them evil.

To the degree that power corrupts judgment, we can see that nuclear proliferation is essentially a balancing game. Once the West acquired the bomb the Soviets had to; once the Soviets had them China had to hurry up; and once India snuck one in, Pakistan had to scramble together a program by any means possible. These juxtapositions (including possession by those old chums Britain and France) have had the effect of freezing total warfare between nuclear-armed powers. As it stands, nuclear bombs have been used as a lever to deter aggression, and acquired to discourage all-out war rather than initiate it.

Israel is still out on a limb for possessing nukes in a neighborhood where no one else has them. Few tears will be shed if Iran eventually developed one of its own, thus balancing the Israelis. One of the world's great civilizations and still a large nation, a "Persian bomb" would not be illogical, with its sole purpose crossing off the equation with Israel, and since the 2003 invasion and occupation of Iraq, the Americans, who often appear to act in concert with their interests.

The more egregious out-on-a-limb case is North Korea, which has developed nukes not to balance its prosperous twin in the South (which has none), or its ancient enemy Japan (which could probably come up with a huge arsenal in a weekend if it had to), but its overseas antagonist, America. Since broadcasting its nuclear achievements, North Korea has demanded face-to-face talks with the United States, instead of discussing its problems with its formidable neighbors.

This is transparently an attempt by Kim Jong Il to elevate his domestic prestige as if he were a great player on the world stage. A huge fan of American movies, Kim may be the self-dramatizing sort and desperate for attention. American policy toward North Korea should be governed by three principles:

(1) Ignore any possible threat North Korea could present to the U.S. homeland. At the same time, allow it to be clear that if Kim ever launched an aggressive attack, the United States would just calmly obliterate him and his state about 20 minutes later. This should be our only strategic view of the matter.

(2) Cut off North Korea's export of weapons technology through a confluence of both regional and international agreement. Toward this end, the United States should guide North Korea to the point where it can earn cash without furtively selling Scuds to the Mideast. Contact with the American economy, as in the case of China, has a wonderful way of relaxing tensions.

(3) Leave direct dealings with Pyongyang to its neighbors, particularly South Korea. The United States—provided its defense industry is not already intent on leveraging Pyongyang's toughness into urgency for missile shields, spaced-based defense systems, ever-more nuclear subs, or a new generation of fighter planes—should just treat Kim's wretched little state with benign neglect.

The Bush administration may continue to build up North Korea as a threat to the United States, thus justifying billions of dollars in missile defense programs and an even greater amount of domestic paranoia. But the truth is that we need to have nothing more to do with the place.

It should be remembered that North Korea is an orphan, abandoned by its Cold War parents and painfully separated from its more prosperous sibling. The United States, acting as the world's policeman, only aggravates the problem by wielding a billy club, since a capacity for violence is the only potential that North Korea still retains. The North Korean people are already imprisoned by their dictator, who is in turn imprisoned by the new international order engendered by the first president Bush after the Cold War. It's now a matter of rehabilitation, and for the more prosperous nations that surround North Korea on every side, it should be a matter of patience.

Fortunately, President Bush turned his other cheek to the truculence, impudence, and downright insults that emanated from the northern half of the Korean peninsula in 2002–03. The problem for Bush was that the North Koreans were tough, and no one in the administration or army wanted to fight them again, much less in a "pre-emptive" war. The NKs are real killers, and in those claustrophic mountain folds there would be no joyrides for mechanized forces.

North Korea's own problem is that it has nothing of value—no oil, no central geographic position, no Israel nearby—so that as fearsome as it tries to be it can just as easily be ignored.

Bush the younger had already settled on Iraq for his first pre-emptive war, and it was a much richer, more important target, its army far easier to defeat in battle. The North Koreans were left once more to stew in the pool of their geopolitical irrelevance. According to Bush's rhetoric it had seemed as if they might once again be the center of America's attention. WMD, terrorism, despotism—what more did this tough-guy U.S. president want? It turned out that Bush and the people who influenced him had wanted Iraq from the start.

10

DRUMS ALONG THE POTOMAC

Regardless of how the merits of the Iraq War are judged in the future, it will remain a serious stain on the American public that it let itself be goaded into an aggressive war under false pretences. The Bush administration's two primary rationales—Iraqi possession of Weapons of Mass Destruction and Iraqi culpability in the attacks of September 11, 2001—were false.

That said, there were other motives behind the invasion of Iraq, some stated publicly and some that lay behind the scenes. Once the Bush administration began flailing to justify the increasing casualties of the venture, moving to plans B, C, and D in the public relations battle, subsidiary rationales reached center stage. With a nod to Sergio Leone, we can divide these into three categories.

THE GOOD

Saddam Hussein was one of the most vile dictators in modern history. This opinion doesn't stem from his failed foreign aggressions, both of which were mistakes he had cause to regret, but from his brutal treatment of his own people. Modeling himself after Stalin, his ruthlessness toward political opponents and rebellious subjects was despicable from the moment he took power in 1979. After his crushing defeat at the hands of Bush the elder, when the north and south of the country revolted, his murderous repression knew no bounds. To its credit America, supported by its allies, stepped in to halt the near-genocidal attacks against the Kurds in northern Iraq. In the south, the Shiites may have fared worse, and though the U.S. and Britain eventually erected a no-fly zone in the south, this did nothing to stop the imprisonment, torture and executions of thousands of Shiites on the ground. It is still debated what the U.S. could, or should, have done to protect the Shiites who rose up against the Baathist regime in the wake of its defeat in Kuwait. The final result was that U.S. troops in 2003 were able to point out mass graves, upon which large crowds of people descended to try to identify their missing.

There is a possibility that Saddam's mass murders have been exaggerated by the current Bush administration to justify its invasion (some of the mass graves in the south may have been Iranian war dead). But a flood of reports have emerged describing torture and other inhuman excesses under Saddam's rule. His eldest son, Uday, was evidently a Bob Guccione from hell, combining brutality with sexual miscreance, to the point where Saddam named his younger son, Qusay, as his successor.

When Bush asks, as he frequently does, is the world better off without Saddam Hussein in power, the answer must be yes. However, the issue was not good enough for the president to stress as a reason for the war at the outset, and if the question had been asked: Would the American public choose to sacrifice thousands of its young men and women year after year in order to remove Saddam, the answer would surely have been no.

Saddam was a brutal dictator, but he was primarily concerned with stability in his own realm. His murderousness reached peaks during times of crisis when he was threatened by rebellion. But now the American invasion has resulted in far more dead and maimed on all sides than he would have bothered to create if he had been left alone. It is a good thing to have removed Saddam from power but it is not yet clear if the U.S. armed forces—replacing indigenous repression with rule by foreign firepower—are a proper substitute.

In Spring 2004, four American citizens were gruesomely killed by Iraqi insurgents in the city of Falluja. The U.S. Marines responded with an assault on the city, and by the end of the week hospitals were reporting over 600 dead Iraqis, most of them women and children. This action was not distinguishable from Saddam Hussein's own punitive efforts when the Shiites and Kurds used to rise against him.

THE BAD

It was suggested before the war that if the United States could effect a regime change in Iraq, the result would be a free-market democracy that would transform the rest of the Islamic Mideast through its example. Specifically, the idea was that the "Arab street," from Damascus to Tripoli, plus the Persians of Iran, would soon look to Baghdad as a model of peace, freedom and prosperity. Downtrodden people throughout Islam would thenceforth overthrow all the dictators, mullahs or autocrats who stood in their way. The region would be transformed by a tidal wave of pro-Western amity.

The first problem with this vision was that invading Christian armies wielding tremendously lethal military technology were not the best agents to achieve it. Despite the average American's conceit that Iraqis are like schoolchildren, not knowing what is best for them, the Iraqis possess both ethnic and religious pride, and even among illiterate Bedouin tribesmen there exists a sense of history. And if it looks like a foreign occupation, smells like one and hurts like one, the people now populating the land of ancient Mesopotamia are especially well qualified to recognize that it is one—and by infidels no less. America's attempt to switch from conquering Iraq to transforming it into a Jeffersonian democracy has stalled beneath showers of blood, and the danger is that most Iraqis will come to see the effort in its more starkly realistic light: subjugation.

How the Bush administration judged that democracy in the Arab world would equate with pro-American sentiment remains a mystery. It was apparently assumed that if given a chance to vote, or "freedom," as Bush terms it, the Arab masses would immediately vow their support of Israeli policies, and of an American military presence in the region that resembles nothing so much as a reprise of the Europeans' and Ottoman colonializations. American freedom manifests itself in a number of ways—not all desirable—while American power manifests itself very distinctly in the Mideast through overwhelming destructive capability. If the object has been to convert the Iraqi state to Bush's evangelical vision of human liberty, that lesson has already been lost on the Iraqi people. Saddam Hussein earned his reputation for ruthlessness largely by fighting the Ayatollah Khomeini, and then by suppressing the extremely conservative Shiites in his own southern territories. Now that the U.S. Marines and 1st Armored Division have taken over the job, along with Halliburton, we have seen that the Iraqis' idea of self-determination has little to do with Judeo-Christian social morés, or the lack thereof, but the will to defend their culture against all comers.

The conundrum is that while the sophisticated armaments of our liberal society allow us to easily defeat an Arab state, it is the very conservatism of those states that prompts them to bristle under foreign rule. As the Soviets learned in the 1980s, there is no length to which a Muslim people, however unsophisticated, won't travel in defense of Islam. And while at that time Americans cheered on the Afghan Mujahideen, calling them, of all things, "freedom fighters," now America is puzzled why Iraqis are not covering our own battle tanks with flowers.

In Vietnam it took a few years to realize we were up against an entire culture rather than just an army. In Iraq this was clear from the beginning and it was foolish to try once again to forcibly mold an ancient people to America's political and cultural will. This is the primary reason why Bush the younger's coalition was only a pale shadow of his father's, while the vast majority of world opinion has stood against it. American military dominance wasn't the question; American chutzpah in thinking that it could use its military to transform a deeply religious foreign nation was. What young man on the receiving end would submit to such naked cultural imperialism? What other nation would support America's aims except through the cold prism of their own self-interest? And through what virtue had the United States come to be an arbiter of other peoples' way of life, except for its unparalleled capacity to inflict violence?

There was a time when America was as conservative as Islam, holding just as tightly to its religious beliefs. Imagine if the Salem Colony of 1632 had been invaded and occupied by the urbanized effetes of Bourbon France. The Puritans in America would have resisted desperately, not just to protect their territory, or even their dignity, but their very souls. In Iraq we have attempted to conquer a religious culture as well as a political state, and while the latter is an easy task, the former will prove impossible. Cultures don't change as a result of foreign firepower, or at least they shouldn't. They must evolve along their own paths, which is part of what "freedom" means.

This is not to say that the United States can't or shouldn't have a positive influence on Iraq by extending peaceful political and economic contacts. The idea of setting up post-Saddam Iraq as a model Arab state in the American image, however, is not something that can be achieved by force.

The second problem with the Iraq-as-model-democracy theory is that in Bush's councils it has not been pushed by idealists such as Tom Friedman of the New York Times, who has envisioned an empowered Iraqi people able to join the global economy, but by the loose-knit cabal known as neocons. The term is short for neo-conservatives, in essence an aggressive foreign policy wing of the traditional conservative movement, and their concern with the average Iraqi's happiness is about as genuine as Dick Cheney's belief that Saddam was about to unleash an ICBM on Pittsburgh. While Bush, along with Britain's Tony Blair, have spouted heavenly phrases of all best intentions, the philosophical architects of the Iraq War—Perle, Wolfowitz, Kristol, Rumsfeld, Feith, Libby—have never been seen to have the Iraqis' best interests at heart.

They have instead looked to the U.S. military as the best vehicle to hammer down their geostrategic goal, which is to neuter Iraq and thence all of Islam. The theory has been that if ancient Mesopotamia can be remade into a larger version of Ohio, other Islamic peoples will fall into line.

As America learned in Indochina, however, domino theories are questionable. And the notion of a "free" Iraq influencing its neighbors to follow suit won't work, or at least not until the U.S. armed forces are able to kill off all the Iraqi men and women in the resistance. It has now become a question of who are the new freedom fighters—the Iraqis who resist the occupation or the U.S. Army and Marines.

THE UGLY

In June 2002 George W. Bush gave a West Point commencement address in which he unveiled a new American doctrine of pre-emptive warfare. "We must take the battle to the enemy," he said, "disrupt his plans and confront the worst threats before they emerge. In the world we have entered, the only path to safety is the path of action." Now one may have thought that capturing Osama bin Laden would be the first course of action. But Bush was now thinking of larger goals.

Interestingly enough, forty years earlier in the same forum, President Kennedy also announced a new phase of warfare, "Ancient in its origins—war by guerrillas, subversives, insurgents, assassins; war by ambush instead of by combat; by infiltration instead of aggression." He, too, recommended a new military doctrine for the United States, and his 1962 speech presaged our war in Vietnam.

A corollary to Bush's pre-emptive doctrine, revealed in the same speech, was that the United States would never allow another nation to match its power. "America has, and intends to keep, military strengths beyond challenge," he said, "thereby making the destabilizing arms races of other eras pointless."

Kaiser Wilhelm II would have blushed. It is of course the ambition of every great power to try to be the strongest in the world, and America has been no exception. But to openly state the aim reveals a new high in hubris that, aside from comprising an open invitation to Murphy's law, is offensive to every nation that prioritizes peaceful relations. And this new combination of pre-emption and pre-eminence in the hands of Bush II was, and is, frightening.

Since its first days in office the Bush administration displayed a unilateralist bent, unceremoniously demolishing the Kyoto Protocol, arbitrarily dropping the ABM Treaty, refusing to cooperate with the International Criminal Court, and resisting accords on bio-weapons and nuclear testing. It has recently defied the UN, ripped NATO asunder, and waged an unprovoked war despite the vast majority of world opinion. In less than two years the United States was able to take the heartfelt support of the entire globe and transform it into widespread fear of both our actions and motives. Bush's confidence appeared to rest on the unsurpassed power of our military, which allowed him to disdain allies, treaties and international law.

But what is the foundation upon which American military dominance stands? If the test is human resolution, the United States did not really appear all that impresive in Lebanon, Somalia, or Kosovo. During the "war that never was" in Afghanistan, the most dynamic combat leader appeared to be the Uzbek leader, Abdul Rashid Dostum. In that conflict, U.S. troops hesitated to engage until "those folks" who engineered the September 11 attacks just sauntered unscathed away from the battle.

The American military is a mighty instrument, and indeed unprecedented in terms of technology, global reach and weaponry. But there is only one type of war at which it is unsurpassed—that which calls for defeating an enemy army through obliterating firepower. When it is a test of willpower, the ability to suffer casualties year after year in a situation beyond the ability of a B-52 or a SpecOps raid to correct, America is not so pre-eminent. And now, thanks to his policy of pre-emption, George W. Bush has placed the United States—stripped of major allies, UN approval, and global moral support—in the exact kind of war in which our military holds no advantage.

There is currently a great deal of literature extolling the "Western Way of War," as if America's military strategies should all derive from the confrontational clash of the Greeks against the Persians at Marathon. But there is also a great deal of history that reveals Western armies being destroyed by Eastern forces, from the Romans at Carrhae to the Germans at Leignitz to the French at Dien Bien Phu. The best example to keep in mind is the First Crusade in the Holy Land, where the Frankish knights found that Muslim forces were unable to stand before a concentrated charge of armored cavalry. The Crusaders then tried to launch such charges at every opportunity, not realizing that the Muslims had learned the same lesson. The Muslims sought to avoid such armored charges, instead spreading out their forces in order to encircle the enemy and eventually to destroy them. When Saladin overthrew the Crusader Kingdom of Jerusalem it was by leading the knights into the desert where they suffered from thirst, lost their cohesion, and finally became easy prey.

The younger Bush's invasion of Iraq resembled a charge of armored cavalry, just as in the Crusades, with the opposing force not willing to stand against the Western onslaught of iron and steel. But rather than giving up, they had only waited for the tactical situation to switch in their favor, once the invaders were surrounded and more vulnerable. On 9/11 Osama bin Laden made a true breakthrough by demonstrating that American military might could be bypassed, and in fact rendered impotent by unconventional tactics. President Bush drew the entirely wrong lesson, and after letting bin Laden escape he launched the first armored cavalry charge that he could. Now the Iraqis, shorn of any pretensions at having a confrontational-style military, have adopted traditional Arab tactics.

Bush may still harbor dreams that Iraq, under U.S. guidance, will resume being a fount of oil wealth and that its transformation to a democratic system will cause its happy people to rise up spouting affirmations of Anglo-American and Israeli points of view. But so far Bush's leadership has resulted in more dismal consequences. The Iraqis have not accepted this latest Crusader charge, and U.S. casualties have outnumbered those in all our wars over the past 30 years put together. Al Qaeda has only been strengthened by our attempt to subjugate the cultural and geographic center of Islam, while the Pax Americana has practically been sabotaged in the attempt. For his part, George W. Bush prefers to persist, as if any self-doubt would divest him of the moral clarity upon which he based his presidency.

Much as a gunslinging cowboy might like to go it alone, there's a lot of Indians in those hills. Superior firepower is a fool's gold if the cowboy ends up all by himself and the enemy that surrounds him tracks his movements with patience. It remains to be seen which will be transformed first—George W. Bush's large-scale ambitions or the Iraqi people, who would prefer not to consider their country an outpost of a newly imperial America.

UNSPOKEN MOTIVES

In the search for the exact reason why the United States invaded Iraq, a number of theories have arisen that ignore official statements and look to other, more under-the-table factors instead. We don't wish to dwell on these at length, and for further guidance the reader can be directed to the internet, Michael Moore books or Al Jazeera for details. Nevertheless to describe them in brief the "hidden motives" school boils down to three main theories. What they have in common is a wealth of facts to justify their existence, albeit in the same way that while peering into a microscope one sees a lot of detail but tends to miss the larger view. To take them in turn:

The Israeli Connection—Right-wing Israelis and hard-line backers of Israel in the United States were enthusiastic about the Iraq war from the beginning. However humbled Saddam Hussein had become after the Gulf War, kept "in a box" by Anglo-American airpower and trade sanctions, the fact remained that Iraq was the largest and potentially strongest Arab state east of Israel. Unlike Saudi Arabia and the Gulf sheikdoms, which practiced a weird combination of medieval social morés and commercial entwinement with Western petro-dollars, Iraq still clung to the Baathist philosophy of stressing education, empowering women, encouraging native industry, and ultimately creating a formidable bloc of pan-Arab power.

The Israelis, unlike the United States, had to take seriously a potential military threat from Iraq. While America was unreachable and Saddam didn't want to provoke it anyway, Israel was just a couple hundred miles away, and during the Gulf War it had already been bombarded by Iraqi missiles. Israel had removed Egypt as a threat through diplomacy, Turkey through shared commerce, Syria and Jordan through intimidation, and the Arabian peninsula was both too wealthy and weak to opt for war. But then there was Iraq, and beyond it Iran, both many times the size of Israel and with evident ambitions to someday be great powers.

Since the Iraq War was primarily a neocon project, it is worth noting that most of the neocons are either Jewish or Christian Evangelicals who subscribe to the policies of the Israeli right wing. During the 1990s the U.S. Christian right, particularly those living in the South, suddenly made common cause with the Israeli Likud, largely for theological reasons having to do with the Second Coming and its prerequisite of the restoration of a united "kingdom of Jerusalem." It is indeed difficult to find a neocon—Jewish or not—who doesn't also support Israel's West Bank settlement program or any other manifestation of a Greater Israel. President Bush has not stood apart from this trend, and according to Prime Minister Ariel Sharon, has become the "best friend" Israel has ever had in the White House. So far this friendship has so freed Israel from U.S. opprobrium that it can not only erect its meandering barrier wall, but use American-made Apache helicopters to assassinate elderly, half-blind quadroplegics in wheel chairs without fear of criticism.

It is not certain, but a definite possibility, that the root cause of the fall of the Twin Towers on 9/11 was Israel's subjugation of the Palestinians outside its UN-sanctioned borders. Even if Palestine is not foremost on Osama bin Laden's list of grievances, the issue inflames every other Arab in the Mideast, making it possible for a fanatic like bin Laden to attract followers. Once the United States had settled its hash with Al Qaeda with every means at its disposal, it should have turned around to achieve a just peace in Palestine, capping the flames that generate nonstop resentment toward America in the Middle East. Unfortunately, the Bush administration did neither. Osama bin Laden has been left at large, now with more recruits than ever, while the Israeli military grip on the Palestinians has only tightened.

But at this point it appears that the Israelis are off the hook. Under George W. Bush, America, too, has defied the UN in order to subjugate an Arab people. And the gradual attrition of lives in Palestine now pales before the scale of bloodshed in Iraq. The next attack on American shores by bin Laden or his successors need not be blamed on the Israeli occupations of Palestinian territory. Rather than projecting our own principles, the United States has followed the Israeli example, and has thus created new hatred, writ large.

The War is Good for Business—With all the other brutal dictatorships in the world, it has raised eyebrows that America decided to bring freedom to the country that possessed the world's second largest oil reserves. That Dick Cheney's former company, Halliburton, as well as other Republican-connected firms, immediately began profiting from the war against Iraq is undeniable.

But all wars waged by capitalist societies create profits, none more so than World War II, which brought America out of the Great Depression. The Gulf War in 1991 was expressly waged for economic reasons, in accordance with the Carter Doctrine that called for defending the Persian Gulf against foreign aggression, and Bush the elder's determination not to allow Saddam Hussein to control the world's oil supply.

The Iraq War differs from the Gulf War in that it was unprovoked—in fact, initiated by America—so that any economic motives would have to do with the ambitions of U.S. individuals or corporations rather than a restoration of world stability. The military-industrial complex, of which we were warned back in 1960, has been re-energized by this new conflict, and the energy industry has opened a new vista for exploitation, even as U.S. domestic oil reserves dry up.

Nevertheless, it is impossible in these pages to countenance the notion that tens of thousands of people could be killed and wounded solely for financial profit motives, so we can best leave this topic to the million or so pages currently being written that claim otherwise.

The War is Good for Politics—The suspicion that Bush's political guru, Karl Rove, was prominent in the cheering section for the Iraq War holds water at first glance. It is possible to see time and again how George W. Bush has modeled his first term on the lessons drawn from his father's inability to earn a second. His father alienated his base by agreeing to tax compromises with the Democrats; Bush 43 responded with the biggest tax-cuts ever seen, and then again, until he had finally achieved the largest national deficit in the history of the world. The elder Bush had been perceived as "out of touch" with regular Americans; the younger Bush has become the most "regular guy" president in memory.

Most importantly, the elder Bush removed foreign policy from politics midway through his term, a fact that led to his electoral doom. For half a century, Republican presidents had been buoyed by their superior ability to face down foreign antagonists, build up U.S. strength, and if necessary wage military action. The father was a successful president while engaging in foreign policy, but then he was so successful he eliminated every reason for the public to retain him as president.

There was thus good reason for the Bush 43 White House to keep foreign policy center stage. This was initially achieved by naming the conflict begun on 9/11 "The War on Terror," according to the business theory, if you have a problem, just enlarge it. Waging war on a few hundred Al Qaeda terrorists was insufficient, because either they would be caught quickly, ending the war, or if they were not caught after a year or two the administration would look inept. Enlarging the conflict into a more vague, ongoing struggle would keep the patriotic fires burning.

Zbiginiew Bzrezinski, former Senator Bob Kerrey and others have complained about the concept War on Terror, because it means fighting a tactic rather than an enemy. Kerrey has said it's as though, after Pearl Harbor, FDR had declared war against Japanese airplanes. And since most terror doesn't take place in the United States but in Palestine, South America, Sri Lanka, Ireland and elsewhere, was America supposed to be warring against those people also?

What 9/11 presented America was a war against certain strains of radical Islam. But to define it as such would mean dealing with the political issues that motivate the radicals, such as the Israeli occupations and the Indian occupation of Kashmir. And that would probably mean sponsoring negotiations, an altogether unwarlike endeavor. It was far better in terms of public consumption to ignore specific Islamic grievances and stick to the simple claim that they hate us for our freedoms—truth, justice, and the Anglo-American way.

The remaining problem was that pitting America's vast military arsenal against scattered groups armed with pocket knives and fertilizer bombs was also insufficiently warlike. The threat had to be expanded, preferably to an opponent out in the open who still relied on a standard, conventional military establishment. Iraq was the obvious choice. Attacking Iraq would allow Bush to remain a war president while trashing a feeble opposing army. The immediate object was to build Saddam up as a threat so that the victory wouldn't look too easy. "Better to fight them over there than fight them over here," Bush said repeatedly, simultaneously enforcing the false connection between Iraq and 9/11, while conjuring up the image of Iraqi troops someday staging a D-day invasion of Jones Beach.

And if the Bush administration could justifiably be optimisitc about the military's ability to crush the Iraqi army, it was equally sanguine about what would follow. "We will in fact be greeted as liberators," said Dick Cheney, while Paul Wolfowitz estimated that within a few months a mere 30,000 U.S. gendarmes would be necessary to watch over the grateful, docile Iraqi population. And then there were the winds of democratic freedom that would start blowing across the Arab world as soon as the U.S. Army occupied Mesopotamia.

It would be far-fetched to say that the invasion of Iraq took place for purely political reasons. However, given the administration's overoptimism—or in other words, the fact that it had no idea what it was getting into—the calculation was made that, politically, a new war against Iraq wouldn't hurt. After all, the last president who defeated Saddam Hussein saw his approval ratings reach 90 percent.

All of which brings us to the final, and perhaps most crucial, factor behind the invasion of Iraq.

THE SINGULARITY OF GEORGE W. BUSH

In terms of prior experience, grasp of detail, and by all accounts, intellectual curiosity, Bush ranks low among recent chief executives. In fact, it is difficult to imagine him being president at all if he were not his father's son. But he does have other qualities, including self-confidence, decisiveness, and a highly tuned sense of moral clarity—all characteristics that amount to the "leadership" principle he cited during the 2000 campaign. In this way he is most similar to Ronald Reagan, who also practiced a hands-off leadership style. Except that Reagan knew when to cut his losses, and he did not thrust the country into huge, prolonged wars.

There are times when moral clarity without experience, or as one can call it, "simplicity," is a dangerous thing. On assuming office, Bush not only lacked a true grasp of foreign policy, he also seemed to lack a familiarity with America's own culture. As a young man he had sidestepped the turmoil of the 1960s, opting to join a jock fraternity and participate in a cheerleading squad instead. As American cultural mores fell like dominos to ever more licentiousness in movies, music and fashion, Bush donned cowboy boots and listened to country music in his small Texas town. Later in life he salved personal problems by increasing his devotion to Christianity. Deep faith is a wonderful thing, and as Jimmy Carter has demonstrated, also helps with moral clarity. But it is not a proper belief system upon which to base invasions of Islamic nations. By April 2004, Bush had been forced to abandon all the hysteria about Iraqi WMD, and at a press conference described another of his reasons for invading Iraq:

> I believe so strongly in the power of freedom. You know why
> I do? Because I've seen freedom work right here in our own

country. I also have this belief, strong belief, that freedom is not this country's gift to the world. Freedom is the Almighty's gift to every man and woman in this world. And as the greatest power on the face of the earth we have an obligation to help the spread of freedom.

So this may explain why our Black Hawks, Apaches, Predators, Spectres, Warthogs and Cobras are in Iraq. While Marines cranked up loudspeakers to blast AC/DC's "Hell's Bells" at Iraqi resistance fighters in Fallujah, 2,500 1st Armored troops waited for the order to attack the Shiite holy city of Najaf, and U.S. jail guards gaily skirted the Geneva Conventions during the nocturnal hours at Abu Ghraib prison, the question had finally been answered. We were stamping our bootprints on the Iraqi people so that they could enjoy freedom. It would be wholesome, pure, and rewarding to the wretched masses enslaved by both Saddam and Islam.

On the other hand, as Bush may or may not have heard back during the 1970s: "Freedom is just another word."

Bush's father was the last of our World War II presidents, a man whose worldview was forged during the 1940s. Bill Clinton was a thoroughly 1960s fellow, while Al Gore, with his earth shoes and self-analytical ways, would have been our first 1970s president. But the United States had somehow skipped a decade, and so backtracked slightly. In 2000 it elected its first 1950s president, a man completely uncomplicated by everything that had come after. When George W. Bush strove mightily to remake the nation of Iraq in the image of America, what he personally had in mind was Eisenhower's America.

The motive behind America's 2003 invasion of Iraq remains difficult to fathom and in all likelihood the decision was made for a combination of reasons. Paranoia, revenge, false intelligence, imperialism, oil, Israel, and politics may all have played a part. No factor appears larger, however, than the character of George W. Bush. Because he lacked a sophisticated grasp of issues, he was a pliable tool for others; because his moral clarity was unsurpassed he was eager to lead the way. In short, between the limited scope of his vision and his enthusiasm to enforce it, he has been America's own radical.

THE COUNTDOWN TO WAR

After President Bush unveiled his new policy of pre-emptive warfare in June, the summer of 2002 saw a swirl of debate.

In July, British Prime Minister Tony Blair came to Washington to convey his support for the upcoming war against Iraq before a joint session of Congress. While the public had gone along with Bush's cowboy talk and Cheney's ominous murmurs, Blair practically lifted the rafters of the Capitol with lyrical, passionate oratory. Invoking God, civilization, and the judgment of history, this former lead singer of the pop band Ugly Rumors caused the entire nation to swoon at his eloquence. And the British PM was also direct. "The ending of Saddam's regime in Iraq," he said, "must be the starting point of a new dispensation for the Middle East."

While Bush was at his ranch on vacation in August, a counterattack came in from an unexpected direction. Brent Scrowcroft published an article in the Wall Street Journal headlined, "Don't Attack Saddam." Now this set off a flurry because former National Security Adviser Scowcroft had been considered Bush the father's alter ego, even to the point that he co-wrote the former president's foreign policy memoir. So far Bush senior had been completely silent, and no one expected to him to utter a word of criticism against his son. It has since turned out that neither did his son consult his father during the run-up to the war. But here was Scowcroft saying, "An attack on Iraq at this time would seriously jeopardize, if not destroy, the global counterterrorist campaign we have undertaken."

Less than two weeks later, Dick Cheney gave a speech before the Veterans of Foreign Wars that amounted to a point-by-point rebuttal of Scowcroft's argument. The personality dynamic was interesting because during the first Bush administration Cheney had served well but had been nowhere near as close to the president as Scowcroft. Now it was Cheney alongside the president and Scowcroft who was on the sidelines.

In the Fall of 2002 the Bush administration came up with a brilliant maneuver to acquire free rein for its future actions from both the U.S. Congress and the United Nations. First it submitted a bill to the Congress to authorize the use of American armed force against Iraq in

support of UN resolutions. In early October the bill passed both houses by overwhelming majorities. Ironically, Bush's father had barely
been able to muster 51 votes in the Senate after Saddam had conducted an all-out invasion of Kuwait; now that Saddam was just sitting
there, the vote in favor of using force was 77 to 23.

In November, the Bush administration pushed Resolution 1441
through the UN Security Council, achieving a unanimous 15–0 vote.
The Resolution similarly sanctioned force if Saddam did not comply
with the will of the UN, specifically the unqualified acceptance of a
new contingent of weapons inspectors.

Little did the UN and Congress realize that no other votes would
be requested, and that regardless of how the inspections went, the
Bush administration would ride the autumn endorsements all the way
to its invasion in March 2003.

The October vote subsequently became a source of embarrassment
to Democratic candidates in the 2004 presidential race. Only Joe
Lieberman of Connecticut continued to stand unequivocally by it,
while other candidates professed to have been hoodwinked. General
Wesley Clark, a late entry into the race, inadvertently summed up the
confusion when on the first day of his campaign he said that he would
have voted for the resolution. The next day he said that he would
never have voted for war. Pundits pounced all over him but Clark had
only made the novice politician's mistake of being honest.

The vote to threaten Saddam Hussein with force if he didn't accept
new UN inspections was justified. Saddam had evicted the last team of
inspectors in 1998, and in the post 9/11 world it was important to ver-
ify that he had not restarted dangerous programs. Given the paranoia
afoot in the land, it was an acceptable idea to force him to accept new
inspections.

The other side of the coin was that Saddam did accept the inspectors, who after months of searching could not find illicit weapons. But
Bush invaded Iraq regardless, without further votes from the Congress
or UN on whether war was truly necessary.

At the end of 2003, Hillary Clinton made the round of the Sunday
morning talk shows after completing a long trip through Afghanistan
and Iraq. Not known as a warmonger, she defended her October vote
by stating that all presidents should receive full authority from the

Congress to defend the nation as they see fit. However, she too had been fooled by the fact that Iraq had turned out to have no WMD, no links to Al Qaeda, and that the October vote had resembled the Tonkin Gulf Resolution in that it disguised what was truly to come.

In the presidential race, Hillary was still only a gleam in the eye of Democratic activists, and meanwhile the remaining candidates (Lieberman aside) were perplexed at having to defend their falling for Bush's maneuver. This was primarily the result of the remarkable candidacy of Howard Dean, whose meteoric rise in the polls was matched only by the rapidity of his collapse.

Dean, an unusually plainspoken politician, said early and often that an invasion of Iraq made no sense. The surprise was that this obscure longshot candidate suddenly began to far outpace the field in the polls and campaign contributions. While the Democrats in Congress had meekly lain down before the Bush steamroller, it turned out that millions of people in the country privately agreed with Dean. Prior to this revelation, only a few idealistic stalwarts like Senator Robert Byrd had dared to oppose the president's war aims. Dean opened the lid to massive, previously unnoticed public opposition. Naturally the other major candidates stopped trying to out-patriot each other and immediately began competing for the revitalized Democratic grass roots that Dean had revealed. Eventually Dean's unscripted ways, on Iraq and other matters, did him in, and the party's nomination went to the more statesmanlike Senator John Kerry.

After the passage of Resolution 1441 in November, a new UN weapons inspection team prepared to return to Iraq. This time the inspectors were headed by the Swedish diplomat Hans Blix, and it was made clear that American Intelligence operatives were no longer in the lead. (CIA and MI6 operatives in the previous teams had only prompted Iraqi resistance.) After several weeks of training, several hundred inspectors arrived in Iraq with a mandate to be as intrusive as they wished, searching Saddam's palaces, apartments or pillow cases. The Iraqis were more cooperative than in previous years, but were still not totally compliant.

In early January 2003 Blix issued an interim report to the United Nations, in which he pointed out continued Iraqi recalcitrance. The

Bush administration perked its ears to the news that Iraq was still trying to foil UN inspectors, thus evidently continuing to conceal WMD.
The cassus belli was still on track. But in reality Blix had only fired a
shot off Saddam's bow. There were a number of reasons why the Iraqis
would instinctively resist foreign inspectors with authority to snoop
into every corner of their country. To the regime, which depended on
a perception of strength for its domestic survival, it looked much like
humiliation, as if it had already been defeated. To average Iraqis it
looked like their country had lost its sovereignty, and to the Arab
world at large, which Iraq had once hoped to lead, the intrusive
inspections combined with the Anglo-American "no-fly" zones were
too pitiful to countenance.

But Blix had correctly sensed that only he and his inspectors now
stood between peace and war. On the one hand his stern report was
meant to signal the Bush administration that he was not accepting any
guff from the Iraqis; on the other hand it was a signal to Baghdad that
they had better come clean, quickly, before America and Britain
launched a major military operation.

Saddam got the message, and during the first few months of 2003,
the UN inspectors were able to go anywhere they desired. They prioritized places recommended by the CIA and Blix later said, "We went
to sites that were given to us by U.S. intelligence and we found nothing. They said this is the best intelligence we have, and I said, if this is
the best, what is the rest?" During their months of searching, the
inspectors encountered signs of old, dismantled programs, but saw no
signs of current ones. They weren't able to find actual weapons at all.

It is a tribute to the Bush administration's PR ability that the failure of the UN inspectors to find WMD was spun so that the American
public now considered Saddam more sinister than ever. The Iraqis
were obviously masters of concealment, and given such treacherous
skill what other evils lurked behind their inscrutable visages? In addition, many Republicans had never had much respect for the UN, much
less for letting it act on behalf of American interests, so Blix's reports
were easily dismissed.

Bush's January 2003 State of the Union address was full of the
now familiar litany of ominous warnings about Iraq. Today it is best
remembered for one sentence: "The British government—has learned

that Saddam Hussein recently sought significant quantities of uranium—from Africa." It was partly the spooky way that Bush said the line, as if all that was missing was a "da-da-duh-DUH" from the James Bond movies. However, as affirmed first by former envoy to Iraq Joseph Wilson, and later the CIA and the British government, the allegation was a long-discredited falsehood, based on clumsily forged documents. A new term gained public currency—"cherrypicking"—as in, the Bush administration was apparently cherrypicking intelligence, whether it was verified or not. And aside from the usual false promises one hears, it was difficult to recall a president including a factual lie in a State of the Union speech before. Little did the public realize that the entire Iraqi WMD scare was a manufactured ruse.

Bush had secretly made his final decision for war in January. Yet those who doubted its wisdom still had a champion they could count on. It was Secretary of State Colin Powell. The public had known him for 15 years, primarily as one of the heroes of the first Bush administration. He was not a rightwinger like Cheney and Rumsfeld, nor a neocon like Wolfowitz and Feith, and unlike Rice, who seemed to interpret her job as maintaining a 24/7 mind-meld with the president, he was not in thrall to Bush. Most of all, the public sensed that the former general, a self-confessed "reluctant warrior," preferred diplomacy to bloodshed and that he could be trusted.

On February 5, 2003 Powell appeared before the UN Security Council. Calmly, convincingly, albeit with a shockingly flimsy collection of evidence, he proceeded to support George W. Bush, making the case that Iraqi WMD still existed, and thus war was necessary. He showed a satellite photo of what looked like a Pennsylvania truck stop and said it was an Iraqi chemical weapons installation. He showed a photo of some mud huts and said they were an Al Qaeda–linked poison factory. He held up an artist's drawing of a mobile bio-weapons lab. He played some scratchy tapes of Iraqis talking, at least one of which turned out to be mistranslated.

Since virtually all of Powell's evidence turned out to be false, thus severely damaging his once stellar reputation, background stories have emerged about his preparations. One has him at a CIA briefing suddenly throwing papers in the air, saying, "I'm not going to read this bull—!" Another has him picking up CIA director George Tenet at his hotel to make sure Tenet sat behind him throughout his speech at the United Nations.

Nevertheless, Powell's presentation took the wind out of the doubtful center. It was not that the evidence was convincing, but if you couldn't trust Colin Powell, then all was indeed lost.

As on previous occasions, it was the French who pricked Bush's balloon. France's Foreign Minister Dominique de Villepin earned a standing ovation at the UN the next day by rejecting Powell's evidence while recommending patience and restraint. On March 6, Bush called for a vote in the UN Security Council to sanction the war. "It's time for people to show their cards," he said. But de Villepin informed Powell that France would veto the resolution. The vote was cancelled.

Another foreign setback occurred on March 1 when the Turkish parliament voted against allowing U.S. troops to conduct operations from its territory. The Saudis had earlier refused to allow their country as a major staging ground and the U.S. had had to set up a huge new base in Qatar. The Turks' refusal caused more disruption because the 4th Infantry Division had intended to attack Iraq from their territory in the north. Thirty-six ships with the division's equipment had been waiting off the Turkish coast, and the flotilla now had to reroute through the Red Sea and thence up through the Gulf.

The American public's resentment of Turkey did not culminate in any attempt to rename the bird that Americans traditionally eat on Thanksgiving. On the other hand, due to animosity against France there was a serious movement to rename French fries "freedom fries." At least no one put major pressure on MacDonald's to rename them "Infinite Justice fries." But many restaurants and bars in America temporarily stopped serving French wine.

In Iraq, Blix's UN inspectors were looking at every place they could think of but were still coming up empty. Iraqi officials were now plainly stating that they had gotten rid of all their chemical weapons years ago. Blix was as mystified as anyone that his hundreds of inspectors couldn't even find an old mustard gas shell. Afterward he thought it was as if Saddam had put up a "Beware of Dog" sign to scare off intruders, but he didn't really have a dog.

The most pitiful sight in the last weeks before the war was of Iraqis destroying over 100 Al Samoud-2 missiles, one of the only sophisticated weapons they possessed. Iraq was not allowed to have missiles that could go farther than 90 miles (150 km), but Blix's inspectors had determined that the Samoud-2s could go about 105 miles. Iraqi scientists protested, saying that once loaded with fuel and warheads they would stay well within limits; however the inspectors insisted. The Iraqis dutifully set about destroying them. On the Tonight Show Jay Leno said, "Gee. George Bush must be the greatest military genius of all time. First he gets the enemy to destroy all their weapons—then he attacks!"

Back at the UN, France, Russia and China had all said they would veto any new resolution intended to authorize war. The United States and Britain could still try for a majority of the entire 15-member Security Council, which would at least be a moral victory. But they couldn't get that either. Not even Mexico would go along. Bush decided not to submit the resolution. Instead he traveled to the Azores, far out in the Atlantic Ocean for a huddle with Britain's Tony Blair and Prime Minister Jose María Aznar of Spain. Within a year Aznar would be voted out of office and Spain would withdraw from the coalition. In London the Leader of the House of Commons, Robin Cook, resigned from Blair's cabinet. The United States no longer had the support of NATO or the UN. Around the world, millions of people took to the streets in protest.

Bush's father had once tied the world together under American leadership in a war against Iraq. His son had just achieved the opposite, leaving America more isolated from international good will than at any time in its history.

And it was about to get worse.

11

THE IRAQ WAR

The invasion of Iraq in March 2003 came off as easily as anticipated. The biggest surprise was that the Iraqi Army caved in from the start so that it could hardly even be found on the battlefield. The fight was waged primarily against paramilitary forces, armed civilians, and ad hoc groups of soldiers fighting as guerrillas. Shortly after the invasion began, Lt. General William S. Wallace told the Washington Post, "The enemy we are fighting is a bit different from the one we wargamed against." Wallace was slapped down by the Pentagon for implying that the U.S. had not been prepared for all contingencies. And the campaign, dubbed Operation Iraqi Freedom, was indeed wrapped up within three weeks.

The 225,000 American troops in the theater had been joined by some 45,000 British, 2,000 Australians and 300 Poles, together called the Coalition of the Willing. The total force was only a third the size of the one deployed for 1991's Desert Storm, and the ground contingents—mainly 130,000 Americans and 25,000 British—were proportionately even smaller. Then again the Iraqi Army was only about a third the size it had been in 1991, and now its equipment was even more obsolete.

During the intervening 12 years American arms had ridden a technological whirlwind, computer-driven innovations arriving faster than arms designers could keep up with them. Imagine the PC one bought in 1991—a clumsy, monochrome device little better than a glorified typewriter. Then look at the device one acquires today—smaller, cheaper, with 1,000 times the memory and power. When one translates this techno-revolution to the military of the world's sole remaining superpower, we find Global Positioning Systems, instant communication between pilots, troops, commanders and the Pentagon (the digital revolution had also sponsored one in telecommunications), and a vast array of high explosives, cluster bombs, fuel-air bombs, and bunker-busters that could now be delivered precisely on target, regardless of darkness, weather, or human frailty. Computer guidance also lent itself well to America's top battle-tank, the M1-A1 Abrams, and to missiles fired from the sea.

While the United States once had to win wars by building the most machines, now it could win them by building the best ones, many with a capability beyond what generals of the previous generation had ever dreamed of.

Still sitting there with his 1970s' Soviet arsenal, or what was left of it, Saddam Hussein was looking at the 21st-century arsenal of the United States. Providing a nice cap to the Cold War, in 1991 the Iraqi army stayed still long enough to prove that U.S. arms, even then, had become far superior to the Soviets'. Now Saddam retained the same rusting, inept equipment while the U.S. had leaped forward with ever more impressive weapons. And in 2003, the Americans were about to attack him again.

Though conquering the entire nation of Iraq seemed like a more daunting task than evicting the Iraqi army from Kuwait, the upcoming campaign opened up new possibilities for American mobility and the element of surprise. Curiosity increased during the weeks preceding the attack as to what form it would take.

CENTCOM commander Tommy Franks had in fact designed a daring invasion plan. Historically, American offensives had consisted of an overwhelming build-up of force, a preliminary bombardment to soften up the enemy front, and then a massive attack. Instead, Franks' plan called for all arms to attack simultaneously, airpower providing tactical cover for the ground troops like flying artillery. The armored columns would avoid cities and opposing troop concentrations to penetrate deep into the enemy's rear areas. This would disrupt the enemy's plans and compel them to fight in all directions while the attackers retained the initiative with concentrations of force at essential spots. In other words, it was a classic German blitzkrieg attack.

There were three main prongs in the assault. On the left was the U.S. 3rd Mechanized Infantry Division (3rd ID), supported by the 101st Airborne Division (Air Assault) and part of the 82nd Airborne. In the center was the 1st Marine Expeditionary Force, some 60,000 strong, and on the right the British 1st Armoured Division, made up of the 7th Armoured Brigade (Desert Rats), an air assault brigade and a brigade of Royal Marines.

On March 17, George W. Bush went on TV and said, "Saddam Hussein and his sons must leave Iraq within 48 hours." It was a curious ultimatum, not just for the usual echo of cowboy talk, in this case, "get out of town," but because it implied that hundreds of thousands of troops were about to wage war over the presence of three people. "Their refusal to do so," Bush continued, "will result in military conflict, commenced at a time of our choosing."

THE INVASION

Fittingly enough, Operation Iraqi Freedom began with an assassination attempt. On the afternoon of March 19, 2003 the CIA received word that Saddam Hussein would be meeting later that night with his sons, Uday and Qusay, in a house on the outskirts of Baghdad. The offensive wasn't scheduled until two days later but Bush took the chance to get Saddam with one blow. Two F-117A Stealth fighters were quickly readied and launched toward the target, arriving at 5:30 in the morning Baghdad time (9:30 in the evening, March 19 in Washington). Each Nighthawk delivered a pair of 2,000-pound bombs, and Tomahawk cruise missiles soared in from ships in the Persian Gulf to make sure. For weeks it was thought that Saddam or his sons might have been killed, and at this point it is still unclear who the unlucky victims were.

The main offensive had to be rushed ahead of schedule due to the assassination try, but by the next afternoon the troops were ready to go. The attack was preceded by U.S. Special Forces, SEALs, and British SAS slipping into Iraq to set up observations posts and to secure the southern oil fields. During the 1991 war the worst damage Saddam had been able to achieve was by creating a gigantic oil spill in the Gulf, and by setting fire to hundreds of wells in the disputed

Rumailah oil field that straddled the border between Iraq and Kuwait. This time coalition commandos prevented the demolition of all but a few wells.

It later developed that Anglo-American aircraft had been paving the way for the attack for months in Iraq's southern "no-fly" zone. Pilots had always had permission to destroy Iraqi anti-aircraft installations if they were fired upon, incidents which generally inflamed the U.S. public as examples of Iraqi perfidy. But since the Fall of 2002, under the cover of these routine clashes, U.S. aircraft had been methodically clearing out essential Iraqi radar or AA sites to prepare for the invasion. This went far toward allowing Franks to dispense with a preliminary bombardment in his plan.

On March 20 the main offensive crashed across the Iraq-Kuwait border, meeting little opposition. The 3rd Infantry, with 270 Abrams tanks and 200 Bradley fighting vehicles, and the Marines, with their own amphibious APCs as well as tanks, sped deep into Iraq. The British headed for the city of Basra, 50 miles due north of Kuwait.

The next night, as per the original schedule, Baghdad was plastered by a gigantic storm of explosives. Bombs from 700 aircraft combined with the power of 600 cruise missiles to bury the city under volcanos of flame. The Bush administration termed the spectacle "Shock and Awe."

When the British arrived at Basra, a city of over a million, they set up a cordon on the outskirts rather than go charging in. As opposed to pre-war predictions, the southern Shiites had failed to greet the invaders as liberators and the British chose to let tempers cool before occupying the city's center.

After three days the 3rd ID, charging through the desert west of the Euphrates, had gotten half the distance to Baghdad. Marine spearheads had crossed the river at Nasiriyah but had encountered surprisingly fierce resistance around the bridges. It did not come from organized Iraqi army units, as expected, but from civilian fighters in the city itself. So far so good. But that weekend, the invasion started to turn ragged.

On Sunday, March 23, the tents of a headquarters bivouac of the 101st Airborne was attacked at the cost of two officers killed and 14 wounded. The assailant had been one of the 101st's own men, a convert to Islam named Asan Akbar. He had thrown grenades into the tents and then opened fire when the officers rushed out.

That night the 11th Attack Helicopter Regiment launched 32 Apaches against the Republican Guard Medina Division. Upon arriving over the target, the airmen saw the electricity grid on the ground click off for a couple seconds, then come back on. It turned out that the Iraqis had traced the helicopters since they had taken off from their refueling depot in the desert. When the lights clicked, a torrent of weapons fire rose from the ground. It was an ambush, and every Apache in the formation was sieved by bullets. One went down, its two pilots captured, and only seven were still operational the next day.

In Nasiriyah, the Marines were assailed by counterattacks, suffering 18 dead and about 50 wounded. They were able to maintain a grip on their essential bridges, but the rest of the city was a free-fire zone. Late that night the 507th Maintenance Company, a rear echelon support unit, tired and far behind schedule, came rolling in looking for a route north. They took a wrong turn, then another, and found themselves alone in the center of the city.

Suddenly they were attacked from all sides, automatic weapons fire and rocket-propelled grenades ripping apart their vehicles. Some troopers fought back while others found their M-16s were jammed with sand. While the convoy desperately tried to race out of the death-trap, a cargo truck hit a wall after being riddled with fire, and a Humvee crashed into it from behind. Iraqis overran the position, killing 11 soldiers and capturing six more. Among the captured was an attractive, 20-year-old private from West Virginia, Jessica Lynch. She had joined the Army prior to fulfilling her true ambition—to be a kindergarten teacher—and had been badly injured in the Humvee crash.

The invasion's spearheads were still charging along, sharing none of the problems of their support units, when beginning on March 24 they, too, encountered unexpected opposition. It was a giant sandstorm that stopped the entire offensive in its tracks. It looked like a truly dangerous moment as U.S. tanks and aircraft alike were blinded. But Iraqi infantry had an even more difficult time in the storm and were unable to take advantage. The 3rd ID, which was now near the holy city of Najaf, was able to beat off a series of attacks.

In northern Iraq the 173rd Airborne Brigade had flown in along with Special Forces teams to join hands with the Kurds. Since 1991 the United States had helped the Kurds maintain an autonomous region in the north, and though somewhat warily, the Kurds welcomed the invasion to remove Saddam.

After the dramatic first few days, the invasion smoothed out into an inexorable flow of armor churning across the desert, preceded by aircraft bombing every target they could find in advance. So far the largest surprise had been the fierce resistance encountered in the Shiite south, where the Americans had expected to be greeted as liberators. Some of the resistance had come from fighters called Saddam Fedayeen, a group led by Saddam's son, Uday. But much of the resistance was plainly instinctive, from the civilian population.

Another surprise was the apparent disappearance of the official Iraqi Army. As the Marines and the 3rd ID closed in on the capital resistance grew ever weaker. "Where are all Iraq's soldiers hiding?" was the title of an article written by the eminent military historian John Keegan for London's Daily Telegraph newspaper. "One of the most mysterious aspects of this highly mysterious war," he wrote, "is the absence of casualties. . . . There is endless television footage of M-1 Abrams tanks and Bradley infantry fighting vehicles driving up the long empty roads of central Iraq, but they never fire their guns."

It was not as though the Iraqis were surrendering. In 1991 Coalition forces had taken 80,000 prisoners in four days. This time, after two weeks there were about 4,000 prisoners. It was as if the Iraqi Army, like Iraqi WMD, did not really exist. After the war it was revealed that U.S. Psychological Operations had been active prior to the offensive, sending faxes to enemy commanders, or even calling them on the phone to advise them not to resist the invasion. There is also the possibility that as much cash changed hands during Operation Iraqi Freedom as in Operation Enduring Freedom, when much of Afghanistan's Taliban was paid to defect.

In the meantime, between hundreds of reporter embeds and non-stop video coverage, the American public got to see its own army in action for the first time. The troops were impressive, extremely well disciplined, and the destructive power they wielded was immense. U.S. forces tried to avoid collateral damage to civilians; however when civilians found themselves in the line of fire the result was devastating.

In contrast to the Gulf War, this one was taking place in a populated region, and the public also saw the people of Iraq for the first time. The little kids were cute and the girls all seemed to wear pretty dresses. The boys wore shirts and slacks. Despite all the talk of Iraq being hopelessly stuck in the medieval period, they looked like American kids in Kansas, circa 1937. An exception was found in a New York Times photo that showed kids lined up along a wall to receive candy from an American soldier. A little toddler on the end was wearing a Batman t-shirt.

On April 1, Special Forces staged a helicopter raid to rescue Jessica Lynch from a hospital in Nasiriyah. Like a reality show, the exploit thrilled the public, until word came out that her doctor had tried to hand her over the previous day but had been turned back at a U.S. checkpoint. There were no enemy fighters at the hospital, and they could have just picked her up in a cab. While the Pentagon leaked stories about how the private had gallantly fought to the last, emptying her M-16 and finally being stabbed in hand-to-hand fighting with the enemy, it was left to Jessica to explain that she had simply been injured in the vehicle crash. While America's affection for Ms. Lynch will ever remain undaunted, the true question that arose was: How well had the Pentagon learned to control public perception through the media?

All eyes were now on Baghdad as the culminating battle of the war approached. Despite fierce fighting by paramilitary forces and civilians, the Iraqi Army had yet to appear in force. It was thought that Saddam's Republican Guard was preparing a final gotterdämmerung in the capital, which was now smoldering from within and ringed from without by smoke from trenches filled with burning oil.

Lead elements of the 3rd Infantry pulled into Saddam International Airport on the west side of the city on April 4. The next day the division's 2nd Brigade conducted what it called a "Thunder Run" into the city, blasting its way through the streets and back out again. Iraqi opposition was intense, but it still consisted of ad hoc groups with small arms.

The Marines had meanwhile arrived on the east side of the city where they forced their way over a bridge. They had encountered a suicide car bomber several days earlier, and had taken to shooting approaching vehicles without being overly careful. A dozen Iraqi civilians trying to escape across the bridge were gunned down by jittery Marines. The fleeing civilians were more jittery, and when one's car is hit by bullets it appeared that one's first instinct is to drive faster.

On April 7 the 3rd ID made another Thunder Run, this time seizing the presidential palace in the center of Baghdad. The Marines came in to link with the Army troops, while the firefights that had flared around the city began to cool down. The Air Force tried to assassinate Saddam and his sons again, based on a new CIA tip. This time a huge B-1 bomber was diverted to smash a restaurant with 8,000 pounds of bombs. The strike was accurate, while whoever the casualties were remain unknown.

Contrary to expectations, the Iraqi Army hadn't fought for Baghdad either. It had more or less disintegrated. On April 9, a crowd of liberated Iraqis gathered around a giant statue of Saddam Hussein in Baghdad's Firdos Square. It was a modest crowd, consisting of about 150 military-age men; however TV close-ups made it look like a sizeable enough throng. In the White House President Bush watched transfixed as they proceeded to try to tear down the statue.

One of the young men climbed up to tie a thick rope around the statue's neck. After this painstaking procedure it turned out the rope was too short for anybody to pull on it. Then a beefy Iraqi came up with a sledgehammer and started hammering in the statue's base. But once he got past the facade there was something harder underneath and he couldn't make a dent. Finally a U.S. Marine engineering vehicle pulled over to the statue and a corporal from Brooklyn named Edward Chin climbed up to wrap a heavy chain around the neck. The Marines had previously been ordered not to raise American flags over captured ground because the invasion was supposed to be a liberation, not a conquest. But now Chin pulled out a U.S. flag and draped it over the face of Saddam's statue. There must have been groans in the White House. In a worse mistake, Chin placed the flag upside down.

The Marine vehicle gunned its engine and pulled Saddam's statue off its pedestal, creating an iconic image that made it to the cover of every newsmagazine in America. In truth, the entire scene could not have been more symbolic.

Operation Iraqi Freedom concluded with 138 American and 33 British dead. At least 2,100 Iraqi civilians had died while the number of Iraqi military casualties remains anyone's guess. From over 36,000 aircraft sorties the Coalition lost two planes, with one pilot rescued by CSAR. In addition, a British Tornado was accidentally destroyed by a Patriot missile battery. In terms of speed, forces employed, and forces lost, it looked like a more impressive performance than the Gulf War. The only question that remained was whether, like the previous conflict, this one had been a genuine victory.

On the first day of their liberation the Iraqi people celebrated with the most relentless orgy of nonstop looting in history. They ransacked stores, government buildings, banks, oil refineries, power plants, office buildings and factories. American soldiers were too few to stop the rampage, but they did place a guard in front of the Oil Ministry. They forgot about the National Museum, which contained hundreds of thousands of Mesopotamian artifacts from the dawn of civilization. By the time the mob was through the Americans might as well have hit it with a B-52.

Mixed with the looters were criminals, because Saddam had emptied his prisons prior to the invasion, and saboteurs, who intentionally tried to shut down the oil industry and public works. Baghdad, Basra and other cities lost electricity, thus their water supply and sewage systems. Among the other things the Americans forgot to guard were arms depots, and Iraqis descended on these for small arms, RPGs and explosive munitions.

Operation Iraqi Freedom's war plan had worked well, as it played to the U.S. military's strengths. But the Pentagon had also been made responsible for the postwar, and there it had false assumptions rather than a realistic plan. 150,000 ground troops had proven more than sufficient to vanquish Saddam's army, especially since it had not shown up to fight. But the troop level was not enough to provide order to a nation of 25 million people suddenly enjoying the freedom of anarchy.

The looting had to die down sooner or later, once there was nothing left to cart away. And fighting all but ended in the last half of April. Saddam and his sons had gotten away, but by now Americans were accustomed to seeing their primary antagonists escaping.

On May 1 President George W. Bush donned an Air Force flight suit and boarded an S-3B Viking jet to make a dramatic landing on the returning aircraft carrier Abraham Lincoln. Stretched behind him was a huge banner that read "Mission Accomplished." The carrier had been held up for a day so that the photo-op could be staged, and when Bush landed the craft was pointed out to sea so that the cameras wouldn't show the San Diego skyline in the background. After claiming that the banner was the sailors' idea, the administration later admitted, to no one's surprise, that it had been the work of the White House press office. By now an Orwellian scent had spread so far across the land that very little could come as a surprise.

In his speech aboard the Abraham Lincoln, Bush said, "We've removed an ally of Al Qaeda," and that "No terrorist network will gain weapons of mass destruction from the Iraqi regime because the regime is no more." During this triumphant moment after the successful invasion of Iraq, Bush could hardly be expected to suddenly drop the erroneous rationales that had led America into an unnecessary war. But the biggest falsehood was inscribed in the giant letters on the banner that loomed behind him: "Mission Accomplished."

THE OCCUPATION

The casualties began immediately after Bush had taken off his flight suit. A U.S. soldier was shot in the head in Baghdad by a stealthy assailant who then slipped away in the crowd. Mortar fire hit U.S. compounds, and ambushes were sprung on convoys. The Rashid Hotel was hit by rockets concealed in everything from pick-up trucks to donkey carts. The most common form of attack was by Improvised Explosive Devices (IEDs), or homemade landmines. These weapons could be pressure-detonated or set off by remote control. When consisting of several artillery shells strung together, the blasts could knock out a tank; but it was the U.S. Army's lighter vehicle, the Humvee, which was most often seen burning in Iraqi streets.

Along with Saddam Hussein's army, the U.S. invasion had also eliminated his police force, so that murder and rape increased multifold. Without electricity and water during the searing days of summer, those Iraqis who had welcomed the fall of Saddam began to turn against the American occupation. The richest country in the world seemed more concerned with repairing oil pipelines than the sewage system. And there was no law in the cities at all.

The first U.S. administrator in Iraq, former Lt. General Jay M. Garner, had done an excellent job organizing the Kurdish region in 1991 but appeared overwhelmed by his new task. The Pentagon had not anticipated the post-invasion challenge, and Garner took the fall for its lack of planning. He was replaced by L. Paul Bremer III, a dynamic career diplomat and troubleshooter. However, Bremer reinforced the original mistaken ideas by disbanding the Iraqi army—thus creating 300,000 angry, unemployed young men—and banning former Baathists, which stripped the country of professional and government expertise. There were too few U.S. troops to keep order, while their own first priority was "force protection."

Bremer organized an Iraqi Governing Council of 25 members, though he failed to give it any power. The only time the Council put its foot down was when the Bush administration arranged for 10,000 Turkish troops to arrive as an occupying force. Iraq had been ruled by the Turks for 300 years and the Council adamantly refused to allow them to return. The Kurds, in particular, must have wondered whether America knew what it was doing in Iraq.

The Bush administration's efforts to find other major countries to help with the occupation came to naught as India, among others, refused to contribute troops until the venture was sanctioned by the UN. Instead the Coalition of the Willing grew through minor contingents from Eastern Europe, Latin America, and some tiny island nations. After much discussion Japan was finally persuaded to send a contingent; on the other hand, Britain started quietly withdrawing the majority of its forces. This did not stop Tony Blair from flying across the pond every few months to continue to lend the White House his enchanting moral support.

The Pentagon had expected that after the invasion it would find a happy population and a functioning, oil-rich society. Instead, the Iraqis were more physically miserable than ever before. Saddam's economic infrastructure turned out to be held together with gum and strings, and the looting had caused it to utterly collapse. As the Americans—suffering some 550 dead and wounded in the first 10 weeks of occupation—tried to figure out who was trying to kill them, the Iraqis became increasingly disgruntled about their liberation. As if to illustrate the surreal nature of the war, the Pentagon had drawn up playing cards with the faces of Baathist leaders on them. It was like the Americans were playing a game. And then, at the very height of the sweltering summer, the U.S. had a success.

On July 22 Saddam Hussein's sons, Uday and Qusay, along with a bodyguard and Qusay's son, were discovered in a house in Mosul. They had been betrayed by the owner of the premises, who earned a $30 million bounty for the tip. U.S. Special Forces and 101st Airborne soldiers cordoned off the neighborhood and then cautiously entered the house. A fusillade of automatic weapons fire burst from the second floor and three soldiers were wounded, the rest retreating.

For the next two hours the U.S. troops, supported by an OH-58D Kiowa helicopter, blasted the house, and then tried to enter again. They met more fire and another soldier was wounded. Finally they ripped the place apart with a salvo of anti-tank missiles and made another entrance. Of the house's occupants, only Qusay's 14-year-old son, Mustafa, was still standing, and after getting off a last burst from his AK-47 he was gunned down by the Special Forces.

Overall, the brothers' Butch and Sundance ending was slightly uncomfortable for the Bush administration, which had spent so much time describing them as evil. In order to convince the Iraqi people that Uday and Qusay were really dead, doctors performed plastic surgery on the corpses to repair distorting wounds, gave them shaves and haircuts, and then the bodies were shown on TV.

The battle also raised questions about the nature of the Iraqi resistance. Until that point the Pentagon had been describing the insurgents as Baathist diehards intent on resurrecting Saddam's regime. But if this was true, finding the brothers living together in Mosul made no sense. If the resistance was being orchestrated by remnants of Saddam's regime, Qusay, who had commanded the Republican Guard, and Uday, who had commanded the Saddam Fedayeen, would not have let themselves be caught together in an ethnically mixed, northern city. And if the resistance wasn't Baathist, what was it?

On August 7 the Jordanian Embassy in Baghdad was blown up by a car bomb. Jordan had secretly cooperated with the U.S. invasion by letting its territory be used as a Special Forces staging ground. In a far worse attack on August 19, the United Nations headquarters was demolished by a suicide truck bomb. Among the dead was the UN's special representative to Iraq, Sergio Vieira de Mello, a talented, accomplished diplomat. The truck had aimed for a spot just below his office. The UN, which the United States had ignored prior to the invasion, had arrived to help with humanitarian issues and, if allowed to by Bush's Pentagon, political ones. Now Secretary General Kofi Annan pulled remaining UN personnel out of the country. At the end of the month still another car bomb exploded in the holy city of Najaf, killing, along with over 100 others, the most prominent Shiite cleric who had cooperated with the Americans.

Saddam Hussein had always built his strength on conventional armed forces, and he had never been the type of dictator people would commit suicide for. This new rash of terrorist attacks on large political targets was more along the lines of radical Islam. President Bush had been warned prior to the war that overthrowing Saddam's tightly held Baathist regime would only create a new environment for radical Islamic violence. Bush responded to the new suicide attacks by calling Iraq a front line in the War on Terror—and indeed, it was he who had made it such.

Going into the autumn of 2003, American forces were still suffering a slow drip of casualties, almost like a one-a-day prescription. In the six months following Bush's "Mission Accomplished" speech, 222 soldiers had been killed, mostly by the ubiquitous IEDs that sprinkled the convoy routes. And then the violence suddenly escalated.

BLOODY NOVEMBER

To improve morale, the U.S. Army had begun a leave program to allow troops to take two weeks off to visit their families. This resulted in a flurry of movement between bases and airfields. On November 2 a large CH-47 Chinook helicopter ferrying troops going on leave was shot out of the sky near Fallujah, west of Baghdad. The missile hit near the back rotor causing the Chinook to explode, and then it exploded again when it hit the ground. Sixteen soldiers died and 21 were wounded. Judging from the wreckage it was a miracle that anyone had survived.

A few days later a Black Hawk helicopter was shot down outside Tikrit with the deaths of six U.S. soldiers. And then on the 15th, near Mosul, two Black Hawks collided in the air and crashed to the ground killing 19 soldiers of the 101st Airborne. It appeared that one helicopter had been hit by an Iraqi missile, lost control, and veered into the second, causing both to crash. U.S. pilots quickly changed their tactics, either staying at high altitudes outside of missile range or speeding low to the ground so assailants would not have time to fire.

And the violence turned international. On the 12th a car bomb exploded at an Italian-run compound in Nasiriyah, killing 19 Italian soldiers and nine Iraqi policemen. A week later, seven Spanish intelligence agents were ambushed south of Baghdad. Their vehicles were hit by RPGs and rifle fire, and a triumphant crowd dragged out the bodies to display them on the street. According to Iraqis on the scene, they thought they had killed a group of CIA agents. That day, two Japanese diplomats were ambushed and killed in Tikrit. On the 19th, the British Consulate and a British bank were blown up by truck bombs in Istanbul, Turkey, killing 27 and injuring nearly 500.

Smelling blood, resistance fighters in the Sunni areas increased their efforts. Attacks and ambushes increased from an average of 15 a day to as many as 50. It was becoming clear that U.S. armed forces had been placed in the one situation in which they did not excel—on the defensive in the midst of a hostile population. America's tremendous firepower was useless when the enemy was invisible, moved in small groups, and blended in with the civilian population.

General John Abizaid, who had replaced Tommy Franks as commander of CENTCOM, and Lt. General Ricardo Sanchez, who led U.S. forces in Iraq, came up with Operation Iron Hammer, in which U.S. airpower and artillery kicked back into action. Heavy ordnance and rocket firing helicopters blasted buildings suspected of being insurgent hideouts. In one action, an A-10 Warthog bombed two mortar sites atop a two-story building. Now one might ask: what is a mortar site—a place from which someone had once fired a mortar? This could probably be as easily done from the rubble of the building once the insurgents returned. Like other actions during the campaign, Iron Hammer seemed to be conducted for the benefit of the U.S. public rather than from any source of tactical logic. And to the degree that indiscimrinate firepower killed civilians, demolishing their homes and businesses, it only assisted the resistance.

On the last day of November, as the U.S. public braced for a summary of what had been the costliest month of the Iraq venture—with 82 American dead, even worse than the invasion months of March and April—the U.S. military announced a triumph. In the town of Samarra north of Baghdad, troops of the 4th Infantry Division had foiled an ambush and slain no fewer than 54 Iraqi attackers without suffering a scratch in return.

So it appeared that the Iraqis, who for months had been ambushing or blowing up Americans at no cost to themselves, had either decided to revert to Napoleonic tactics, marching in lockstep toward U.S. machine-gun fire, or had decided to imitate Japanese Banzai assaults. Skeptical journalists made appointments at Samarran morgues and hospitals, and could find only eight bodies, including an elderly man and a woman who had been shot on her way home from work.

Earlier in Operation Iraqi Freedom, General Tommy Franks had said, "We don't do body counts." But evidently when the Pentagon needed to create a headline, it proved to be flexible.

WASHINGTON, DC

By early December President Bush was showing signs of frustration that the neocon agenda to which he had subscribed was leading him nowhere. An early indication came when a reporter asked Bush if the U.S. had found any evidence of links between Saddam Hussein and Al Qaeda. "No," he replied, "we have found no evidence."

The bluntness of his answer was breathtaking. The entire war had been launched on the premise—stated or unmistakably implied—that it was a response to 9/11. "It's better to fight the terrorists over there than over here" was the most constant refrain. The whole WMD issue only made sense if it was connected with further assaults on America such as 9/11.

Bush's response was all the more surprising since he could have easily evaded the question. Just a week earlier Vice President Cheney had fielded a similar question on Meet the Press by answering with ominous profundity, "We don't know."

By just saying "no," Bush was hardly attempting to give the lie to two years of his own rhetoric (and press attention was indeed muted); instead he was firing a warning shot at his neocon advisers, up to and including Cheney. There was something in the impatient frankness of his response that seemed to say, "No, we have not found evidence yet—but there had darn well better be some."

Bush's statement was immediately followed by a document known as the Feith Memo, in which leading neocon Douglas Feith, the number three man at the Pentagon, listed 50 separate pieces of evidence connecting Saddam Hussein's Iraq with Al Qaeda. The memo produced a huge ho-hum as the incidents cited were speculative, unsubstantiated or already proven untrue. Feith most earnestly tried to resurrect the story that the lead hijacker in the September 11 attacks, Mohammed Atta, had once met with an Iraqi intelligence officer in Prague.

Though the rumor had already been repudiated by both Czech and U.S. intelligence, at the root of the Atta-in-Prague scenario was a commonsense truth: that Al Qaeda's 9/11 operations depended on absolute secrecy. The 19 hijackers had to simultaneously penetrate every layer of U.S. security, from the CIA and NSA through the FBI, Customs and local law enforcement to airport security. The idea that Al Qaeda would have brought an entire national government into the plot—especially a secular, defection-ridden regime such as Saddam's, which was no doubt already penetrated by the CIA, MI6 and Mossad—was beyond belief. This is entirely apart from the fact that bin Laden considered Saddam a socialist apostate.

Few in the government or public were willing to rally to Feith's new list of outdated events or quasi-facts. The exception, of course, was that part of the neocon press that jumped to annoint Douglas Feith the world's new arbiter of truth.

After November ended as the bloodiest month in Iraq yet with no end in sight, Bush decided to switch gears. On December 5 he announced that James Baker III would return to the government to act as his new special envoy to seek international cooperation on Iraq.

As secretary of state in the first Bush administration, Baker had engineered the grand coalition for the Gulf War in 1991. His new role was to coordinate the handling of Iraq's debt between concerned nations, including the ones that George W. Bush had recently estranged. But that official role fooled no one. Bush hadn't brought back his father's foreign policy vizier to act as a croupier. Instead it was the clearest sign yet that the President had become displeased with the neocons. It appeared, in fact, as if grown-ups were returning to the White House.

The neocon countermove arrived with amazing speed. On that same day Deputy Secretary of Defense Paul Wolfowitz signed a directive stipulating that $18.6 billion of reconstruction money the U.S. had set aside for Iraq would only be available to contractors in countries that had taken part in the invasion coalition. Notably excluded from this list was Canada, France, Germany, Belgium, Russia, China and India.

Thus, not only could the United States appear aggressive and unilateral to the rest of the world, it was now determined to seem vindictive and petty. And just as Jim Baker was packing his bags to visit Paris, Berlin, Moscow and other capitals, Wolfowitz had pre-empted him by cutting those countries off from participation in Iraq's reconstruction.

Perhaps the most embarrassing thing about Wolfowitz's directive was the part where he expressed his belief that withholding contracts from nations would provide an incentive for them to join the coalition. In other words, this conflict was not to be a case of "blood for oil." It was to be "blood for construction work."

Bush was reportedly displeased that Wolfowitz's directive became known just as he was scheduled to call the leaders of France, Germany and Russia on the phone, not to mention that it chopped Baker at the knees just as he was about to visit them in person. Nevertheless, on the following day Bush stood up for Wolfowitz's decision at a press conference.

What I'm saying is . . . the U.S. people, the taxpayers, understand why it makes sense for countries that risked lives to participate in the contracts in Iraq. It's very simple. Our people risked their lives, friendly coalition folks risked their lives, and therefore the contracting is going to reflect that.

The President's mistake was in assuming that the American people cared whether huge U.S. construction firms profited from the invasion of Iraq. On the contrary, the prospect of seeing firms such as Halliburton and Bechtel quickly start profiting from the war was one of the public's greatest fears. It didn't help that Halliburton, which Dick Cheney had run before becoming vice president, was found to be price-gouging gasoline and overcharging for meals it provided to soldiers in Iraq.

As for James Baker, he traveled to the foreign capitals and performed his mission. And then he returned to private life.

SADDAM

On December 13, American forces found Saddam Hussein. He was hiding in a hole in the ground near his hometown of Tikrit. His capture set off a wave of jubilation in the United States, not least in Washington. In Baghdad, Paul Bremer appeared before an audience of military personnel and simply said, "We got him!" The cable news channels in the U.S. began 24/7 coverage.

It was left to the maverick Democratic presidential candidate, Howard Dean, to mention that the capture of Saddam didn't make the United States any safer. Like a skunk at the garden party, Dean was hounded, criticized and shunned for his remark—described by most pundits as a "gaffe"—but as in several other cases he was perfectly correct.

Saddam had not attacked the United States; in fact, it was quite the reverse. He didn't even have the Weapons of Mass Desetruction that the administration had claimed. So after America had invaded his country, killed thousands of people, and opened up Iraq as a newly chaotic playing field for Arab nationalism and radical Islam, it was unclear how finding the 67-year-old former dictator hiding by himself in a hole made America any safer.

One result of Saddam's capture was that the United States could finally no longer demonize Iraqi insurgents by connecting them to the dictator. In fact, for many Iraqis inclined to resist the U.S. occupation, Saddam's capture came as good news. The Shiites, in particular, had no wish to ally themselves with Saddam or his Baathist party. But now the issue had become far larger than the figure of Saddam Hussein. It was no longer a Baathist fight—it was an Arab one.

In an extremely ill-advised move, the United States managed to sully its capture of Saddam by broadcasting a scene of the former dictator being manhandled by a U.S. Army dentist. At first this was interesting to see; however, once it had been shown millions of times on the air, veritably every time the dictator's name was mentioned, it served to degrade the captors as much as the prisoner. Most of the world did not have direct contact with Saddam's brutality and did not share the visceral hatred that he seemed to provoke in George Bush. All they saw was the abusive manner in which the United States treated a conquered Arab leader.

Hopefully the American decision to humiliate Saddam in captivity will not rebound to its detriment. Should bin Laden ever be captured, however, the U.S. would do well to keep the tongue depressors out of it. The difference between Saddam and bin Laden is that while the former spent his life trying to increase his own power, the latter gave up riches and comfort in order to fight for a puritan strain of Islam. Whereas the Iraqi dictator gained minions through intimidation, bin Laden commands genuine loyalty, however misguided, throughout the Middle East. Humiliating a captured Saddam was dangerous, but publicly abusing a captured bin Laden would be deadly, gaining the United States nothing at all.

3/11

Contrary to the Bush administration's hopes, attacks by Iraqi insurgents did not decrease after the capture of Saddam, and U.S. forces suffered another 87 dead through January. The only silver lining was that while the U.S. conducted its largest transfer of troops since World War II—replacing units while flying in others—the insurgents were not able to hit a large transport plane, though not for lack of trying at Baghdad Airport and elsewhere.

The worst setback came when suicide bombers blew up the Erbil headquarters of both Kurdish political parties simultaneously. Hundreds were killed and wounded, including a number of Kurdish leaders. As usual, it could not be determined who was responsible for the attacks, but their large scale with multiple targets were reminiscent of Al Qaeda. The world's most dangerous terrorist organization had not been present in Iraq prior to the invasion, but signs were increasing that it may well have arrived.

February saw only 20 American deaths, the lowest monthly total yet. The reason was that U.S. troops had cut down on patrols, withdrawing to their bases in an attempt at benign neglect. Another factor was that as part of Rumsfeld's program to pare the military by outsourcing functions, as many as 20,000 private contractors had arrived in the country to take over convoy duties and provide security. Even Paul Bremer was guarded by private security guards. By the spring of 2004 about 100 of these had been killed by insurgents, including 33 of those hired by Halliburton.

On March 11, 2004, precisely 30 months after 9/11, ten trains were blown up simultaneously in Madrid, killing nearly 200 and wounding about 1,700 people. The government of José Anzar attempted to blame the attack on Spain's own Basque separatists, even as evidence pointed to an Arab group based in Morocco. In elections three days later the Spanish threw Anzar out of office. The new prime minister announced that Spain was withdrawing from the Coalition of the Willing, of which it had been a founding member. As 1,400 Spanish troops prepared to leave Iraq, Honduras and the Dominican Republic followed suit with a combined 700 of their own. The prime minister of Poland, which had been another original member of the Coalition, said, "We cannot turn a blind eye to the fact that Spain and others are leaving Iraq."

Just as the American public had previously seethed at France and Germany, it now ridiculed Spain for being weak-kneed in the face of terrorist attacks. However, a large majority of the Spanish public had been opposed to involvement in Iraq to begin with, as was the case with most other members of the Coalition. In fact, according to Zogby and other polls, it was unclear if there was a single country on earth whose public approved of America's action in Iraq, except Israel, the U.S. itself, and, on every other day, Britain.

In Iraq, America's circling-the-wagons policy had not worked out as the insurgents only seemed to be getting bolder. By now, new units had been acclimated, and the Army and Marines resumed their aggressive patrols. The result was 52 dead U.S. soldiers and several hundred more wounded, making March the second worst month of the occupation. President Bush appeared on TV and restated his determination to "stay the course."

UPRISING

April 9, 2004 marked the first anniversary of the toppling of Saddam Hussein's statue in Firdos Square. And now Iraq was aflame with explosions and gunfire as native militias seized back cities and the occupying U.S. army rushed to counterattack like a Paul Bunyan stomping out a forest fire. The Americans' worst nightmare had arrived: Shiites had joined the rebellion.

Two events precipitated the uprising. On March 28, U.S. soldiers in Bagdhad shut down and padlocked a weekly Shiite newspaper called Al Hawza. The Coalition Authority had accused it of printing incendiary rumors, such as that a bomb that killed 50 Iraqi police recruits in February had really been an American missile. Al Hawza also happened to be the organ for Moqtada al-Sadr , an ambitious 31-year-old cleric who commanded a militia called the Mahdi Army. Sadr's father, for whom Bagdhad's Sadr City section was named, had been a respected Ayatollah until 1999 when he and his two eldest sons were killed on orders from Saddam Hussein. Moqtada had since come to epitomize the phenomenon the United States encountered in Iraq, that no matter how much the people appreciated the downfall of Saddam, their greater wish was for the Americans to leave.

Thousands of people gathered to watch U.S. soldiers put padlocks on the doors of their newspaper. Most Shiites had been inclined to wait for the elections the Americans had promised, after which they, as a majority, would finally be able to assume power. But now they saw the true nature of democracy under American occupation. Urged on by Moqtada, the Mahdi Army gathered its weapons.

The second event occurred three days later in the Sunni stronghold of Fallujah. Reportedly with the help of Iraqi civil defense forces, insurgents set an ambush for a group of American private security guards. These men, all former Special Forces soldiers, worked for a firm called Blackwater USA. In the minutes before the attack the insurgents cleared the streets of other traffic, and when the Americans arrived in SUV's they opened fire, shooting four men. A crowd gathered and set fire to the SUV's, possibly with one man still alive inside. Then they dragged out the burnt corpses to kick and dismember them, and strung up two of the mutilated bodes from a nearby bridge.

The American public woke up the next morning to the ghastly sight as recorded by Arab videocameras on the scene. Thoughts immediately raced back to Mogadishu, Somalia, where a crowd had dragged a U.S. soldier through the streets. Then, as now, it was not so much the losses, or even the barbaric mutilation, but the expressions on the faces in the crowd—they showed pure joy. For months Paul Bremer and his spokesmen had described the resistance as Baathist diehards or foreign fighters, together comprising only a tiny minority. But here were hundreds of Iraqis, many of them teenagers, dancing in the streets while blackened American corpses swung in the wind. We thought we had been coming to liberate this people—to bring them freedom. Did they really hate us this much?

On the following Sunday, a week after the closing of his newspaper, Moqtada al-Sadr launched his Shiite forces in a coordinated offensive. Eight U.S. soldiers were killed in Baghdad and the revolt spread south to Kufa, Najaf, and as far east as British-held Amarah. The insurgents overran Iraqi police stations, only recently set up and equipped by the Coalition Authority. The newly recruited policemen either joined the rebellion or deserted to their homes. The shiny, blue and white civil defense vehicles provided by the Americans were now being driven by Moqtada's men. And the Mahdi Army, once estimated to number 3,000 fighters, had turned out to be much larger. In some Shiite areas it appeared that every man was a secret member. Jeffrey Gettleman of the New York Times described how Baghdad's Khadamiya bazaar erupted in frency when news arrived that U.S. soldiers had torn down a poster of Sadr's revered father. "Shopkeepers reached beneath stacks of sandals for Kalashnikov rifles," he wrote. "Boys wrapped their faces in black cloth. Men raced through the streets, kicking over crates and setting up barriers. Some handed out grenades. Within minutes this entire Shiite neighborhood in central Baghdad had mobilized for war."

Not to be outdone, on April 6, Sunni fighters in Ramadi staged a coordinated ambush on a Humvee convoy, killing 12 Marines and wounding two dozen more. That day the Marines launched an offensive into Fallujah dubbed Operation Iron Resolve, in response to the prior week's mutilation of security personnel. A battalion of the newly formed Iraqi defense force refused U.S. orders to participate. After three days of house-to-houe fighting, the Marines controlled a quarter of the city and then suspended their operation in order to open talks with the defenders. By that time hospitals in Fallujah reported 600 dead and at least 1,200 wounded, most of them women and children who had fallen to U.S. fire. A fuel convoy heading for Fallujah from Baghdad was ambushed by Iraqis on the highway with the loss of nine Americans, one of whom later escaped captivity.

In the south, the surprise Shiite uprising forced Ukrainian soldiers out of Kut, while a nearby Bulgarian contingent called for American assistance. Shiite fighters seized a number of hostages, including three Japanese nationals who were threatened with death unless Japan withdrew its forces from Iraq. They were later released without harm, while some 40 other foreign hostages were seized around the country.

Ayatollah Ali al-Sistani, the most revered Shiite leader in Iraq, had been considered a moderate, willing to wait for the Shiite majority to gain power through the ballot box rather than bloodshed. Now that Moqtada al-Sadr had chosen violence, Sistani still recommended calm and negotiation, but pointedly failed to condemn the uprising. It is possible he would have lost his influence had he tried to stand in the way of the rebellion.

The Sunnis and Shiites appeared to feed off each other's success, and Shiite fighters were reported slipping into Sunni Fallujah to help defend that city against the U.S. Marines. In Basra in the far south, men from both sects began attending prayers together. General Sanchez, the Coalition military commander, said, "The danger is we believe there is a linkage that may be occurring at the very lowest levels between the Sunni and the Shia. We have to work very hard," he said, "to ensure that it remains at the tactical level."

For a year the United States had struggled with an insurgency centered in the Sunni triangle north and west of Baghdad. This was diffi-cult enough; however the Sunnis comprised only 20 percent of the population, and the greater fear was that the Shiites, who comprise 60 percent, would join the fight against the occupation. In the first week of April 2004, it happened. Or, as British Foreign Secretary Jack Straw told the BBC, "The lid of the pressure cooker has come off."

Oddly, it was at this juncture that Tom Friedman, one of America's leading Mideast experts, headlined his column in the New York Times, "Are there any Iraqis in Iraq?" He posed the question: "Is there a critical mass ready to identify themselves—not as Shiites, Kurds and Sunnis—but as Iraqis, who are ready to fight for the chance of self-determination for the Iraqi people as a whole?"

Apparently the answer was yes. Just as the Mujahideen of Afghan-istan had laid aside their ethnic and tribal differences to resist the Soviet invasion, disparate groups in Iraq had finally found a common cause. It was to drive the Americans from their country.

President Bush pinned his hopes on a "transfer of sovereignty" to Iraqi leaders scheduled to take place on June 30, 2004. With the coun-try wracked by ever-increasing violence, the concept involved in trans-ferring sovereignty was not exactly clear. The U.S. had already stated that its troops would remain in Iraq after the transfer. The new gov-ernment would neither control its own military nor have the ability to pass legislation. Rumsfeld had said that America would never accept a theocratic regime. In an April interview from the safety of the "Green Zone," the heavily fortified U.S. headquarters in Baghdad, Paul Bremer was asked to whom America was planning to hand over sovereignty. "That's a good question," he said. On May 17, Izzedin Salim, the president of the Iraqi Governing Council, America's previ-ous puppet government creation, was killed by a suicide bomber while waiting to enter that Green Zone.

STRANGER THAN TRUTH

April 2004 concluded with the United States suffering more losses in a month of occupation than during the army's entire drive from Kuwait to Baghdad the previous year. On the last day of the month the Marines began to withdraw from Fallujah, abruptly dropping their demand that the city's resistance fighters hand over their arms. Instead the Marines decided to rely on a force of Iraqis led by one of Saddam Hussein's former generals. Though criticized by American hawks, this decision was wise in that the Marines' only other option was to "destroy the city in order to save it," one of those old Vietnam dilemmas that the Bush administration was now anxious to avoid.

The 1st Armored unwisely persisted in its attacks against Moqtada al-Sadr in the holy cities of Karbala and Najaf, at the great risk of further inflaming the Shiite population. In fact the Shrine of Imam Ali, one of the most precious mosques in Islam, was damaged during the fighting. It also appeared that the U.S. Army had returned to the body-count business, as each day's briefing, conducted by Brigadier General Mark Kimmit, contained news of up to 30 fighters in the Mahdi Army killed in action. These reports of deaths among the Shiite militia, though they could not be independently verified, were presumably intended to bring cheer to the U.S. public.

That public had become sorely in need of good news because by the first anniversary of Bush's "Mission Accomplished" speech the airwaves had become flooded with photos of American troops sadistically abusing Iraqi captives. The scenes from Abu Ghraib prison, which need not be described here, could not have been more damaging if they had been staged by Al Qaeda propagandists. Suffice to say that between the hoods, shackles, attack dogs, bullying violence and sexual humiliations—all framed by grinning U.S. troops—it was as if the Arabs' darkest suspicions about America's true nature had come to life. In the United States, even those who possessed a sense of the ruthlessness of warfare were shocked by the gleeful sadism. It was like Larry Flynt had introduced Jim Crow to the Nazi SS, with helpless Iraqis their mutual victims.

The Bush administration and its apologists correctly claimed that the vast majority of U.S. troops were not brutal perverts, and that Saddam's tortures in that same prison were worse. This was a thin salve on an American psyche that remembered how so recently the United States had been the most admired nation in the world. Aside from the misguided invasion of Iraq itself, something else appeared to have slipped, and the battle lines between good and evil were not as clear as some had thought.

The American occupation of Iraq is an ongoing story, albeit one that gets more bizarre with each passing day and also more dangerous, as the sense grows that the United States is due for a counterattack. As Churchill would put it, we have only seen the end of the beginning in Iraq, not the beginning of the end. Having shorn ourselves of allies, UN approval, the Geneva Conventions, and a great deal of international respect, it only remains to be seen how and where the counterblows emerge.

President Bush, for his part, delivered a speech on May 24 in which he outlined his new plans for the occupation. In it he expressed a newly keen desire to coordinate closely with the United Nations, NATO, and the Iraqis themselves in order to reduce American responsibility for the fiasco. In this otherwise reasonable speech, which practically mirrored the views of his opponent in the 2004 presidential race, Bush revealed his former self only by repeatedly referring to the Iraqi resistance fighters as "terrorists." His goal to restructure Iraq "will be a decisive blow to terrorism at the heart of its power," he said. But to anyone watching the conflict unfold, it was unclear how young men fighting to resist a superior army that had suddenly invaded their country could be despised.

In fact, it was not only the Iraqi resistance, but the majority of the Arab world that remained determined not to accept George W. Bush's occupation of Iraq. This should by no means have come as a surprise in Washington, since it goes without saying that Americans would do the same if the tables were ever turned, and a foreign culture ever attempted to subjugate us to its will.

CONCLUSION

In examining these wars waged by the Bushes, we can see a huge difference between the military leadership of the father and son. A chasm has opened not only in the way they have waged wars, but in their attitude toward allies, and their vision of America's role in the world.

The father achieved clear-cut victories with short, decisive campaigns, expertly matching America's military capability with its geopolitical goals. He combined overwhelming force with superb diplomacy, and did not wage war until a combination of American interests and objective principles of justice finally required action.

In recent years, the term "exit strategy" has unfortunately entered our discussions of military affairs, as if the United States needs to identify a line of retreat before it even attempts to achieve a victory. The elder President Bush took an opposite approach, in that he identified clear strategic objectives for which there was no substitute for a decisive result.

The invasion of Panama is often underestimated because people forget how many things could have gone wrong. There was every chance, and even a likelihood, that it would turn out to be another sloppy, prolonged operation such as America had become used to since World War II. Instead, President George H.W. Bush launched a combined-arms attack that in a number of respects was unprecedented in history. After an eight-hour splash of violence, democracy in that strategically vital nation had been restored.

It is difficult to say which was more impressive about the 1991 Gulf War—the military victory or the diplomatic achievement of uniting nations from every continent under American leadership. In military terms the United States was not certain what to expect, and casualty estimates beforehand wildly exceeded the final total. It was a time when the president needed moral courage rather than superficial bravado, and it was an enormous credit to American leadership that over 200,000 allied troops stood with us.

Both Panama and the Gulf War serve as excellent tributes to the first President Bush's grasp of military skill. However, his greatest victory may have been concluding the Cold War without violence at all. Again, one must consider how many things could have—and under a number of other U.S. presidents, would have—gone wrong. Volatile, ambitious, or simply misguided elements on either side could have created tragedy for untold thousands of people. Instead, the collapse of the Soviet Union, marked by a phone call on Christmas Day from its leader to President Bush, left the United States with all the opportunities inherent in a true Pax Americana.

It had been achieved through courage, through battle, and most of all through the projection of universal principles abroad so that the majority of the world held respect for American leadership. After World War II the United States had assumed a similar role as world leader, but at that time it was opposed by a powerful, opposing bloc. Now there was no other bloc. America stood alone with its principles and its power, and it had assumed an even greater responsibility. The first President Bush was more than equal to this challenge, and he handed his successor an admired nation, at peace.

In Bush the son we have hardly been able to recognize the father. And looking at the wars he has waged it is difficult to see a pattern in his military leadership, except for the fact that he seems to have possessed no skill whatsoever.

On September 11, 2001, the United States suffered an incredibly devastating attack. It was not just the worst in American history— exceeding Pearl Harbor—it was the most egregious attack suffered by any great power in the modern era. The younger Bush talked toughly, instilling the public with confidence. But then barely 300 soldiers were incrementally dispatched to avenge the aggression. Stand-off airpower was also employed, together with bribed Muslim fighters. And in the end the atrocities of 9/11 went unavenged. Osama bin Laden and his Al Qaeda organization escaped, as did the leaders of the Taliban. It is not that the United States lacked the power—and certainly not the willpower—but that its leadership attempted to fight a low-risk war on the cheap, with a lack of results that equalled the price.

Bush the son claimed victory though he had not really defeated anyone. Three thousand U.S. citizens had died while the most formidable elements of the U.S. armed forces were left idle. And as opposed to a quick, decisive war such as his father favored, leaving stable nations behind, the son has let Afghanistan fall into chaos while over 14,000 U.S. troops belatedly roam the territory, sidestepping newly grown poppy fields while supposedly searching for bin Laden.

One would assume that after effectively ignoring the greatest cassus belli in American history, George W. Bush had revealed himself as a timid military leader, lacking the courage to commit troops to battle. But then came the invasion of Iraq, a project undertaken without any apparent reason, and which has so far cost the U.S. armed forces more casualties than all our wars since Vietnam put together.

We have already discussed how Bush the son's rationales for the Iraq War resembled a three-dollar bill from the start. Suffice to say that the United States has recently become estanged from many of its traditional allies, has ruptured NATO, become divorced from the UN, and is now looked upon askance by the majority of world populations. Bush has become the anti-Bush, in that while his father lifted America to new heights of international respect, the son has managed to portray the United States in the eyes of the world as an aggressive state with motives that are still unclear.

As for military judgment, while in Afghanistan George W. Bush failed to fight a war, in Iraq he has fought an entirely wrong one, placing American troops in a situation that has stripped them of all their advantages. The Navy's weaponry, the vast reach of the Air Force, and even the fighting power of the Abrams tank have all been negated in an occupation effort that leaves infantry to fight on all sides against a native population which we can barely understand, much less have the ability to mold in our image.

At this writing our dead and wounded number over 5,500, some ten times the total that was incurred during the invasion itself.

America is unsurpassed in its ability to project confrontational might on a battlefield, and our SpecOps forces possess skills that allow for flexibility against smaller, specific objectives. But in an occupation role amidst millions of civilians, our troops may as well be the Ottomans. In the case of Iraq there is little hope of persuading the population of American virtue through our firepower, while it not just the rest of Islam but the rest of the world that has begun to stare at America as if it has lost its senses.

The invasion of Iraq made for a fascinating spectacle, as in the way that boys like to play soldier. But the occupation has become a serious problem, costing many lives with no discernible end in sight. Rather than blindly adopt Bush the son's advice to "stay the course," it has become time to think seriously how to handle the problem, regardless of how or why it was begun.

America's first task at this juncture is to increase our intelligence capability and homeland security mechanisms so that we don't suffer a repeat of 9/11. Osama bin Laden has unfortunately been left free and now has more recruits than ever due to the U.S. invasion of the geopolitical heart of the Arab world. It is now no longer a matter of "what if" but when the United States will next be attacked, as it drew the entirely wrong lesson from 9/11, and instead of quelling the conflict decided to increase it.

The other most urgent task is to close down the Israeli-Palestinian conflict without further delay. It can be debated whether the Twin Towers fell as a direct result of America's support of Israeli occupation policy. What cannot be debated is the fact that America will be unable to claim moral superiority in the region as long as it enables Israel's principle of "might makes right." The United States, which more than any great power in history, rests its strength upon a credo of multicultural tolerance, has no inherent argument with Islam. It has been put at a disadvantage, however, by Israel's imitation of ancient Sparta, holding a Helot population in thrall with brute force while denying its subject people a semblance of dignity. In specific terms the United States was surprised by 9/11, but strategically it should have expected that the Arabs would take the lead in exploring asymmetrical warfare against Western technological superiority.

Israel's lordship over the Palestinians has lain at the root of anti-American sentiment in the Middle East, and an equitable, two-state solution—already favored by majorities of both peoples and the world at large—is long overdue. Bush the father was the firmest of all U.S. presidents in opposing Israel's expansion outside its UN-sanctioned borders. As if to be contrary, the son has been the most compliant of all presidents to Israel's right wing, including its fanatic settler movement. An end to the Israeli occupations is not only a worthwhile political goal for the United States—and would be a major contribution to our self-defense—but also a worthwhile moral goal, as Bush the father and other presidents realized, but Bush the son has not.

The most difficult question is how exactly the United States can extract its forces from Iraq now that it has blown the lid off the country, opening new dangers. Comparisons to Vietnam have now become acute, in that we may well have entered a situation in which victory cannot be defined, and may already be out of reach. Hearts and minds cannot be won by Apache helicopters hovering over the population centers of Islam, while the progression of flag-draped coffins returning across the Atlantic to the United States are becoming increasingly difficult to justify. There is much talk that America can't withdraw its forces for fear there will be an Iraqi civil war, or a domino effect of Arab theocratic power. Yet the U.S. military is not welcome in the region, and the longer it remains the more it will aggravate the situation. Enjoyable as it would be to offer a solution to this dilemma there is only one that comes foremost to mind.

It wasn't long ago that the United States had a president who possessed a masterful grasp of foreign policy, combining American military strength and courage with high-level diplomacy, and above all a loyalty to essential American principles. It has now become necessary for the current President Bush have a talk with this former president: It was his father.

ACKNOWLEDGMENTS
AND SOURCES

I would like to thank my primary research assistant, Daryl Horrocks, whose speed and thoroughness in responding to my inquiries was more than impressive throughout the writing of this book. In addition to providing specific data, Daryl, who is now at the University of Illinois, responded to requests for overviews with an acumen surprising for the possesor of a Masters in English literature. His grasp of foreign affairs was as useful as his grasp of detail.

I would also to like to thank my long-time friend and colleague, military analyst Sam Southworth, for his information, insights, and indefatigable spirit. Along with Sam's missives from New Hampshire I very much appreciated the input of Janis Cakars from Latvia, where he is currently on a research project, Simon Forty from the UK, and Dr. Pierre Th. Braunschweig from Switzerland, all of whom responded promptly to questions, and who each possess in spades the informed common sense that this book has intended to represent.

I would also like to thank copyeditor Irene Cummings Kleeberg for lending her skill to the first draft, and publisher David Farnsworth, not only for his confidence, which soon needed to morph into patience, but for his overall guidance of the manuscript. Above all, I would like to extend my gratitude to two brilliant Cornell University students, Emily and Annie Smith, without whose selfless curiosity and support this work could hardly have been accomplished.

Since this book has dealt to a significant degree with unfolding events, the sources have been various, ranging from TV news, special reports

and documentaries to radio talk-shows and a great number of contemporary newspapers and magazines. Of the 700 or so of the latter
now comprising a serious fire hazard in this office, from Military magazine to Time and National Review, the New Republic, Naval Institute
Proceedings and many others, the largest piles consist of some 400 section A's of the New York Times dating back to the days just prior to
the Iraq War..

In this work, which deals with current events more than most of
my previous, I have consulted the internet more than before, and during the process have found it more useful than I imagined, even from
a couple of years ago. One could expect that by now JFK's inaugural
address would be posted for those who want to check the exact word-
ing. But I have been genuinely surprised by how much else has been
made available, so quickly and with easy accessibility. If one wants to
read Tony Blair's July 2002 address to Congress, simply type in "Blair
July speech." Likewise for Bush's September 20, 2001 address to the
nation, or his "Axis of Evil" State of the Union. If one wants to examine Douglas Feith's paper of 50 points about Al Qaeda, simply type in
"Feith memo," or PNAC for its 1998 recommendation to Clinton.
The George H.W. Bush Library in Houston has posted not only the
former president's speeches but full transcripts of his press confer-
ences. AOL constantly updates news from AP and Reuters, while the
Guardian Unlimited site provides takes from the UK. If one forgets
exactly what Churchill said about how to deal with primitive tribes, it
is only necessary to type in "Churchill poison gas" and seven sites pop
up. At least five sites have been tracking casualties in our current war,
from the Department of Defense to a site called "Iraq Bodycount,"
which is probably liberal. When one wants to check on the population
of a country or the length of its coastline, the first site that pops up is
the CIA's, with its series of country studies.

Nevertheless, data is one thing and analysis another, and there is
no substitute for books. Following is a list of those whose authors all
contributed to this project and to whom I owe a debt. Rather than a
comprehensive bibliography, the following can be considered a list of
publications that were physically consulted during the timeline Fall to
Spring 2003/04, including some that were published and quickly
acquired during that period.

Atkinson, Rick. Crusade. *The Untold Story of the Persian Gulf War.* New York: Houghton Mifflin Co., 1993.

Baker, James A. III (with Thomas M. DeFrank). *The Politics of Diplomacy: Revolution, War & Peace, 1989–1992.* New York: G.P. Putnam's Sons, 1995.

Blix, Hans. *Disarming Iraq.* New York: Pantheon Books, 2004.

Bush, George, and Brent Scrowcroft. *A World Transformed.* New York: Alfred A. Knopf, 1998.

Clancy, Tom, and Carl Stiner. *Shadow Warriors: Inside the Special Forces.* New York: G.P. Putnam's Sons, 2002.

Clark, Wesley K. *Waging Modern War: Bosnia, Kosovo, and the Future of Combat.* New York: Public Affairs, 2002.

Clarke, Richard. *Against All Enemies: Inside America's War on Terror.* New York: Free Press, 2004.

Cooley, John K. *Unholy Wars. Afghanistan, America, and International Terrorism.* London and Sterling, VA: Pluto Press, 2000.

Corn, David. *The Lies of George W. Bush. Mastering the Politics of Deception.* New York: Crown Publishers, 2002.

Daalder, Ivo H., and James M. Lindsay. *America Unbound: The Bush Revolution in Foreign Policy.* Washington, DC: Brookings Institution Press, 2003.

Donnelly, Thomas, Margaret Roth, and Caleb Baker. *Operation Just Cause: The Storming of Panama.* New York: Lexington Books, 1991.

Dunnigan, James F. *How to Make War: A Comprehensive Guide to Modern Warfare in the 21st Century.* New York: Quill, 2003.

Eitan, Raful. *A Soldier's Story: The Life and Times of an Israeli War Hero.* New York: Shapolsky Publishers, 1991.

Esposito, John L. *Unholy War: Terror in the Name of Islam.* New York: Oxford University Press, 2002.

Ewans, Martin. *Afghanistan: A New History.* Richmond, UK: Curzon Press, 2001.

Frum, David. *The Right Man: The Surprise Presidency of George W. Bush.* New York: Random House, 2003.

Frum, David, and Richard Perle. *An End to Evil: How to Win the War on Terror.* New York: Random House, 2003.

Halberstam, Davd. *War in a Time of Peace: Bush, Clinton, and the*

Generals. New York: Scribner, 2001.

Hanson, Victor David. *An Autumn of War: What America Learned from September 11 and the War on Terrorism.* New York: Anchor Books, 2002.

Hastings, Max, and Simon Jenkins. *The Battle for the Falklands.* New York: W.W. Norton, 1983.

Hiro, Dilip. *War Without End: The Rise of Islamist Terrorism and Global Response* (rev. ed.). London and New York: Routledge, 2002.

Hiro, Dilip. *Secrets and Lies. Operation Iraqi Freedom and After.* New York: Nation Books, 2004.

Houlahan, Thomas. *Gulf War: The Complete History.* Westport, CT: Schenker Military Publishing, 1999.

Huchthausen, Peter. *America's Splendid Little Wars: A Short History of U.S. Military Engagements: 1975–2000.* New York: Viking, 2003.

Goodson, Larry P. *Afghanistan's Endless War: State Failure, Regional Politics, and the Rise of the Taliban.* Seattle: University of Washington Press, 2001.

Graubard, Stephen R. *Mr. Bush's War: Adventures in the Politics of Illusion.* New York: Hill and Wang, 1992.

Greene, John Robert. *The Presidency of George Bush.* Lawrence, KS: The University Press of Kansas, 2000.

Kagan, Robert. *Of Paradise and Power: America and Europe in the New World Order.* New York: Alfred A. Knopf, 2003.

Karsh, Efraim. *The Iran-Iraq War, 1980–1988.* Oxford, UK: Osprey Publishing, 2002.

Kempe, Frederick. *Divorcing the Dictator: America's Bungled Affair with Noriega.* New York: G.P. Putnam's Sons, 1990.

Marquis, Susan L. *Unconventional Warfare: Rebuilding U.S. Special Operations Forces.* Washington, DC: Brookings Institution Press, 1997.

McConnell, Malcolm. *Just Cause: The Real Story of America's High-Tech Invasion of Panama.* New York: St. Martin's Press, 1991.

Miller, Judith, Stephen Engelberg, and William Broad. *Germs: Biological Weapons and America's Secret War.* New York: Simon & Schuster, 2001.

Munthe, Turi (Ed.). *The Saddam Hussein Reader: Selections from Leading Writers on Iraq*. New York: Thunder's Mouth Press, 2002.

Murray, Williamson, and Robert H. Scales. *The Iraq War: A Military History*. London and Cambridge, MA: The Belknap Press of Harvard Univ. Press, 2003.

Parmet, Herbert S. *George Bush: The Life of a Lone Star Yankee*. New York: A Lisa Drew Book/Scribner, 1997.

Powell, Colin. *My American Journey*. New York: Random House, 1995.

Purdum, Todd S., and the Staff of the New York Times. *A Time of Our Choosing. America's War in Iraq*. New York: Times Books, 2003.

Rampton, Sheldon, and John Stauber. *Weapons of Mass Deception: The Uses of Propaganda in Bush's War on Iraq*. New York: Jeremy P. Tarcher/Penguin, 2003.

Russian General Staff. (Trans. and ed. by Lester W. Grau and Michael A. Gress.) *The Soviet-Afghan War.: How a Superpower Fought and Lost*. Lawrence, KS: The University Press of Kansas, 2002.

Schwarzkopf, H. Norman. *It Doesn't Take a Hero*. New York: Bantam Books, 1992.

Sifrey, Micah L., and Christeropher Cerf (Eds.) *The Iraq War Reader: History, Documents, Opinions*. New York: Touchstone, 2003.

Southworth, Samuel A. *U.S. Armed Forces Arsenal: A Guide to Modern Combat Hardware*. New York: Da Capo Press, 2004.

Southworth, Samuel A., and Stephen Tanner. *U.S. Special Forces: A Guide to America's Special Operations Units*. New York: Da Capo Press, 2003.

Smucker, Philip. *Al Qaeda's Great Escape: The Military and the Media on Terror's Trail*. Washington, DC: Brassey's, Inc., 2004.

Tallesen, Charles N. "Secret World War II Biological War." *Military Heritage*, December 1999.

Tanner, Stephen. *Afghanistan: A Military History from Alexander the Great to the Fall of the Taliban*. New York: Da Capo Press, 2002.

Thatcher, Margaret. *The Downing Street Years*. New York: HarperCollins, 1993.

Venter, Al J. *The Iraqi War Debrief. Why Saddam Hussein Was*

Toppled. Hermanus, South Africa: Earthbound Publications, 2004.

Walker, Greg. *At the Hurricane's Eye. U.S. Special Forces from Vietnam to Desert Storm.* New York: Ivy Books, 1994.

Woodward, Bob. *The Commanders.* New York: A Touchstone Book, 1991.

Woodward, Bob. *Bush at War.* New York: Simon & Schuster, 2002.

Woodward, Bob. *Plan of Attack.* New York: Simon & Schuster, 2004.

Yousaf, Mohammad, and Mark Adkin. *Afghanistan—The Bear Trap: The Defeat of a Superpower.* Havertown, PA: Casemate, 2001.

INDEX